# A City's Finest

*Reflections, reminiscences and revelations of the Norwich City Police*

## Maurice Morson

Illustrated by
Terry George

*Published by Redbridge Books of Norwich*
*British Library Catalogue-in-Publication Data*
*A catalogue record for this book is available from the British Library*

ISBN 0 9520192 0 5

Computer set and printed in Great Britain by
The Gallpen Press Limited, Starling Road, Norwich, NR3 3EL

This book is dedicated to all who served in,
or with, the Norwich City Police—whenever.

All best wishes

Maurice Morson

## Acknowledgements

There were many who assisted and encouraged the formation of this book. I am grateful to every one of them, whether they be named below or not.

A special thank you to those tireless administrators of the Norwich City Retired Police Officer's Association—Stanley Limmer and Cecil Mason, for their industrious research and correspondence to members.

Ted Mileham was a major contributor and I record my special thanks for the privilege of reading his personal recollections, and also the time he spent discussing details and proof reading the formative chapters.

Special thanks to Donny Martin who contributed, discussed and checked details, at the same time provoking memories with unique photographs.

Ernie Croxson was a significant contributor with much historical detail and I gratefully acknowledge his invaluable assistance.

Johnnie Johnson led the campaign for this book and I am very grateful for both his support and material.

To Bryan Veriod of the Norfolk Fire Service, who had already trod the same thorny path for the sister service, my special thanks and very sincere appreciation of the time spent reading the draft and advising from the bedrock of experience.

I am grateful to the Chief Superintendent, officers and staff of the Norwich City Division of the Norfolk Constabulary for the facilities and assistance provided in tracing and examining records.

Finally, the great majority, my special thanks to the ex-Norwich City Police officers, their wives, friends and associates, who through correspondence, interview, discussion, even interrogation, revealed or confirmed details that will now, hopefully, be preserved in the memories of others. This is their book. Grateful thanks to L. Abley, A. Anderson, L. Bacon, A. Bartram, R. Bass, A. Blyth, D. Bishop, R. Brighton, D. Brook, A. Brown, P. Brown, E. Bussey, R. Bunting, C. Cable, A. Chisholm, T. Comer, K. Dennis, P. Fleming, N. Garnham, J. Green, K. Grist, M. Goffin, J. Groombridge, B. Horrex, T. Jones, B. Kybird, J. Lester, E. Mann, M. Monument, L. Pearce, R. Pitt, R. Porter, C. Potter, F. Riches, B. Rouse, C. Scott, K. Statham, B. Tester, A. Turner, A. Watkins, R. Woodhouse. Whether you contributed, confirmed or inspired, it was appreciated.

# List of Illustrations

# Contents

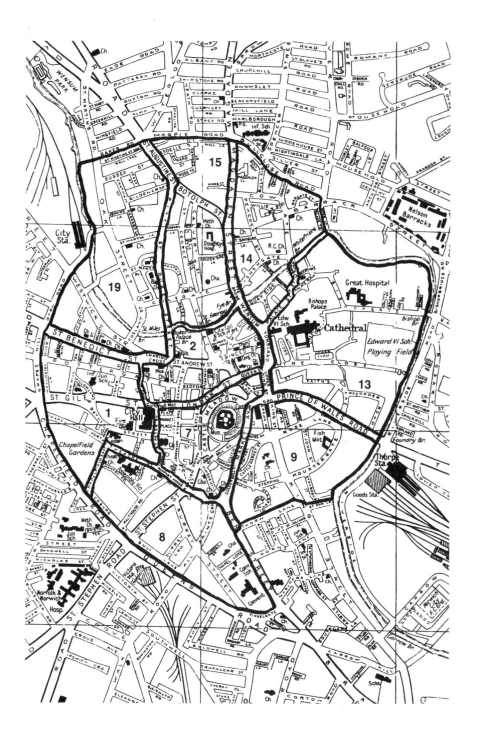

# Introduction

HISTORY, and a number of vociferous campaigners, called for this book. It was rightly claimed that a fine city should have a record of its own Police Force, especially through its closing era when the respect and esteem of the police was at its highest, for these were times which moulded characters and created opportunities in the inter-relationship of police and public.

The result is not a definitive history but a representation of the Norwich City Police, and a revelation of the final thirty years or so when the 'bobby on the beat' was an integral part of the British way of life. Police stations, procedures and equipment varied through these years and where it is considered helpful some dating guidance is given, the 1930's and the Second World War are examples, but mainly the subject matter is contained within the period from the late 1940's to the early 1960's, a significant and closing era in the life of a Police Force.

The Norwich City Police was formed in 1836 with just 18 untrained recruits, and it ceased to exist in 1968 when its 271 trained professional officers became divisional members of the Norfolk Joint Police, an amalgamation of Norwich, Norfolk County and Great Yarmouth Borough forces, later to be renamed the Norfolk Constabulary.

The text that follows cannot possibly do justice to all that went before, but it should stand as a monument to a system that evolved over 132 years and began a process of extinction with the amalgamation of a city into a county.

Although surnames are not used there is not generally a deliberate attempt to hide identities, and first names and nicknames are real. In some cases the subject prefers anonymity and in others the identities add nothing to the account. Some incidents are left without character identification because it is not an auto-biographical book. Personal experiences which are fairly reflective can be noted in the context of joining the Force and the C.I.D. The humour is real, although more evident in retrospect. A police officer without a sense of humour has a serious disadvantage, both then and now.

Finally, the intention is not to eulogise or criticise but to record with descriptive comment. The reader will form an opinion, may even yearn for a return to the yesteryears, or rejoice in the passing of such an era, but be assured: that is the way it was, is no more and can never be again.

M. MORSON
July 1992

# So you want to be a Policeman

JOINING the Norwich City Police was not unduly difficult, provided you were physically within certain dimensions, apparently fit, reasonably literate and could answer the obvious question as to why you should nurture such an ambition. A short but confident speech on serving the community in a job of varied interest was calculated to satisfy that question, but the would-be recruit did have other obstacles to overcome, and, however much he rehearsed his serving the community speech, he could not possibly anticipate some of the trauma that was to befall him when he made his first exploratory visit to the Police Station.

Bethel Street Police Station was modern and imposing to the ambitious young civilian who, in the 1950's climbed the steps under the blue lamp. Pushing open the swing doors he found a public enquiry desk on his left with another set of swing doors barring further access to the inner depths of the station. The Constable behind the counter dealt swiftly with a stated desire to join the Police Force.

"Through the swing doors. Ask at the wicket."

The instructions seemed innocent and straightforward enough and the wicket, which was closed, provided no clue to the obstacle that lay behind. A conveniently placed bell was obviously the secret to further progress.

Ring the bell and wait. Study the names on the Roll of Honour on the wall and become even more enamoured of a police career. The potential recruit is feeling less nervous and more hopeful with each passing second.

The crash of the wicket door opening brings the candidate down to earth. Before he can adjust to the suddenness of the noise a gruff voice demands to know his business. He is aware that the voice belongs to a large face which fills the wicket. It is not a face of benevolence and patience.

"I would like to join the Police Force."

Slamming of wicket door and silence. Then the opening of a real door a few feet away. The owner of the voice emerges. The first obstacle to a career in the police appears—the tallest man in the force. All six feet seven inches of uniformed Sergeant. This is the first introduction to 'Stumpy', a nickname that speaks for itself as an opposite. It is not just the height; he is well built with a determined look of enquiry that serves only to break down the mental script of the puny civilian standing before him.

In a strong Norfolk dialect, and with tones of intense suspicion, Stumpy asks the question reserved for all aspiring recruits, especially those less than six feet tall.

"What do you want to join the Police Force for, boy?"

The 'boy' begins his explanation which mainly relates to helping people.

"Can you fight?"

The force and directness of the question raises the suspicion that a trap has been prepared. Is it a trick to discover bullying tendencies? An attempt to weed out those joining with the sole intention of knocking the locals about. No such guile. The answer, "If I have too", is barely out before Stumpy moves on.

"How tall are you?"

Half expected this one, but as the answer is trotted out Stumpy is on the move and the applicant is obviously expected to follow. He is ushered into a side corridor and pushed up against a wall containing a height ruler. The measuring rod is pulled down with a degree of briskness that invites a headache and threatens to take a quarter inch off the true height of the subject.

Stumpy announces the measurement to all within earshot which is the

*A degree of briskness that invites a headache*

Station Office, telephone room, front desk, adjoining corridor and possibly the first four underground cells. The tone of the voice indicates less than complete satisfaction with the midget reading.

Having gleaned all relevant, and some irrelevant, information from the not so tall, and now not so confident, applicant, Stumpy instigates the next phase. A small side room with table, chair and examination paper. This test of intellectual ability covers a broad spectrum of mathematics, English language and general knowledge which include such demanding questions as "Where are Rowntrees chocolates made?"

There is an unnerving transition to solitude and concentration as the applicant wrestles with chocolate and other problems. The sudden absence of Stumpy's towering presence and booming voice is itself a test of powers of recovery and adjustment; but for the time being the only barrier is a piece of paper. Later, he will learn that Stumpy is a kindly man with an uncomplicated approach to life and a predilection to oranges, usually supplied by the errand boy duties of the office Cadet who saw the less kindly side of the man the day he returned with four threepenny oranges instead of three fourpenny ones.

The candidate for police status knows nothing of oranges and the true nature of his first police obstacle. He is more concerned with how long it takes to mow a lawn if it is of a certain size and is tackled with a mower of certain dimensions, at a certain speed. These and other profound questions are safely negotiated before Stumpy returns to announce that time is up. The manner of the announcement leaves no room for discussion.

The examination paper is collected, examined and marked in front of the hopeful applicant. A differing tone of grunt indicates right or wrong answers. Stumpy then gives the police version of the theatrical "Don't call us we'll call you". He returns to the General Office to peel an orange and reflect upon the falling standards of recruits, and the recruit with the falling standards escapes into the outside world wondering if he has just made an error of judgement.

More visits to the Police Station follow. The applicant sees another very large policeman, almost as tall as Stumpy, but he speaks differently and sits behind a desk in an office of impressive size. He is the Chief Constable and he makes a very short statement.

"I am prepared to give you a position as a Constable on probation".

A career begins. A number is allocated. That number will be well used in future years, principally by those above who wish to communicate with the one below, but also, of course, as an announcement of self identification.

Another visit collects enough uniform for a campaign in Upper Siberia and includes an overcoat that a Russian General would have been proud of. The recruit will learn that this garment and a batman like cape are very warm but exceedingly heavy in wet weather, though the cape does have other advantages in that the wearer's arms are hidden from view—a boon to smokers; but see later for certain disadvantages accorded to the careless types. Leggings and mackintosh are issued for wet weather protection. They achieved their objective but they also combined to create a rustling noise that was enhanced by slopping through puddles, thus removing any possible image of stealth or surprise in approaching persons or premises.

High neck tunics for night duty had to be checked for free movement otherwise there was a danger that a sudden neck turning movement would produce a garrotting effect. Shirts and ties brightened up the day appearance but were unavailable to the pre-1950's officer. Two helmets, black badged for night duty (apparently under the delusion that they were inconspicuous), silver (and later a comb type) for day wear. White gloves and barathea uniform for summer, black gloves and serge for winter. These seasons were decreed by Force Orders and with the vagaries of the English weather could result in shivering or sweating beat Constables. Daring decisions concerning shirt sleeve order were made by the Chief Constable, usually just as the heatwave was finishing.

Accoutrements, or appointments—there are both references in police terminology, are issued. The pocket book is obvious and will be produced many times: with deliberate emphasis before the eyes of despairing wrongdoers, and great alacrity for an impatient Sergeant or Inspector. Various other documents, dealing with missing persons, dogs and traffic accidents, are included with the real bible of knowledge, the Beat Book— a parable of ringing-times, beat boundaries and scheduled working on nights. It told the Constable where he should be but gave no clue to the whereabouts of Inspectors and Sergeants—a bit one sided.

Next, a truncheon, or staff as Force Orders referred to the length of wood that was inserted in the special pocket in the trouser leg; comforting, but painful if that leg was banged against something or fallen upon. It was used mainly for throwing at nocturnal animals (sometimes with unexpected results, as will be detailed later) and achieving entry to houses where the sole occupant had not been seen for some time, evidenced by the growing pile of newspapers and milk.

Holding the truncheon is another lesson to be learnt. The strap wrapped round the wrist prevents someone pulling it away, but in truth it is unlikely ever to be drawn in defence or to effect an arrest: too much writing afterwards. If in trouble it was better to subdue the aggressor with something that had not been issued, hands preferably.

The recruit finds that handcuffs are heavy, with a ponderous key that would, apparently, do service as a thumbscrew. Fitted into the back pocket they also can give a painful reminder to the officer who slumps back onto a hard chair. It cannot be denied that they were a useful appointment in that they restrained prisoners who would wish to use their hands for other things, such as strangling or punching the arresting officer, but as they required the co-operation of the prisoner to place them on the wrists, or a battalion of assisting officers sitting on all potentially moving parts, their use was of limited value.

The whistle was a decorative part of the uniform, or the chain was. In real terms it was used to referee football matches and hardly ever in the

4

pursuit of criminals. Examples of ineffectiveness are readily found. The Constable who chased a suspect from St. Giles into Bethel Street, past the Police Station, found enough breath for several short blasts without stirring the inhabitants of the station to any form of inquiry. When he later indignantly called for an explanation he was met with an indifferent response, although one comfortably installed officer admitted that he thought he had heard something outside.

The Constable who climbed twelve foot high gates in Malthouse Road with the aid of a ladder (apparently he heard a noise in a building) came to grief on the downward side when the ladder broke. With a broken ladder, not to mention a wrist and four ribs, he spent three quarters of an hour blowing his whistle before giving it up as a bad job. He struggled back to the station to report sick and comment on the deafness of others. So much for the power of the whistle.

Other accoutrements were necessary but not issued. They had specific uses and the young policeman learning his trade would acquire them through experience, as will be seen.

Folders of byelaws and something called Consolidated Orders are issued. He learns from the latter that he is required to discharge his duties with "energy and promptitude".

The Police Surgeon has previously pronounced the recruit fit to serve Queen and country. A visit to a small city shop now produces a Magistrate and the reading of the oath affirming this aim. He has been examined, kitted out, sworn in and numbered; all that remains is the process of change from civilian innocence to police realism. Training!

Our recruit of the 1950's will have Home Office inspired training with national guidelines; he will meet other fresh faced aspiring Chief Constables and he will essentially learn from both instructor and colleague with follow-up training in-force rather than just the incestuous and localised guidance provided to his predecessor of years before.

A thirteen week sojourn at an Oxfordshire mansion, rejoicing under the title of No. 5 Regional Training Centre, prepares the new Constable for life on the streets. He learns parrot fashion the definition of larceny, false pretences and other heinous crimes. He delves into the inner mysteries of embezzlement, fraudulent conversion, agricultural tractors and heavy goods (as opposed to light goods), whilst the dramatic difference between breaking into a house before and after nine p.m. is emphasised time and time again. (A question as to whether the burglar has a watch is treated as facetious). An unrelenting torrent of knowledge overwhelms him as he fruitlessly searches for some order and logic in the thinking of the lawmakers.

The fine difference between a hawker and a pedlar is assimilated along with the intricacies of betting, gaming, liquor licensing, goods licences, trade plates and a multitude of other simple subjects that the parliamentarians had managed to complicate. He learns that an 1824 Act of Parliament forbids the exposing of certain things from wounds and deformities to certain parts of the anatomy. Finding that this same act

5

classifies offenders as idle and disorderly, a rogue and vagabond or an incorrigible rogue, does little to increase confidence in the modern law. He gives up a quest to reconcile a person as both idle and disorderly.

Other gems of working knowledge are that works trucks should not be stopped because they are exempt from just about everything, identifying a public place is not so simple and has nothing to do with the public being there, you stand in a bucket of disinfectant before serving Form D, and Essex policemen are the shortest in the country. And he must not forget the agricultural tractor—the simple rule is that if one is seen approaching move smartly in an avoiding direction: to question the driver on the vehicle's legal complexities would require an IQ of 200 and a degree in philosophy.

The name 'Moriarty' creeps into everyday language and is used to settle arguments and force home points of law. If Moriarty says something, that is the end of the debate. Nothing to do with Sherlock Holmes' adversary. This Moriarty wrote a book called 'Police Law'. Personal copies, every policeman had one, became well thumbed in training, and in later stages of a career were in danger of falling apart before promotion examinations. At the police training centre it was the student in danger of falling apart.

Before the regional training centre was in being new recruits stayed within their Force, were given a copy of Moriarty and told to learn it. Additional training was provided in the form of saluting—a most important aspect of a policeman's career. Norwich recruits were required to enter the Fire Station yard and salute the petrol pump. It was without a doubt the most important petrol pump in Norfolk and it must have been a wonder that it actually condescended to provide petrol with the status it was given.

Marching and saluting were consistently practised at the training centre as was cross country running, presumably under the theory that criminals have to be chased. What happened to the "It's a fair cop guv"?

The cross country run singled out the unfit and deceitful. The second because of the first. Running briskly out of the main gates and into the Oxfordshire countryside a number of runners would make sudden diversions into the undergrowth, leaving the main pack to stream away into the distance. Later the perspiring leaders would approach the gates and struggle along the main drive to be rewarded with congratulations and an earnest comparison of running times.

The main body of runners would then appear but as they approached the gates their ranks would be swelled by others materialising from the adjoining countryside. Well tucked into the centre these new runners would gasp and struggle in unison with their colleagues, eventually collapsing with the majority in front of the mansion. Not really deceitful because they did not seek to win, just get back without doing irreparable damage to a system already suffering from the excesses of training, not to mention smoking and alcohol.

Other tortures were inflicted in the gym where a physical training

6

instructor of doubtful parentage and Gestapo like leanings would encourage recruits to "Come at me with a knife".

With a real knife the temptation would have been irresistible, but in a play acting situation the recruit could only approach half heartedly. That was a mistake because the instructor obviously believed a real knife was somewhere in existence and he regularly flattened the timorous recruit. Upon reflection he did not often invite the really big ones to attack. This meant of course that the sons of Essex were frequently in a winded condition.

It was always possible to nurse a tortured physical condition by relaxing through lectures, not the kind where an instructor would suddenly demand the definition of larceny in acid tones (he had detected the relaxation) but the sit back and absorb kind provided by visiting experts of one type or another. One of the favourites was obviously designed to inure the unseasoned individual to the coarseness of the outside world for slides of murder victims, and persons who had lost an argument with an express train, were shown in great detail.

Instructors enacted scenarios for accidents, arrests and giving evidence in court, with recruits in the starring and embarrassing roles, but it was inconceivable that any member of the public or judiciary could be as awkward as they were. The entertainment provided to the watching class was tempered by the knowledge that someone else was going to get a turn in dealing with a 'drunken' motorist, suspected 'thief' or insulting 'solicitor'.

The recruit is eventually returned to his force, moving like a clockwork soldier, filled with apprehension that he should meet a rogue and vagabond driving a works truck in a non-public place or, worse still, an agricultural tractor out of control.

The scene moves to Magdalen Gates Police Station, otherwise known as B Division Headquarters, a grand title for a brick built box within which, half is devoted to reception of the public (no more than three at a time or others cannot get in the door) and half to assembling three footbeat officers in the rear. A little annexe to the back room would make a useful cupboard but is euphemistically known as the Sergeant's Office. The fact that the building was purpose built as a Police Station causes some wonderment concerning the budget that must have been available. It offers little space over the house next door which used to be the Police Station and goes back to the time when recruits were advised that the station key was kept under the mat. In those days the Superintendent and his wife lived above and accessed through the station to their quarters, much to the discomfort of sandwich munching policemen who were required to spring to attention.

Quarter to ten on a bitterly cold winter's night and the Sergeant emerges from his cupboard like office to call the numbers. A light bulb that struggles to provide any measurable light reveals four Constables assembled to protect a portion of the city until six the next morning. Easily distinguishable from their day brethren they sport black helmet

7

badges and closed neck cheese cutter tunics.

The Constables hold up their truncheons, handcuffs and pocket books to prove they are suitably armed to give the aforementioned protection.

One five two. One five one. Fourteen.

The numbers are called out and identify two policemen and a beat. The Fourteen Beat man has a recruit for the night. (A coincidence of near numbers in this case). They add up to the release upon an unsuspecting public of a brand new policeman, finely honed from Stumpy to Oxfordshire and back, carrying the fight into the streets. It also means he is not going to be loose on his own. Two months of night duty lie ahead, closely supervised by brother officers. No way is an untested product going to be inflicted upon the public in broad daylight.

At Bethel Street Station a similar scene is enacted, but with more men and in a larger room actually known as the parade room. In this case the Duty Inspector takes the parade from a rostrum. His entry will have brought the assembly to its feet and short circuited all speculation concerning his identity, bringing forth subdued groans and exclamations of "Oh no!" as he makes his way to his speaking point.

The Inspector at Bethel Street, or A Division Headquarters to give it proper definition, orders "Put appointments away", reads the duties and exits, leaving the accompanying Sergeant to read outstanding pieces of information form the briefing board. This will include stolen cars, missing persons and break-ins. There is much sympathy for any Constable who has failed to find a break-in on his beat.

At both stations the Constables are ahead of the Sergeant for they have been reading the briefing board since just after half past nine. At Magdalen Gates there are less to share the board and the Sergeant does not surprise anyone with information that requires frantic scribbling and a muttered "What did he say?".

The scene is slightly different at the outlying stations at Ketts Hill, Mile Cross, Earlham and Tuckswood where more relaxed Constables, with suburban cycle beats responsibility (plus Thirteen Footbeat at Ketts Hill), are self serving with information which has been supplied by the internal ferry system of motor cycle beat men. They are relaxed because they know that the 'powers-that-be' are elsewhere. The telephone will ring at about twenty to the hour and a familiar voice, the Inspectors, sometimes the Sergeants, will allocate the beats and any other instructions he thinks pertinent to the occasion. It is then up to them to leave the station on time. Inspectors have been known to make a fast trip from Bethel Street to catch those lingering.

Lamps are issued and the Magdalen Gates strike force collects the metal rechargeable Wootton lanterns from a wooden box that has all the marks of considerable service and innumerable journeys. The light from the lamp comes a pathetic second best to the starved light bulb in the ceiling. It is also very heavy and recruits quickly find that the strap leaves a red weal across the shoulder, even through a greatcoat. They also learn that turning the lamp upside down streaks the greatcoat with acid. It is not long before an Ever Ready torch is purchased.

The Fourteen Beat man leaves the Station with his recruit accompanied by the recipients of the Fifteen and Nineteen Beat awards. Cycles, carelessly propped outside the station on arrival, are now lodged in the store in Bull Close Road and a chorus of "See you later" precludes the dispersal with the Nineteen Beat man making rapid ground in the direction of St. Augustines Gates and a beat generally regarded with disfavour, even called a punishment beat by some, mainly because of its large uninspiring area through to St. Benedicts and a night schedule that required some fairly quick progress.

The Fifteen Beat man, moving at a more leisurely pace towards Leonard Street and Rose Yard, can look forward to the questionable delights of a myriad of courtyards and alleys in St. Georges Street, Calvert Street and other similar Victorian highways. One side of Magdalen Street is the best part of the beat, which sums up the rest. The bright spot is that the schedules are not demanding, just depressing; unless you are a film producer wishing to portray Jack the Ripper scenes, then you could do worse than the inner depths of Fifteen Beat.

The recruit, chaperoned by the Fourteen Beat man, sets forth along Magdalen Street with the wonders of Peacock Street, Fishergate and Quayside still to behold. Exploring this latter area was akin to moving into a time warp. It was antiquarian and vintage Dickens and the impression was that door handles should be shaken with care in case the buildings collapsed.

Whatever the locale, modern or Dickensian, a new policeman was being served up for public consumption. Admittedly, it would be some time before the public would be allowed to get too close but that did not matter. He had arrived all the way from Stumpy's wicket to the black depths of Quayside. And who knows what might lay ahead.

For the time being it was a succession of door handles with a guide to ensure that he was properly acquainted.

# Follow My Leader

LAUNCHING a new policemen was not a sink or swim exercise for him, or a take it or leave it gesture to the public. It was a carefully constructed and staged programme of initiation designed to deliver an all round comprehensively tuned specimen to public duty at the end of two years. So much for the theory. What about the practice?

The first two months of supervised nocturnal activity would teach many things, not all of them with the approval of those in higher positions who frequently made derogatory comparisons with the policeman of their day. However, the recruit would get his geography sorted and learn the beats.

Schedules A, B and C dictated different routes and ringing-in points from the Beat Book. Decided each day by the Early Turn Inspector, they were designed to confuse the enemy who apparently studied policemen's movements before embarking upon a well planned criminal enterprise. Good thinking but it is doubtful whether any of the local criminals ever applied that amount of thought to what others were doing; they had enough difficulty in working out their own courses of action.

Walking beats and, therefore, an early introduction to fixed scheduled walking in the first half of the night, starting with his own Division; then cycle and motor cycle beats, repeating the performance on the other Division. Allocated to different colleagues he would progress through twenty five beats, some joined together for regular working, and would discover different guiding personalities, giving him cause to reflect upon attitudes that, basically, either accepted him or regarded him as a nuisance.

Some of his guides would be friendly, chatting consistently as they moved along the street rattling door handles and generously spraying a torch over succeeding lock up premises. Every so often there would be a quick dart to the pavement edge followed by a neck craning view of upper windows. Teetering on the kerb edge, flashing the torch and talking to his uniformed colleague, little acknowledgement was given to elements of stealth or surprise.

There were a number of complications attached to one policeman showing another the way, not the least of which followed the guides sudden right angled progress from the pavement edge across the front of the recruit desperately trying to keep out of the way. Only the fading voice gives a clue, showing that the black hole into which the conversation maker has disappeared is in fact an alley.

The recruit hastily making time down the alley realises the voice is getting stronger and meets his guide on the way out: sharp about turn and he disgorges back onto the main pavement causing sudden changes of course by pedestrians wending their way home from the nearby cinema. They are moving quickly to catch the last bus and do not appreciate the dramatic appearance of a policeman who appears to be talking to himself. Suitable apologies are offered, and accepted, before they move on muttering something about not being able to find one when you want one.

Some chattering leaders welcomed the company and spent the night forging a noisy course in which the fortunes of Norwich City Football Club, usually at a low ebb, were discussed and the listener's choice of career was roundly condemned. Others offered a grunted greeting before maintaining a consistent silence, occasionally broken by a terse comment which included the words "Keep up".

Enthusiasm and a desire to keep up with the leader could be inconvenient, embarrassing or even disastrous. A certain recruit, who found that all three applied, was very keen to make a good impression. He was smart and tall, passing Stumpy's critical eye with ease, and he was ambitious enough to stick closely to his guide for both verbal and visual

*The recruit meets his guide on the way out*

11

tips. (This recruit later transferred his keenness to the Essex Force, making a significant difference to the average height of that force).

Working Thirteen Beat on nights the two officers approached the riverside near Prince of Wales Road and became aware of a scuffling noise accompanied by other sounds of frenzied activity. The recruit dutifully took up a secondary position as the guiding Constable approached the source of the noise on the river bank. A sudden dart to the river's edge and the Constable's torch revealed a couple locked in a passionate embrace. Everything in order, just a courting couple, in fact a vigorous courting couple. The Constable switched his torch off. Unfortunately, the recruit was making up ground fast to discover what had already been apprised by his leader and the loss of illumination did not help him to keep his bearings. He arrived on the towpath but, with insufficient room to maneouvre, he had to bypass the other Constable. This he did by plunging into the river. One considerably wet and deflated Constable was taken to the Police Station to dry out. The views of the courting couple must have been interesting—if they noticed.

Refreshments at Bethel Street Police Station (there was hardly room for leverage on the sandwiches at Magdalen Gates) was time staged via the Beat Book to accommodate all nine walking beat policemen, but allowed sufficient overlap to learn the art of snooker in direct competition. The recruit also learned how to falsify the booking-in book to gain an extra few minutes, precious on a cold winter's night or when you still needed the pink to win and refreshment time was officially finished.

There was a deflection tactic, specially reserved to thwart those poised to make the winning shot. This was a cry of "Adcock's alarm" and it effectively emptied the station as available Constables leapt down two flights of stairs and swarmed out of the front portal aiming for the well known tobacconists in Davey Place. Sometimes it was a false call engineered by a bad loser, but more often it was a real call from the most unreliable alarm system in the city. Some of the veterans, with very long memories, could remember when the call was genuine and a burglar was caught.

Eating could precede or follow snooker depending upon table availability but, invariably, a satisfied stomach came first. Sandwiches left by the recruit at Magdalen Gates would reappear at Bethel Street canteen, courtesy of an internal transport system that sometimes reshaped them in the process. Proper identification was also necessary and much ill feeling was created by incidents in which cheese or marmite owners mistakenly ate another's ham or chicken. The Constable who ate the Sergeant's sandwiches kept his head down and was never identified, well, not for forty years.

A War Reserve Constable served tea of an approximate 20/50 viscosity and incinerated anything that required any form of cooking, and old stagers garrulously told recruits how lucky they were to be allowed in the station for refreshments. In their day sustenance was taken on the G.P.O. steps.

After forty five official minutes of conversation, indigestion, snooker and warmth, it was back to the streets and the war against crime and disorder.

Being shown round a beat did not mean the recruit would learn everything about the area; that depended upon the guide and whether he was inclined to share trade secrets with an unknown and untested colleague. A natural caution might prevent him revealing some of the perks of the beat, which meant he was looking at eight hours of self denial. It would explain a degree of grumpiness in furthering the education of the new man.

Sid had no such inhibitions and working Seven Beat in the city centre with his recruit, Cyril, dutifully following his footsteps he showed no inclination to reveal other than door handles until late at night they met a man walking his dog. Sid brightened considerably at this very ordinary sight and the animated conversation that followed did much to advance Cyril's education of Seven Beat. There was nothing wrong in the landlord of the 'Walnut Tree Shades' walking his dog, or being friendly with the beat officer, but the conspiracy took on a whole new meaning when much later that night, after tiresome schedule working was over, Sid led Cyril to a hiding place near the 'Walnut Tree Shades' and retrieved two bottles of brown ale. The next port of call was St. Stephen's Church which was unlocked and, therefore, a convenient refuge for two ale swigging Constables.

Cyril noted that Sid was unmoved by the risks attached to leading a new officer astray and wondered over his ability to cross the landlord's path on further occasions, irrespective of the designated schedule. The fact that St. Stephen's Church was on Eight Beat appeared to be of little consequence in the light of other transgressions.

A strange twist to this story is the revelation in Cyril's family history of his great, great grandfather's service in the force from 1850 to 1870 which included an admonishment in 1864 for seeking a glass of ale whilst on duty in Gentleman's Walk. The very same beat. Did it really need Sid to lead Cyril astray? Had he inherited the taste and instinct for the locality?

Just when the recruit believes his feet will never be the same again, probably correct, he moves into the suburbs and acquires a cycle. Although policemen do not tear around on cycles two together can be problematic, especially if one does not know where the other is going. A sudden turn by an uncommunicative escort either means one peeling away and the other swiftly employing a U turn to recover ground or a coming together of men and machines with an unhappy relationship for the rest of the night.

The cycle beat man had no fixed routes to learn in advance which meant that the sudden arrival at lock-up property could disadvantage the recruit who has not been in verbal contact and suddenly needs a convenient propping place for his machine. His escort has already dumped his cycle in the usual place and disappeared round the back of the premises. By the time he recruit is organised and heading in pursuit of number one that uncommunicative gentleman is returning and the alley syndrome is repeated. Apologies and high speed collection of a machine that had taken so long to carefully park.

Cycle beats meant refreshments in a Section Box which were, and still are, small brick built Police Stations at Mile Cross and Ketts Hill on B Division, and Earlham and Tuckswood on A Division. Dating from 1952 they were the suburban policeman's operating and rest centre. Refreshments in a Section Box was a more cosy and intimate affair than Bethel Street, but no snooker. Make your own tea and no worries about upsetting a colleague because of an inability to sink a simple red. Perhaps steal a few minutes extra refreshments period, but with one ear cocked for the Inspector's car. If he arrived you were trapped with the documentary evidence against you in the form of the booking-in book, signed and timed upon arrival—or perhaps after the first sandwich provided it was not too far from the Beat Book stipulated time.

After being shown the motor cycle beats, much to the disgust of the motor cyclist who had to transfer to a cycle for the occasion, the recruit repeats the whole process on the other Division, from walking beats onwards. His overview of the two Divisions, more industrial and old world on the B side, main features, shops and city centre on the other, is concluded.

Near the end of the recruit's owl like existence daring decisions are taken. He is allowed half a shift without company. He may even be loose from six p.m. onwards. Peering tentatively at the outside world from beneath a helmet with a silver badge the new officer of the law is conscious of his solo performance and thankful that his severest test is identifying the location of the Odeon Cinema to inquiring citizens who are totally unaware of his newness. After all, a policeman is a policeman.

Comes the day, as opposed to night, comes the man. Unescorted and with a beat to himself, viewing traffic in quantity and without lights, he sets out to put the world, or a small part of it in the shape of Norwich City, to rights. His status moves from 'shown round recruit' to 'probationer', usually spoken with an intonation of voice which indicates that the subject is still not a real policeman. The next target is confirmation of appointment after two years.

He still has to be shown things. Probationer training at the Lads Club is a temporary relief from beat work and provides more opportunities to play snooker. Under the benevolent eye of Harvey the Training Sergeant, later Inspector, the probationer learns of matters peculiar to Norwich; the byelaws of the fine city which prohibit all manner of things which the parliamentarians forgot. Mousehold Heath is particularly well protected and a day out on unspoilt heathland could result in a multitude of sins. Pages of 'no unauthorised person shall' show that it is a difficult place to negotiate and delving into history reveals that a vast amount of unauthorised 'goings on' centred around this area.

The complexities of traffic law are not only probed but traffic control is taught, working on the well known principle of 'there it is, go and do it'.

The 'it' in this case was Thorpe Station crossroads. A small group of probationers would walk from the Lads Club, and after Harvey had explained, in his usual courteous and very polite way, that he would turn the traffic lights off, he did just that, retreating very quickly to the safety of the pavement. "And don't forget the station yard" was the parting shot.

If the Thorpe Station yard was not forgotten it was a five road junction on the A47 with many bus routes and a continual stream of impatient taxi drivers from the station. Bus drivers knew it was a training ground and smiled sympathetically, or was it a mischievous grin? Taxi drivers muttered and were less than kind over the quality of signalling whilst the public asked why the lights kept breaking down and wasn't it handy there was always a policeman to take over.

If the probationer of the fifties thought he was hard done by in being subjected to the pressures of Thorpe Station crossroads under supervision he would have done well to listen to the tale of the probationer of the late 1930's who, without the benefit of a training centre initiation, found himself, with only ten nights supervised experience, directing traffic at Thorpe Station crossroads at eleven p.m. on a hectic August Bank Holiday with a complaint of a drunken driver and obvious trouble in a nearby public house. His guiding Constable was absent, the only consolation being that he was dealing with the public house trouble. The probationer had been ordered to sort out the heavy holiday traffic streaming into the city whilst his leader sorted the public house, but the principle of a divided force was to cause some heart stopping moments for both; the guiding Constable's came when he returned to find the traffic unsorted and his probationer missing. He was unlikely to find him because he was on Mousehold; that place again.

Bert was the probationer faced with what appeared to be a conspiracy of fate. On this occasion of sudden indoctrination into a policeman's need for instant initiative he was mastering the traffic when an excited citizen ran forward to inform him that a car driver was drunk and had proved it by hitting a steam roller and succession of red lamps, presumably intended to protect the steam roller which was parked in Riverside Road. The driver had compounded his misdeeds by driving off. Bert felt compelled to abandon his crossroads and go with his witness who readily agreed to use his own car to transport him in the direction taken by the offending driver. Their diligence was rewarded for the drunken driver was found on Mousehold with his car embedded in a tree. The first real bend after Thorpe Station had caught him out and a broken whisky bottle lay at his feet as he slumped over the wheel. The obliging citizen made a 999 call on Bert's behalf with the result that a drunken, relatively uninjured motorist was removed to become an ex-motorist the following day at Magistrates Court. The Inspector actually told Bert that he had done well. All part of the training.

The training interlude at the Lads Club was followed by two more visits to the Oxfordshire mansion to confirm that marching and larceny had not been forgotten. There was also attachments to specialist departments and supervisory reports by a nominated Sergeant and Inspector to contend with. The Sergeant was delegated to the reporting responsibility for the period of probation, but the Inspector was the one found by the Sergeant who would admit knowing the probationer and was prepared to find the time to write something about him.

The supervising Sergeant would have a well used game plan to keep his charge on his toes and the opener would come during a street visit.

"How are you getting on lad?" Moved up a stage—only a boy when Stumpy was doing the assessment.

"All right Sarge". Offer nothing—wait for the next move.

"How many non-indictables have you had?" Every probationer knew this one. It came at not infrequent intervals and was an opening gambit used by several Sergeants, not just the one who had to write a supervisory report.

"Quite a few Sarge". Suitable details then supplied of unfortunates who had parked in the wrong place, too long or did not have the necessary documentation to cover their vehicular movements. There may have been something really exciting like a dangerous dog, or a drunk and disorderly. (Bert's drunken driver would have been worth a lengthy response and could not fail to have impressed).

"What accidents have you dealt with?" Different tack, but also anticipated. No problem because the total was not within the expertise of the Constable. You did not look for them. They found you. Every passing citizen would advise the Constable of an accident "down the road", although their interest evaporated when asked if they had witnessed the contretemps.

The probationary Constable supplies details of various motoring bumps and shunts knowing that the next question will have a similar overriding criteria.

"Been to any sudden deaths?" Policemen always prefaced the word "death" with "sudden" on the grounds that if there was any other sort they did not have to deal with them. Not strictly true as the young Constable would find later.

Having replied to the death question with any such information that may possibly relate the probationer feels that he has survived the interview rather well, especially as the conversation is taking place in a busy street and he has capably dealt with two enquiries for Elm Hill and one for the Cathedral in that time. He sees another "Excuse me officer" approaching and thinks he has sidelined the criticism seeking probe by his supervisor.

"Straighten that tie and that helmet should not be at an angle. Smarten yourself up if you want to get through your probation".

The Sergeant departs having justified his probationer responsibility and the said probationer, nursing feelings of injustice, fields another enquiry for Elm Hill.

Specialist attachments were a passport to the inner workings of Bethel Street Police Station, the heady atmosphere of the C.I.D. and Traffic Department, a ride in a Wolseley, a visit to the mortuary; fingerprints and photographs—all things that had been spoken of but remained distant. All will be revealed for the benefit of the probationer now nearly half way through his probationary term. Revelations are not, however, always straightforward.

It was back to being shown around, but now there were occasions when you could lose your guide without any effort at all. This was the C.I.D. It starts with an introduction to a stony faced and apparently disinterested detective who is to show what has to be shown. It is followed by the immediate disappearance of the detective. A fruitless search only draws attention to this new C.I.D. attachment and he finds himself in possession of a large bundle of stolen property circulars for delivery at listed city dealers.

The importance of the circulars is stressed and they are delivered. The detective who should have delivered them, and was fortunate to find an aimless probationer attachment, is happy. The dealers are happy because they now know what not to put on display. The deliverer is unhappy and when he returns to the station he finds the stony faced detective is also unhappy and is complaining that he looked for him before he, the detective, went out. Where "out" happens to be is not made clear, but it later transpires that detectives leave the station to make "enquiries", go to a "break" (burglary) or see an "informant". The informants are all well trained because they tend to meet in the 'Walnut Tree Shades' or 'The Plough', where, strangely enough, most of the enquiries are centred.

It is a more worldly wise young officer who moves on to learn the mysteries of hackney carriages, public house licences, aliens registration and other fascinating subjects that will reappear later in his career should he ever contemplate taking the bumpy road to promotion.

There is, however, one point in the series of attachments which is anticipated by probationers, in some cases dreaded, and in which losing the guide would be considered a bonus by some.

"Seen a PM yet?" Why were policemen so adept at asking questions to which they knew the answers? Lennie, the Coroner's Officer, would pose the question knowing that initial training in Oxfordshire included a visit to the Oxford mortuary to view the lay out (appropriate term), but it was very much a hit or miss affair as to whether a post mortem was being conducted at the time. Even if it was, a class of twenty large policemen (including Essex) would be hard pushed for a view in the less than generous space of the Oxford mortuary.

The reply to Lennie's question was, therefore, in the negative. He knew it would be and it gave his next sentence greater emphasis.

"Well you're going to see one now". This came as no surprise because it was one of the reasons for an attachment with the Coroner's Office.

Lennie was another variety of large policeman, but jovial with it. Perhaps it helped to deflect the nature of the job which involved an almost daily routine with corpses of varying history and quality.

Seasoned policemen well into their careers would count a post mortem as one of the many indifferences that life, or death, presented.

17

Not callousness, but a shield of experience and inevitability. Younger and untainted colleagues tended to be more sensitive. Too early to acquire the shield. It soon came with the "in at the deep end" philosophy.

The mortuary at the Norfolk and Norwich Hospital was a small outdated disinfectant reeking room, and our "deep end" attachment officer would be introduced to the pathologist as a "watcher". The pathologist's assistant would be present, and knowing looks would be exchanged all round. The usual greeting would be "If you feel faint fall towards the door not over the table". This does little for the watchers' confidence.

The routine that follows is well scripted with a regular plot within which probationers, who later compared experiences—"What was yours like?" etc.—found very few differences. Only the subject and the result changed.

The table is covered by a large white cloth from beneath which protrude two very white feet, one labelled. Lennie removes the cloth with a flourish, as if performing for the Magic Circle, and the object of everyone's attention is revealed. The post mortem commences and Lennie darts around passing instruments and conversation. The probationer takes up the poorest viewpoint possible, near the door.

Suddenly the animated conversation pauses and the figure by the door is recognised as one of the living. One who is not sharing the joys of discovery on the table.

"Come and look at this" cries Lennie with great enthusiasm.

The probationer does as he is bid and looks at a mass of unidentifiable tissue and listens patiently as certain marks and discoloured (or it could even have been coloured) parts are attributed to the cause of death. He nods and thanks Lennie for the information before retreating to his preferred position at the door. He responds slowly to further invitations to the table as other degenerating and abused organs are brought forward as competitors for the cause of death award.

Apparently, Lennie was a dab hand at sewing up but visiting probationers are not privy to such an exhibition. The pathologist's assistant is entrusted with the task and the watcher leaves with Lennie's mischievous enquiry concerning luncheon intentions ringing in his ears.

The circuit of specialists is completed with administrative visits and a reunion with Stumpy—still intimidating potential recruits and pursuing a love of oranges. Then it is back to the beat and learning by experience.

The end of two years, final reports submitted, comments noted—then an entry on Personnel Orders. The appointment is confirmed. No longer a recruit or a probationer. A fully fledged Police Constable, but the public never did know any different.

Only another 28 years of learning.

# Backbone of the Force

A REGULATION pace of two and a half miles per hour: that was the progress expected of the walking beat Constable. He was informed of this measured tread at training school and when he returned to home territory he found affirmation from those who provided guidance and supervision. He was, of course, allowed to break into a trot to catch felons and was expected to stand still when directing traffic and the public. Routinely, he studied vehicles by day and business premises by night.

What the new policeman did discover was that he, the policeman on the beat, was the backbone of the force. This had been impressed upon him at training school and his Chief Constable repeated the news, several times, publicly.

A backbone is a central, stabilising and joining feature. If it disappears everything else comes adrift and fails to work. Armed with this new sense of importance the new man set forth upon his beat at the indicated two and a half mph only to find that some of the connecting parts worked very well independently, sometimes to the backbone's disadvantage. If he disappeared from view some of them worked quite hard to find out why.

Equipped, armed is not quite the right word, with a whistle, piece of wood, handcuffs and pocket book our uniformed paragon moved between ringing-in points, chatting to the public, pursuing cups of tea and playing fast and loose with senior ranks who had moved on from the backbone stage.

Ringing-in points every hour and twenty minutes brought the beat Constable to the surface for examination by both peers and public. During intermediary periods his expertise was available through being in the right place at the right time (some would say the wrong place), unless of course he was tracked down by a conscientious ratepayer who would inform him that "his light was flashing".

Drunks, motorists, complainers and offenders all appeared with great regularity, sometimes all in one. Variety was present within a theme that rolled through the three shift system and could be expected to offer particular interests, or problems, depending upon your point of view, at certain times and places.

Early turn was from six a.m. and it saw off the black badged helmets and closed necked tunics of the men who had been studying doors and windows throughout the eerie and still hours of the night. It had not been very still when they had started their shift and it was now beginning to stir again for the benefit of the early turn.

The first buses and occasional early traffic cause newsagents, tobacconists and small general shops to open; the enticing smell from innumerable bakeries triumphs over carbon monoxide fumes, and the regular chink of milk bottles is all part of a city coming alive. Its uniformed protector shows similar signs of life and suitably fortified by some early tea he moves two points up the tedium/interest scale.

The rush hour begins; expressionless faces hunched over handlebars or peering from bus windows, some through car windscreens as they edge their way through the morning traffic jam tapping the steering wheel with a finger and looking helplessly at the uniformed figure on the pavement. Most of them are not wanting to go where they are going and the aforesaid uniformed figure can only supervise their frustration at not getting there.

As the traffic increases, the beat men take up various traffic points; not through a sense of public duty but because the beat book says so. This dictatorial tome either places the Constable in the road in direct conflict with the incoming tide of traffic or has him patrolling the pavement of the main road along which it flows. Either way, he is on offer until it is all over.

As soon as the nine o'clock workers have reached their destinations, and stopped clogging up the streets, the beat men start a sequence of refreshment periods at Bethel Street Station. More snooker—the daylight version. The main streets, and some not so main, will shortly have the benefit of the ten a.m. to six p.m. foot patrols, intended to harry the motorist and keep the traffic moving.

By eleven thirty a.m. all the early turn pavement pounders should be refreshed and out again. A motoring period begins. The stationary sort. Cars parked too long or where they should not be. Lorries lost or blocking the road to make a delivery. It is now difficult to observe the passing city life from a doorway. They are required for customers. Tea places are visited but they no longer qualify as hiding places. If something happens outside there are numerous persons available to bring it to the attention of the tea sipping figure in the back of the premises.

Early turns could provide their extraordinary and unnerving moments. The young Constable who left Magdalen Gates Police Station at six a.m. without his torch, on the grounds that daylight was only an hour away, came to regret the decision very quickly. Passing Magdalen Close he was assailed by a frantic woman screaming that her husband had hung himself. She led him to a first floor balcony in a block of flats, pointed into the inky blackness and then shot into a nearby flat, slamming the door with considerable force. The disadvantaged officer peered tentatively into the gloom and inched his way along the balcony with arms extended, eventually discovering the unfortunate man by tripping over the chair he had stepped off. Feeling over the dangling figure the Constable remembered his training—preserve the knots. He was now doubly inadequate, no knife.

Groping his way back to the flat he knocked on the door and asked if he could borrow a knife. The shriek that rent the air aroused the whole block and added to the Constable's embarrassment. It also brought the Sergeant to the scene, arriving shortly after a blunt kitchen knife has brought the victim to earth. That Constable learned that appointments ranged beyond a whistle and truncheon. He never again worked a beat without a knife in his pocket.

A Constable who set off along Magdalen Street one Christmas morning got as far as Stump Cross before his early morning dormancy was interrupted. The stunning silence and absence of life on the streets at just after six on this important day had to be experienced to be believed; but on this particular morning the Fourteen Beat man's attention was polarised by an inhabitant of Stump Cross.

A white rabbit sat contentedly in the road totally oblivious of the festive season and police interest. Not a top hat or magician in sight.

On any other morning he would have been competing with the occasional vehicle but on this important day he had the splendour of Stump Cross, adorned with a light covering of snow, all to himself; until the policeman arrived.

The Constable had enjoyed a very good Christmas Eve and was not feeling on top of the world. Perhaps white rabbits had replaced pink elephants. A quick examination showed that the rabbit was real and unconcerned by its surroundings and the inquisitive policeman.

Satisfied that the previous night's ale was not hallucinatory, a curious Constable returned quickly to Magdalen Gates Police Station and acquired a wicker basket which had a doubtful feline history. Returning to the scene he captured a very relaxed rabbit without opposition. So far so good. But what next? Station Sergeants did not welcome livestock in the station at any time, never mind Christmas Day: but an enterprising Constable was not looking in that direction, he was studying rabbit tracks in the snow. They led for nearly a mile to Albany Road and he followed them to an alley between terrace houses. Sure enough in the back garden was a hutch with an open door. One rabbit returned, but one Constable walking on a cycle beat and a very long way off his own beat.

On the way back to Fourteen Beat the rabbit saviour met not just the Sergeant but the Inspector with him. Explanation time. To be fair both senior ranks showed great interest in the story of Brer Rabbit (new version), possibly wondering if the Police Surgeon was qualified in psychiatry. Corroborative evidence was needed and there was only one way to obtain it. All three trooped back to Albany Road, crept up the alley and stood silently viewing a white rabbit through a wire meshed door. The rabbit stared back unimpressed by the array of police power before it.

The householder who cared to look out of a window, perhaps

checking for Santa Claus, would have seen a Police Inspector, Sergeant and Constable standing in line before a rabbit hutch gazing solemnly at its occupant. It is possible someone did view this strange scene and went back to bed to finish their dream.

All was well; returning runaway rabbits was accepted as a police duty although there was some unhappiness that it should have traversed beats, but of course rabbits did not have beat books.

Two o'clock and no problems, hopefully. Late turn arrives and has the privilege of the run down to the evening rush hour when the same expressionless faces will repeat the contest for road space from the inside going out. Refreshments will be early—five p.m., or late—six thirty p.m., then cinema queues and pubs.

People began to look a little more animated in the evening, especially if they had had a few drinks when they could be very animated. Drunks on late turn had to be dealt with in an official manner because the public was watching. The night man could tow the stupefied obstruction into a convenient alleyway to sleep it off. The late turn man would have to bring him round or call up transport to take him in. Smelly, vomiting, awkward drunks were not very popular with the Station Sergeant, and the provider of the specimen in question would achieve a similar popularity rating.

Jack was a well known character in the city, to policemen and the courts anyway, and he added a specialism to his intoxicated meanderings—boot throwing. His boot, without him in it, went through an extensive list of windows within the city of Norwich in the 1950's. Outside the local glazing industry he was regarded as an infernal pest, particularly by shopkeepers opposite Bethel Street Police Station who wished he would travel further afield every time he had a dispute with the Station Entrance Officer. There was no ill feeling on Jack's part. He simply required a bed for the night and after he had executed a little dance in the Station Office and been told to take himself off, he would do just that and also take his boot off as he arrowed across Bethel Street to hurl the footwear through the shop window. He would then hop back into the police station and repeat his request for accommodation. Immediately granted.

If Bethel Street was too far from the scene of his drunken revelry he would select a window and await the arrival of his policeman, but more frequently he went looking for the beat man to ensure the shattering event was properly witnessed.

The occasion arose when a Sergeant and Constable decided that Jack's antics should be nullified at an early stage. Preventive policing was called for and they were just the men to apply it. Patrolling the city centre in a police van, which was euphemistically shown on the duty sheet as 'Riot Squad' (of which more anon), they came upon Jack working himself into his usual frenzy. It would seem that the scene was set for a very familiar sequence of events.

At one a.m. in the morning there was some scope for unethical police work, as Jack was quick to find out. His song and dance was snuffed out

*An infernal pest—outside the local glazing industry*

without any preliminary dialogue as he was swept off his feet and propelled inside the van by two large policemen. At that point there was no reason to believe that Jack's bed and meals were not booked for some time ahead; but even his befuddled brain suspected that something was amiss when he was deposited on Dunston Common, several miles form the city. He became even more uneasy when his shoes were removed and thrown away. The rapid disappearance of the police van confirmed his suspicions.

The police conspirators drove carefully back to the city congratulating themselves on their initiative. A great deal of trouble had been averted, for Jack's presence in the Police Station was potentially disruptive; he was noisy and very free with opinions on a wide variety of subjects which included the work of the police force. Both the Station Sergeant and Inspector tended to be bad tempered when Jack was around.

The police van cruised into St. Stephens Street with its crew rejoicing in the additional knowledge that they had not been observed on their journey. No other traffic had passed them. A good job well done; that would teach the old reprobate a lesson. The only sign of life now visible on the streets was a man standing outside Samuels the jewellers.

The van slowed as the Sergeant cried, "I don't believe it"

Two pairs of incredulous eyes fixed upon a barefooted Jack who responded to the approaching van by seizing a litter bin and hurling it through the jeweller's window. Two bemused policemen made an arrest and, although he told them many things, most of which they did not want to hear, he never revealed how he had managed to get back.

Drunken disorder often manifested through personal dislikes and imaginary slights suffered by alcoholic crazed customers whose robust response to an issue of minor importance—a query concerning who or what someone was staring at—was a frequent point of ignition. It would ensure a domino effect of shouted abuse, bloody noses and staggering bodies. On Saturday nights the Riot Squad, two or four officers troubleshooting in a van, would be dispatched and pillarphones would start to flash. If the beat man was walking past at the time of the eruption it was a holding action until others ran, cycled or drove into the melee. Heads would be banged together, ears cuffed, behinds kicked. If the disturbers of the peace actively responded to this positive police action it was arrests and police cell accommodation.

Unfortunately, some of those captured would still want to take on all comers in the Police Station and the narrow corridor fronting the cells was the scene of many skirmishes in which numerous uniformed persons struggled to secure a handhold to persuade the screaming, windmilling, octopus like figure that he really should go through the door into the cell.

Certain well built policemen were considered very suitable for the front line approach to recalcitrant prisoners but the day a black American of world heavyweight proportions went berserk in his cell it was a case of volunteers to open the door to let him out, especially as his stated intention was to add homicide to the list of charges against him. Some took the view that he should not be let out, not until the next shift came on anyway, but this was rather short sighted—taking into account the level of noise emanating from the cell.

Donny was freshly back from war service with commando status. He was also very fit with proven stamina as an outstanding swimmer (later to be Traffic Sergeant and the first police frogman). The fact that he did not seem to mind also helped in his selection to tame the fire breathing American. Of course he would have a back-up squad, which immediately backed up round the corner to await events. Donny had the freedom of the corridor.

What happened next in this Anglo-American exercise greatly enhanced Donny's reputation. The back-up squad listened and prepared to charge to the rescue as the cell door swung open. There followed the obvious exit of the roaring American, then a crash, then silence.

Peering tentatively around the corner they observed an unperturbed Donny contemplating an unconscious American sprawled across the corridor floor. Admiration knew no bounds, but what Donny never told them was the sequence of action which began with the enraged American's head down rush from the cell and culminated with him missing his target, Donny, and crashing head first into the corridor wall. Easy if you know how, and have a narrow corridor.

A police presence at public house disturbances was not always so speedily arranged when the antagonists were hard at it in one of the suburban hostelries. The Earlham area was home territory for members of some well known warring families who sometimes met on sociable terms, but, if the venue was a public house the evening's increasing intake of alcohol would arouse the baser instincts and, by closing time, all the old prejudices would have come to the fore. The inevitable result was a battle royal from which the landlord, knowing the track record of the persons involved, would smartly effect his own strategic retreat.

These family feuds often resolved themselves as soon as a contingent of police arrived. Officers would rush into the pub and find a smiling assembly of bruised and bloodied customers standing nonchantly amongst broken glass and overturned tables expressing surprise as to the general untidiness of the premises. A re-emerging landlord knew nothing and could not help the officer concerning that man lying under the table with a rapidly closing eye and an urgent need of a dentist. Oh well! Another occurrence report.

Disorder often came in multiples and without any sign of cheeriness. Not all drink related either. In pre-Second World War days the market place was cleared of stalls at the weekends, and political organisations held rallies before they marched through the city accompanied by policemen who had quickly been turned out of Bethel Street Station. Prince of Wales Road, through London Street to the market place, became known as a marching route and in later years it attracted groups of troublesome youths when it became known as the 'chicken run'.

After the war the 'chicken run' was applied to Prince of Wales Road only and the name was well known to the younger more fractious elements of the community.

On a late turn, Prince of Wales Road was the busiest and noisiest place in the city with cafes, pubs and cinemas all vying for business, and with small groups of teenagers prowling from Thorpe Station at one end to the Royal Hotel at the other. This prowling was generally a desire to be part of the bustling life of the road and not beyond the supervisory capabilities of the beat men.

Prince of Wales Road was part of the A47 and a boundary between the two divisions. Nine Beat shared one side with the rather obscure delights of King Street, Rose Lane, Mountergate and the dreadful Oil Mills Yard, whilst Thirteen Beat had the other side with the more salubrious backing of Upper King Street, Tombland and the Cathedral Close. It was, therefore, not unusual for two officers to be in evidence in the road in the evenings. Just as well because into this area of high life came a foreign power.

A Chinese restaurant opened near the junction with Cathedral Street, almost immediately opposite a cafe whose customers rarely progressed beyond baked beans on toast and did not support the view that our policemen were wonderful. Another cafe, and a fish and chip shop, was not too far away and the Regent and Norvic cinemas were on the same side, only a few yards along the pavement. If Prince of Wales Road needed a new and livelier interest, which it didn't, it could not have been placed in a more active part, nor provided a greater curiosity value.

Foreigners running restaurants and offering strange sounding alternatives to chips needed to be investigated. That was the view of an ignorant minority that thought that anything outside the British Isles was a sub-human culture. It followed that supporters of this view sought to put the polite oriental gentlemen in their place by becoming the awkward customer, with the transparent intention of embarrassing the staff and obtaining a free meal. They not only failed, they failed abysmally. One such failure came to the notice of the Nine Beat man (it will be seen that he could not possibly have missed it) and served as a turning point in the cumbersome efforts of local intimidation.

The Nine Beat man was occupying a doorway near the baked beans cafe, looking across the road towards the glass fronted Chinese restaurant. That is the way the police report would be worded—the power of understatement. His attention could not avoid being drawn because the front door of the establishment exploded into glass fragments and a customer, presumably now ex-customer, landed on the pavement.

Subsequent debate never resolved whether he arrived on the pavement by direct oriental hand or by his own action motivated by sheer terror. The latter view became generally acceptable because he had barely staggered to his feet before a procession of orientals followed him through the door, or the hole that was the door, and they looked distinctly unfriendly.

The hole left by the ex-customer, who was now setting off at a fast speed, was ample for the slight frames of an assortment of staff which included waiters, cooks and what appeared to be an element of management. Later, someone opened the door but the size of the hole made it an academic exercise.

The Nine Beat man noticed that the pursuers were very excited and extremely voluble but what really attracted his attention, and obviously that of the fleeing ex-customer, was the array of cleavers and knives that were held aloft.

The glinting steel no doubt accounted for the astonishing turn of speed of the ex-customer, but rescue was at hand because he hurtled into the approaching Thirteen Beat man and immediately became a supporter of the "our policemen are wonderful" theory.

Policemen often approach these kind of situations with a "What's going on here?", which is a traditional greeting when it is painfully obvious what is going on. In this case it needed to be obvious for a multitude of voices eagerly provided explanations in rapid Cantonese. The English version was not much better, due mainly to a state of imbalance in the nervous system of the ex-customer who now had to add the cost of a quarter inch plate glass door to noodles and bamboo shoots.

Word soon went round that Chinese, Hong Kong or similarly related restaurants, were not to be trifled with, but the police had to advise the hard working gentlemen who ran these establishments that non-paying customers could not be offered to the long knives of the kitchen staff. What really finished it was the opening of a second Chinese restaurant at the top end of Prince of Wales Road thereby realising reinforcements and, with the aid of the telephone, a flanking company that could outsmart terrified customers fleeing from the other restaurant. It was not known if the second restaurant was opened for business or tactical reasons.

Business disputes, if that is what the abortive attempt to obtain free Chinese meals was, were rare; but domestic disputes were common and a danger area for the unwary officer. A flashing pillarphone was often the instructing source.

"Go and see Mrs. (whatever her name was) at (whatever address). Domestic dispute". End of message.

From then on it was all downhill, or should it be uphill. First thing the uniformed marriage counsellor had to ascertain was whether the dispute was still ongoing. The amount of crockery in circulation would provide a useful guide. If violence and damage had ceased then it was a patient listening approach to accusation and counter accusation. Attempts at neutrality were frequently sidelined by a united front to this interfering policeman whose advice was not wanted, and who should leave forthwith. Another occurrence report with the classic line, "I advised both parties of their civil remedy and warned them as to their future conduct."

Not every officer went to a domestic dispute via a flashing pillarphone. The Constable working the cycle beats of Twenty Three and Twenty four was pushing his machine through Philadelphia Lane (known to the locals as "filthy dirty" lane) when, suddenly, a house window, frame and glass complete, left its anchorage and landed in the front garden revealing a circling mass of differing generations hotly contesting various family issues. The noise was such that the Constable was forced to discount the tempting claim that he had not noticed.

Entering the front garden he decided that ringing the door bell would look foolish in the circumstances. He, therefore, stepped through the hole in the side of the house to confront the remonstrating company who seemed totally unaware that the overall structure had altered. The genie like appearance of an officer of the law, combined with the sudden realisation of unwanted ventilation, successfully diffused this dispute.

It was not just relatives that developed aggressive or unsympathetic attitudes to the pressures of gregarious living. The other version of the domestic dispute was the old age saga of territorial intolerance in which the officer's adjudicating love thy neighbour speech usually fell on very stony ground.

Bonfires, dogs, children, fences, abuse and noise all appeared as the bones of contention between neighbours who aimed to use the police as the ultimate weapon. The complainant's version usually bore little resemblance to the defendants, although there might later be some common ground as their irretrievable dislike for each other was qualified by the joint acknowledgement that the police were worse than useless.

Dogs and children were tricky for neither could do anything wrong in the eyes of the owning side. Is it possible that the misty eyed tousle haired collection of offspring assembled by the fond parent could possibly have

27

loosened the wheel nuts on the neighbour's cycle?

"No mister" they all lisp as the question is put.

"There you are" cries the fond parent in triumph. "What more do you want?" Quite a bit actually, but it is not prudent to say so. After making a farewell speech, which contains some references to future behaviour, the Constable moves next door to advise the bruised owner of a mangled cycle that English Law contains a presumption of innocence. The victim of the juvenile enterprise is unimpressed and advises the Constable accordingly.

Later the fond parent, who is not completely stupid, conducts an in-depth interrogation in a manner that would have lost the Constable his job, and metes out summary jurisdiction to the principal nut remover on the grounds that he was not clever enough to divert suspicion elsewhere. Fond parent does not mind the next door neighbour looping the loop from his cycle, but objects to the police being drawn to the parent's abode.

Dogs were guilty until proved innocent. Any other view could be injurious to the enquiring officer. They either aimed to bite, made passionate love to a blue serged leg, or stood alongside on three legs with a satisfied expression on the canine countenance. Sometimes they leapt upwards without malicious intent, succeeding only in leaving muddy paw prints and a collection of hair that would later cause the Sergeant to draw comparison with a hearth rug as a prelude to a rollicking for untidy dress. The leaping up sessions were invariably accompanied by a fond cry of "There he likes you", although sometimes it would be a totally ignored command of "Do get down Rover" followed by a lying "He's normally quite obedient".

Following up a dog enquiry required a reconnaissance with a mental note of the best escape route. Sometimes an empty garden was suddenly no longer empty; the Constable knocking on the door realises too late that (1) the house is unoccupied, (2) the garden isn't. At this point the height of the garden fence becomes very relevant and a number of officers can claim to be holders of unratified high jump records.

Some dogs disliked uniforms, a feeling quite often reciprocated by their wearers. It followed that dog lovers who found strays really needed to know who was on duty before handing in their charge. Some of the dogs had a fair idea and left their mark before being delivered to the Dogs Home, or if the wrong one was on duty, ejected. An officer who received a stray at Magdalen Gates Police Station was lacking in subtlety when he left consecutive reports "Dog Found" and "Dog Escapes". The escape was planned, and not by the dog.

Late turn was the shift with outgoing traffic jams, the tendency to disorder and disputes, lively public houses, evening social pursuits and gathering gloom—not all related to darkness. It remained potentially active until the Constable had cycled into the driveway of his own house. If he came upon anything on the way home it was his, in the police sense of course. Paid overtime? No such thing. Avoid getting involved in the last hour and get home unscathed. Tomorrow is another day.

# All Through the Night

FROM LATE turn duty to nights, black badges and closed neck tunics again. Fixed schedules for the foot men; the city traffic running down and dwindling with pedestrians to nothing in the early hours—silence and inactivity nearly complete by this time: cats, rats and policemen ruled. Occasionally, a criminal wandered across the scene.

The eight hours of night duty polarised upon a principal and demanding subject—property. Lock-up property, meaning unoccupied business premises. The man on the beat was responsible for all insecure doors, windows and lights, inasmuch if they were there he had to find them. Lights? They required an explanation, the most unlikely being a burglar wanting to see what he was doing.

Norwich was a great city for alleys, passageways, courtyards and other interesting but exhausting by-products of a main street. These yards and alleys rejoiced in grand sounding names and the dourness of Nineteen Beat could, with a little imagination, be enlivened by moving along St. Benedict's Street from the Queen of Hungary to Lord Camden in a few hundred yards whilst the Fourteen Beat man would explore sixteen different alleys or yards in traversing from one end of Magdalen Street to the other.

Some beats were OK by day but, because of the disposition of lock-up property, they became models of exertion and depression by night. Nine Beat qualified both day and night. It contained Oil Mills Yard, a dismal and depressing enclave of a desolate area. Accessed from Mountergate, a similarly unattractive thoroughfare, it comprised a collection of decrepit stores and ramshackle buildings of dubious intent and content, approached over potholes of varying depth within an all enveloping degree of blackness not experienced since the Second World War. Its sinister appearance was not helped by the knowledge that one prospecting beat Constable had found a person hanging in one of its sheds.

Many parts of this gloomy area leant themselves to vivid imaginations fired by the loneliness and lack of vision at night. Half past three in the morning, with the Sergeant's visit out of the way and no problems on the horizon—the Nine Beat man chose to lay a course along Thorn Lane and to relax by leaning on the fence bordering a derelict area. Everything was so peaceful but, suddenly, the hairs on the back of his neck started to tingle with the eerie feeling that he was not alone. With a cold chill running down his spine he glanced over his shoulder into a green eyed hideous face only inches from his; with steam coming from the nostrils and condensing in the night air the face emitted an ear splitting bellow, causing the beat man to leap across the pavement which, in turn, caused his Wootton lamp to swing on its strap catching him a direct blow in that most tender part of the male anatomy. The horse peered over the fence and watched the Constable stagger away in a crouched position.

Nine Beat had a twist in the tail for night duty officers, just in case some form of relaxation was envisaged. Traffic signs in Rose Lane had to be changed. They allowed parking on one side only; very reasonable. But which side? The city fathers had decreed that justice would be served by alternating this mammoth concession to the motorist, therefore, the signs were placed on both sides with flaps which showed either "Waiting" or "No Waiting" according to even or odd dates. All very complicated, especially as he could not reach the flap without obtaining a hooked pole which was kept in One Box (a blue shed with a telephone) at Thorpe Station for this very purpose.

It was a major offence not to change the Rose Lane signs, as it was to change them without realising that it was the 31st day of the month. It was also a chore to have to go to One Box to get the pole. Some of the

*It was discovered that cape straps were not strong enough*

30

taller Constables found that the cape strap could be formed into a loop and hooked over the flap, bringing it down to its new reading. This new wheeze was passed on until it was discovered that cape straps were not strong enough to support a swinging policeman. First hand evidence was provided by a winded night duty officer. Quite a dangerous beat was Nine Beat.

Refreshments was the halfway, or near enough, part of the tour of duty. Time to take second wind, refresh and plan the passage of the following hours, the part with no schedule and time to be surprised by horses or attacked by road signs—amongst other things. Delaying refreshments could reduce the initiative required in the second half but a very good reason was needed.

If appearing late for refreshments needed a reason, turning up early could not possibly have an excuse. Therefore, the night duty Constable who found himself ahead of time decided to rest in front of the City Hall; more specifically he climbed onto one of the ornamental lions and enjoyed the view across the market place. This view quickly included the Sergeant coming round the corner intent upon his own destiny with food. This was relaxation time and the Sergeant's unconcentrated and unconcerned progress only hesitated with the realisation that something was different with the front of the City Hall. He stopped to focus upon the lofty and disconcerted Constable. The Sergeant's question was obvious, but the Constable's explanation that he was "seeing what it was like to ride a lion" was not well received and the verbal address that followed contained some pointed references to a circus and the dignity of the office of Police Constable. The rollicking was, however, of sufficient length to prevent an early arrival for refreshments.

Night work was lonely and policemen hiding in the shadows contacted adjoining beat men by soft whistles, or more often, owl hoots. Any ornithologist abroad late at night could easily have been led astray by the number of hoots emerging from doorways. It is even possible that the genuine article was confused, for some of the old stagers were extremely accomplished in their renderings.

Learning the beat was one thing but learning the tricks of the trade was another. To avoid the inconvenience of re-examining property various ruses were employed, mainly relating to the use of markers: sliver of wood against a door or cotton across an alley, thereby giving an indication of subsequent entries to the area concerned. This marker system had its uses for selected places, and dustbins also had a useful role to play.

When it was pouring with rain, and the guardian of law and order was warmly placed in a tea supplying bolt hole, this everyday household article was exactly the right size to receive a police top coat draped around the circumference. The theory was that meeting the Sergeant at the next ringing-in point would show that the rain had not deterred the Constable from doing his duty. Actually it didn't show any such thing because the Sergeant had adopted the same ploy in his beat working days. It did, however, prevent questions prompted by a dry top coat.

Policemen's capes sometimes suffered from excessive dryness because they caught fire. This was not induced by any form of speed or friction. It was a calculated risk for smokers. The cape was a useful covering garment, much appreciated by Constables with sweets to unwrap, pipes to fill or cigarettes to smoke: but extra caution was needed. The sudden and unforeseen appearance of the Sergeant could make life difficult, especially if he prolonged his visit by chatting. Pity the dilemma of the patiently listening Constable as he began to exude smoke from beneath his uniform and was faced with the alternatives of hoping the Sergeant had not noticed, thereby risking an on the spot conflagration, or revealing all as he opened the cape to deal with an overheated interior caused by a hastily hidden pipe or cigarette.

It was not only the cape that permitted covert opportunities. The Sergeant who came upon the Constable at the market place immediately noticed a strained expression, which did not improve as a thin red line emerged from beneath the helmet and trickled from the Constable's forehead towards his nose. Fearing some grievous injury sustained in the course of commendable police work the Sergeant ordered removal of the helmet to obtain more detail. What he saw provided a complete answer. A fresh 'hot dog' balanced on the Constable's head, oozing a tell tale streak of tomato ketchup.

Other parts of the uniform could cover unusual items, even if the wearer was not exactly a party to the concealment. This statement leads to the most famous example of the diversity of a police uniform and the perils of standing still on the beat. Jimmy was a Constable working One Beat and, deciding it was time to rest awhile, he placed his ramrod like figure in a shop doorway in St. Giles Street. Suddenly, he realised he had company. A rat ran up the inside of his trouser leg, presumably as a spontaneous reaction to having its tail stood upon. Jimmy, who had not previously noticed the rodent and had no desire to stand on its tail, or any other part of its anatomy, shook it out before its journey reached a critical point; but he was sufficiently put out by the experience to wear cycle clips for his remaining tours of night duty on that beat. A career that might have been nipped in the bud, so to speak, continued to the rank of Sergeant.

Ted was a Constable working Nineteen Beat in the second half of the night and he also found himself in a stationary position that proved embarrassing. Wandering through New Mills Yard he came upon a fisherman on the river bank and engaged him in conversation. This led to the offer of a spare rod, which was accepted. The uniformed protector of the area from St. Benedicts to St. Augustines settled down to some serious fishing.

There is always someone ready to spoil the pleasurable pursuits of others, and in this case the spoilsport was also in uniform; and he had three stripes on his arm. Johnnie was a very large and vociferous Sergeant. Coming upon this early morning scene of peace and tranquility he began to disrupt it by addressing Ted at some length on the subject of fishing on duty. In the absence of any defence or mitigating circumstances (it would have been difficult to think of any) Ted contented himself with listening carefully, not aggravating the position, and putting it down to experience and bad luck.

The following night there was every sign of an uneventful shift with Ted being assigned to Fourteen Beat. Not much scope for irregularity there. It had a low rating for interest, mainly due to the previously mentioned abundance of alleys and yards. Ted was, however, pleasantly surprised to find an object of great interest at the end of a yard in Magdalen Street: there, standing in all its glory, was a sit upon knife grinding machine.

With time on his hands, again in the second half of the night when shaking door handles was another robot like extension of boredom, Ted got to work on the machine, producing two pocket knifes (he was not going to be caught out as others had been) intent upon testing the power of the contraption. The necessary friction was obtained by pedalling and Ted was working up a fair speed, his knife sparking against the revolving wheel, when Johnnie appeared in the yard drawn by the sounds of activity.

The conversation that followed was again one sided and made some reference to the previous night's fishing expedition. The diversity from fishing to knife grinding allowed Johnnie a fair amount of scope in his castigation of the errant beat man, but his references to the knife grinding machine drew him closer to the offending article. His overall

*He was sufficiently put out to wear cycle clips*

33

condemnation became interposed by queries concerning the machine's capabilities, resulting in speech tailing off and action taking over. The end result was two policemen happily grinding knives at the rear of Magdalen Street.

The majority of beat men occupied the second half of night duty by window shopping, chatting to a neighbouring beat man (a dangerous occupation because someone must be off his beat, unless of course they were shouting across the road, as did happen in St. Benedicts Street one night between One and Nineteen Beats, until a window opened and a weary voice told them to shut up), drinking tea (some beats had access, others were not so lucky), and trying the occasional door handle. If it opened there was a problem, either a break-in or it had been missed on schedule.

Nocturnal bolt holes were a comfort to the cold, weary and bored officer. Tea, warmth and company were much appreciated; if they came together so much the better. Some beats were better endowed than others and some had fringe benefits—bakeries were a comfort to the inner man, as were certain dance halls where the remains of an executive repast could be shared with the watchman; and an early morning newspaper warehouse provided magazines to absorb a waning interest in police matters.

The freezing cold of the early morning in winter could be numbing to mind and body, hence the warm bolt holes; never mind the tea, get the circulation going before the whole body went the way of the mammoth in the Ice Age. Caravans and parked coaches had their fair share of defrosting beat men, but they had inherent dangers created by the desired change of temperature. When comfort reached the soporific point a ring-in could be missed or, worse still, the Constable who gratefully climbed aboard a coach parked at the Cattle Market but awoke to find himself going through Newmarket.

Night duty could be hazardous, not because of the criminal element but more the unforeseen. A Constable who probed further than usual at the rear of the Bus Station arrived at the Police Station covered in grease muttering about the inappropriate siting of a vehicle inspection pit.

Incapable drunks were less of a nuisance on nights, mainly because they could be removed to places other than the Police Station. Many a reveller collapsed in the city centre and woke up on Mousehold Heath wondering as to the power of the brew that put him there. Others spent the night circulating between beats as discovering Constables towed them over appropriate boundaries only to find them returned by less than receptive colleagues. One paralytic, blissful and semi-conscious specimen covered three different beats in one night as beat men unsympathetically shuttled him around in their version of pass the parcel.

The reproving Constable who had found the neighbouring Constable towing an unwanted drunk over the beat boundary was less than fair in his condemnation of his brother officer because he had earlier dragged this particular specimen onto his neighbour's beat.

The Constable walking back towards Bethel Street to report off duty at six a.m. found a drunk sprawled in the road at St. John Maddermarket. This made Two Beat look untidy and the custodian of the beat was certainly not going to get involved with drunks at leaving off time. He, therefore, dragged the slumbering reeking man up an adjacent alley and carried on to the station where he reported "all correct" before escaping to the cycle sheds. Riding down St. John Maddermarket towards Charing Cross he suddenly remembered the drunk because he rode over him. Insensible or not, he had crawled back to his original position in the road.

Some incidents of river rescue occurred at night with the officer who jumped off Foundry Bridge making the biggest impact; although his heroic rescue of a woman received less comment from the Station Sergeant than than did the pools of water he subsequently left around the Police Station. News that this keen officer had thrown himself in the river left the Sergeant relatively unmoved. Apparently, the woman did not want to be rescued either. Police work could be very unrewarding.

An occasional nocturnal pastime was the sport of truncheon throwing. It was occasional because the targets were furtive and fast moving, and the accuracy of the thrower often left something to be desired; but such incidents did occur, and more than one truncheon finished its service with numerous scars without ever being used in the line of duty. History has at least three occasions when a policeman threw this handy piece of wood at a fast moving rodent and saw it miss, skip of the pavement and disappear through a shop window. The truncheon would be recovered and the subsequent report would draw reference to passing traffic and the likelihood of a stone being thrown up. Logic and improbability were noted together. It was said that one officer, whose aim had been less than accurate, abandoned the traffic theory and, after reclaiming the offending piece of wood, ran up the road blowing his whistle.

What is known is that an officer working near Guildhall Hill wished to attract the attention of another and, not being an owl hooter, he threw a stone. His next report related to finding a broken window in the Guildhall.

The loneliness of a night shift could be enlivened by confrontations with wild animals, although most of them only became wild after they met the beat man. The rat that favoured Jimmy's leg as an escape route was merely panic stricken; it was probably aware that detection would invite some kind of missile, for policemen, in common with most people, despised these scavenging, scurrying creatures that shared their night routine.

Chasing and throwing things was more a gesture of distaste than a practical attempt to dispose of the rodent, but on the rare occasions that one was cornered the brave officer was prompted to a re-appraisal of the situation by the sight of the target standing on its hind legs hissing fury at its tormentor. There were two recorded occasions, one on a day shift, when the intrepid uniformed rat catcher went into battle against an oversized specimen the size of a small dog—finishing with the glory of a newspaper photograph showing the victorious hunter posing over the kill, which turned out to be a coypu: a South American beaver like rat—now extinct, in Norwich anyway.

Mention has been made of the unreliability of dogs in a police presence. Strays crossing the beat were, therefore, best left alone. They tended to have little respect for interfering policemen. However, Basil was not only a beat Constable he was an animal lover, and, more importantly, an opportunist. He frequently collected his own dog, a lurcher, from his home, and took it to run with him on his cycle beat for the last four hours of the night shift. The dog was usually concealed in some convenient shed or outside toilet shortly before the next appointed ring-in.

Basil came unstuck early one morning when he was late for his ringing-in point. With no time to conceal the animal he cycled furiously to the appointed place to find the Inspector patiently waiting.

Basil breathlessly reported "All correct Sir" and then, before this statement could be queried, the dog arrived, panting, to sit at its master's heel.

There followed a marvellous recovery. Basil disowned the animal, totally ignoring the obvious delight of the reunification and the devotion of his pet, complaining "That thing has been following me all night."

He then had to talk his way out of not appropriating it as a stray.

On another early morning run this unofficial police lurcher took exception to a railwayman cycling to work and gave chase. Basil quickly vanished around the nearest corner, whistling and imploring the mischievous animal to follow, which it did, eventually. The fate of the railwayman is unknown.

Only a few shifts later the same maligned creature caused Basil further embarrassment by chasing a rabbit across Mousehold Heath, resulting in panic at B Division because a beat Constable was fifteen minutes late off duty. Not long after this latest incident a quiet verbal instruction put paid to the "Volunteer Dog Patrols".

Horses were another much loved animal, but not by policemen during the night, indeed, many officers subscribed to the view that a horse was dangerous at both ends and uncomfortable in the middle. Having one loose on the beat spelt trouble. They were large and, in the quiet of the night—noisy. Hooves clip clopping through deserted streets would inevitably result in a telephone call to the Police Station with the familiar by-line, "What are the police doing about it?" This would result in a command to the beat Constable to do something about it.

"Go and sort it out" was the usual definitive command. The Sergeant issuing the order would be satisfied that he had carried out his duty, needing only to deliver a follow-up rollicking when the beat man's initiative failed to resolve the situation.

Horses fell into this no-win scenario quite easily but there was a golden period when the problem of where to take them was resolved. The 'Buff Coat' public house was inhabited by horse lovers who would receive and look after emergency captures. The problem was getting the beast to this unofficial pound. Horses were not only big, they were obstinate, and, in the hands of a uniformed policeman of doubtful equestrian ability, they were very obstinate.

Kenny was a Constable in the majority group that had no wish to be associated with a horse at any time; this wish was even more pronounced by the time and place he found himself in the company of an animal whose unimpressive appearance showed an itinerant bloodstock rather than any show or racing distinction. It was simply a scruffy horse. It was loose in Bracondale and Kenny, who was about to go off duty at six a.m., had no desire for the unpaid overtime necessary to coax it towards the 'Buff Coat'. Anyway, the horse did not look to be the coaxing type.

Kenny was not the horsey type but this would cut no ice when reports of a horse loose on the beat reached the station. He was, however, a steady and determined officer; determined that he was not going to waste time over a mangy horse that he suspected belonged to local carter of awkward disposition. The horse was likely to prove to be of similar temperament and was almost certainly the animal that lived in Thorn Lane, with a known propensity to escape. It was no more attracted to Nine Beat than the delegated policeman and it had already incapacitated one of those worthy officers by merely peering over the fence.

If the geography of the situation was a handicap it was also the solution. Kenny was a philosophical person and he believed that horses rightly belonged in the countryside. At the bottom of Bracondale was Trowse Bridge and over the other side were the highways, byways and green fields of the Norfolk County Police. The horse had to be persuaded to explore fresh pastures. This persuasion came in the form of Kenny leaping up and down, hallo'ing, clapping hands and generally behaving in a manner unbecoming a police officer.

With the maniacal performance taking pace at the city end of the horse it was not surprising that it decided to head towards the county. Breaking into what horsey persons would call a brisk canter and what Kenny, panting along behind, called something different, the horse went across Trowse Bridge into Trowse village, leaving the flapping, puffing Constable further and further behind.

Success. The horse was still moving in what Kenny considered the right direction and he could now afford to slow down, watching it depart well into the area of another responsibility; county policemen were better suited to dealing with horses.

The best laid schemes of mice, men—and policemen. The horse was slowing, but still moving briskly as it passed a row of cottages when, suddenly, a man appeared from a front garden. He ran alongside the horse and, firmly gripping its mane, brought it to a halt. Swinging the panting animal round he trotted it back to a thunderstruck Kenny and observed, "I could see you were not going to catch him. Here you are."

Kenny thanked the man.

That this horse should appear again in Bracondale on another night can be of no surprise, but on this occasion it was captured by two

Constables who, in a well planned conspiracy, placed it in a field of lush grass some way from the beaten track. No one is sure when, or if, the owner persuaded it to return to the Thorn Lane scrub site, or whether he even found it. What is known is that there was a witness to this horsenapping enterprise. As two uniformed officers pushed and cajoled the animal past Trowse Mill an upper window opened and a voice asked what was going on, claiming that he thought he had heard a horse. The instant response from the darkness was that everything was all right and the questioner must have had a 'nightmare'.

Dick was a Constable who found a horse wandering loose near the Cathedral; too far from the County boundary, although it is doubtful whether this course of action was even considered. As an ex-artillery man Dick could handle horses, and he proved it by riding this lost specimen bareback to Bethel Street Police Station where he was redirected by an unenthusiastic Station Sergeant to the 'Buff Coat'. No problem—Dick rode the horse there.

Straying cattle were more docile than horses but no less a problem, day or night. On Saturday mornings, hordes of youngsters ran alongside the herds being driven into market along the main roads from that place called the county. Bullock whopping was a juvenile pastime which simply meant acting as an unofficial drover. Any bovine that exhibited the slightest desire to explore a side street would immediately be set upon by a gang of stick wielding youngsters giving forth the traditional cry of "whoa", or something similar.

Maxie was a Constable who would have appreciated some traditional assistance when he peered outside Nine Box (Dereham Road by Bowthorpe Road) to investigate persistent mooing noises. It was very early, the quiet hours of the morning, and the enclosed windowless police box had prevented him seeing his impending company. Slapping hooves and mooing left him in no doubt that he had a stray cow or two outside; but he was hardly prepared for the sight of a complete herd milling around in Dereham Road with every apparent intention of heading into the city. There was no market and no drover. Another "sort it out" situation.

Maxie telephoned for assistance knowing that any that was forthcoming would not be specialised. He then made the first move; placing himself and his cycle in the path of the herd he commenced shouting, using a very limited but forceful vocabulary the majority of which could not be found in a dictionary.

The herd moved slowly back along the Dereham Road with Maxie encouraging their progress from the rear. Early morning workers who cycled past brightened up considerably, making unfavourable comparisons with the wild west before swiftly increasing their pace away from a fuming Maxie.

Help arrived in the form of a younger, and compared with Maxie, more slimline Constable. He immediately declared a paucity of knowledge of bullock whopping and adopted a peripheral role.

As the herd moved along Dereham Road towards the Ring Road they showed a side street curiosity which caused Maxie to scamper from the rear with threatening gestures accompanied by a high crescendo of verbal instruction. He continually accelerated their progress with repeated assaults, using both cycle and truncheon to achieve the desired effect, at the same time calling directions to his young assistant who was junction hopping to prevent any slippage at the front.

The herd ignored the 'Keep Left' sign at the roundabout, turning into Sweet Briar Road to escape the assaulting dervish at the rear. No more side roads; straight on accordingly to plan, for there was a convenient field further along the road. They were successfully corralled by two exhausted officers.

The next part was easy. Wait for someone to report they had lost a herd of cattle.

Extraordinary abilities sometimes came to the fore at night and it can now be revealed that the holly wreath found draped over Thomas Browne's statue in Hay Hill one war time Christmas, which took two council workmen and a ladder to remove, was placed there by an agile beat officer.

Other diversions were less demanding but also uplifting, albeit in a different sense. The sounds of organ music from the spiritualist church at four a.m. may have seemed the first introduction to heaven for any chance passer-by, but further enquiry would have revealed the coming together of two Constables with one playing and the other pumping.

Sometimes a cruel streak came to the fore. As the middle of the night moved into the early hours an occasional early worker would appear. Postmen, milkmen and bakery workers were examples. They moved slowly on cycles through the city centre with a heavy degree of sleep apparent in movement and appearance. Surrounded by an oppressive silence, with no competing noise or movement, some were in danger of sleep riding. A certain Constable, with a wicked sense of humour, brought these early travellers to a state of maximum alert by hiding in a recessed doorway and crashing two dustbin lids together. The result was an involved pattern of progressive cycling with took in both sides of the road and, almost certainly, an accelerating pulse rate.

No less cruel was the beat Constable who crept up to a night watchman's roadside hut and placed a sack over the chimney, resulting in a change from internal slumbering to outside coughing.

Some policemen were not averse to misleading fellow officers. The Seven Beat man spent a considerable time in the early hours searching Castle Meadow for the origin of breaking glass without ever realising that another officer, of cavalier temperament and roguish reputation, had hurled milk bottles against the castle wall before hiding nearby to await results.

Were policemen 'peeping toms'? Curiosity was their stock in trade and a thirst for knowledge cannot be criticised, but perverted prying was not part of the make up. There were, however, stories, and it was difficult to explain to the householder who telephoned the Police Station exactly what the officer was doing sitting on top of his garden shed.

A further problem arose when a lighted window at the rear of Plumstead Road shops caused a patrolling Constable to seek more elevation to ascertain the cause of the light and to this end he borrowed a ladder from nearby premises. Propping it against a convenient tree he climbed upwards. Initiative or enterprise it may have been but what he saw so unbalanced him he fell out of the tree, giving rise to the suggestion that he should have anticipated seeing the occupants of the flat above the shop in the first place.

Whatever the night duty beat man saw, pursued or threw things at; whatever he rode, drove or shouted at; wherever he hid, drank tea, window shopped, fished or ground knives, or however he occupied his eight hours, six a.m. eventually arrived—the hour of happy release.

A full circle has been completed and the early turn is back on the streets. The night shift is off to bed for a full morning's sleep, unless of course a break-in has been missed; then sleep is interrupted by a recall to the Inspector's office. You can never be sure how far away police duty is. It doesn't always appear in shifts.

# Insecure and into Trouble

THE MAN on the beat had the responsibility of preserving the peace, persons and property. Without detracting from the former the importance attached to bricks and mortar was something he ignored at his peril. Lock-up property was intended to be subject to the most rigorous examination by the patrolling officer; if it wasn't he was liable to rigorous examination, which could include being hauled from bed at eight or nine o'clock in the morning following a night shift. The interview that followed would directly relate to a break-in on his beat; and it was no use saying he did not know who had done it, not finding it was a much more serious matter.

Why had he not found the break-in?

Because it had not happened when he inspected the building. One might think this to be an obvious answer.

What time did he go round? What was the state of the building? What route had he taken? And so forth and so on.

The Constable leaves the interview desperately hoping the burglar is never found, and if he is, he does not admit entering the premises before six a.m. Burglars could get policemen into a lot of trouble.

Another trouble making group was, of course, Inspectors. The night duty variety was very sensitive to any state of impropriety amongst premises on the beat, especially if the beat man had not found the abnormality. His routine should have found what was there to be found, but it could not be guaranteed. The routine? Door handles and windows—front and rear, lights—up and down, all in order—move onto the next building. If it wasn't in order then off to the pillarphone for a keyholder. Later, when the Inspector visited, usually in the second half of the night, it was "All correct Sir", or a detailed explanation of what had been found and what had been done about it. The commitment to "All correct" was the road of no return and, sometimes, the prelude to a dialogue that should have been banned by the League Against Cruel Sports.

Know your Inspector was the first rule. If he accepted the salute and the "All correct Sir" without comment then everything was set fair, but if he started a conversation the Constable would have to be on red alert with the grey matter finely tuned for further danger signs.

"All correct you say". This spelt trouble. He knew something.

"Yes Sir". What else can the Constable reply—he is committed.

The Inspector sits back in the seat of a very comfortable Wolseley and addresses the windscreen whilst the frozen and apprehensive Constable stoops to peer through the half lowered driver's window.

"Are you sure?" The worst is feared. What does he know? Whatever it is will not be revealed immediately. Verbal torture will precede the final denouement.

The answer to the last question is that he is no longer sure, but he is committed to a defensive "Yes Sir" through the window.

The Inspector asks, via the windscreen, if the Constable has been up a certain road. All is now revealed. The Constable has obviously been up the road in question because the schedule says so, but what is also obvious is that the Inspector has been up there and has seen something. He has decided to extract the maximum satisfaction and inflict extended pain from his incidental observation.

The Constable is trapped and can only reply "Yes Sir. Went up there on schedule."

"See anything?" Stupid question. He saw a road, buildings, street lights, cats, traffic and so on. What he meant was did he see anything that should be reported and the answer is obviously "No" because he has already said "All correct".

"All secure Sir". The Constable is wriggling as the end approaches.

"Didn't ask you that." No mercy is to be given. It must be a light. The Inspector has seen a light in a building and is going to make the most of it; a not infrequent occurrence when the beat man's neck craning antics extend only to the kerb edge. Alternatives are leaning into the road and being decapitated by passing traffic or crossing to the other side with a risk of being found off the beat, an offence more serious than missing a light. The Inspector is nicely placed to see lights, sitting low down on the other side of the road.

The Constable, resigned to his fate, advises his inquisitor that nothing irregular was seen. He waits for the indictment.

"Look for lights?" Of course he did. The trouble is he did not see any and the two pipped uniform talking to the windscreen did.

"Didn't see any Sir". Wait for it. Here comes the kill.

"How come I saw it then?" How dearly the Constable would like to answer that one in the fullest terms possible.

"Don't know Sir", comes the lying reply.

"Because I keep my eyes open. You would do well to do the same". The Inspector has finished questioning the windscreen and is now adding emphasis by staring directly out of the driver's window at the expressionless Constable. It allows him to observe for suitable signs of mortification as he follows up with an analysis of the Constable's abilities which have nothing to do with lights.

*The routine of door handles—a loss of concentration*

Some Inspectors would have mentioned the light in the first few seconds, some would never have seen it. Know your Inspector when examining property—better still, find the lights that had been left on.

The routine of gripping door handles, peering through, or at, windows, trudging down alleys, rattling padlocks—all whilst moving at a steady pace thinking half thoughts about anything other than police work could, and did, lead to a loss of concentration. The Constable working Magdalen Street from St. Saviour's Lane to Fye Bridge had a consistent run of lock-up properties until he arrived at the junction with Fishergate, and an appointment with Twenty Nine Pillarphone at eleven p.m. The night he was thinking of other things was the night he forgot that one door handle in that long stretch of door handles did not belong to something that should be locked; not at a little after half past ten.

His rhythm was even and uninterrupted by other matters challenging for attention: turn door handle, lean weight on door—move on, repeat at next building—move on. He forgot the 'Jack of Newbury' public house and a crowd of last minute drinkers were astonished to see the door fly open and a uniformed policeman dive into the saloon bar and sprawl full length at their feet. The landlord must have wondered if it was a raid using new tactics but the now thoroughly alert Constable mumbled some kind of explanation, or it may have been a threat related to closing time, and left to find a door handle that didn't open a door. He wasn't the first policeman to stagger through a door that opened unexpectedly. But not everyone had an audience.

Some officers were not so adept at finding an opening door and this included 'the mobile' (traffic car), C.I.D. and other assorted upholders of the law dispatched to Mountergate in response to a report that there was suspicious activity on the wharf. A strong metal fence of formidable height prevented immediate entry, which was exactly its intention, and a number of eager officers crowded outside the padlocked gates debating the dangers to life and limb inherent in scaling them.

The C.I.D. were the keenest, or the Crime Car driver was. He had reached the top of the gates and was anxiously negotiating the metal prongs in a straddled position, bringing feelings of acute discomfort to an attentive circle of spectators, whilst a brave uniformed Constable was spreadeagled in spider fashion half way up the fence wondering how he could return without loss of face, when, the beat Constable arrived having been apprised by a flashing pillarphone of happenings on his patch.

The beat Constable studied the assembly at the gate, taking particular note of a plain clothes officer who appeared in grave danger of being impaled, and walked past—along the continuing fence. As a number of eyes watched, including a pair that were beginning to water, he moved towards the fence and then suddenly reappeared on the other side before moving back to offer assistance from the inside to one perched on the main gate. A startled group of police officers shuffled sheepishly through a small gate inset in the fence and pretended not to hear the strong language coming from the top of the main gate.

Irregularities did not always involve doors, windows and lights. The night the electricity failed at the Co-op in St. Stephen's Street the keyholder (he was also the manager) attended and mournfully pronounced the inevitable loss of all refrigerated products. They were perfectly all right, and would be for some time, but he would not be allowed to sell them. Would the officer like to take some away?

If the Co-op had been the scene of the greatest criminal enterprise in the annals of the city it could not have attracted more police attention than it saw in the three quarters of an hour following the condemnation and offer. Mobile, C.I.D., Sergeants, the Inspector, adjoining beat Constables wishing to assist the search for intruders (but also acting as proxy shoppers for those ordering through the switchboard): they all came and went and the manager found that he didn't have a disposal problem.

Billy was the War Reserve Constable working in the canteen on this bountiful night and he was over employed cooking prime steak, choice cutlets and the like, as the night shift dined as never before, or again. At six a.m., cycle pannier bags were bulging as the riders headed homewards to announce a housekeeping supplement. The early turn shift were driven frantic by the smells that lingered in the canteen.

Giving assistance to a keyholder was all part of the service but it was not always required and the best of intentions could sometimes have unfortunate results. 'Rimp' was a keen Constable who did not ignore his property responsibilities and had proved it by his studious attention to

44

'Ruymps', the ironmongers, and his subsequent identification of the premises as 'Rimps'—hence the nickname. He was a very popular officer; well known for his humour in unusual situations, of which he had a fair share; but it was his calm, philosophical, what could be called matter of fact, approach to difficult circumstances that endeared him to colleagues and public. He adopted this realistic reasoning when faced with the problem of finding an insecure in the second half of the night, because the most likely explanations were an intruder or a less than adequate turn of the door handle in the first half of the night.

Rimp was at the rear of a small office building in Vauxhall Street, accessed via a yard which belonged to a different century which was in turn flanked by minor outbuildings of doubtful origin. The front, inside and rear of the building appeared to be in order—no forced entry and no disturbance or sign of interference, but, the rear door was unlocked. This was not something to discuss with a Sergeant or Inspector, they would not understand, probably go on about dereliction of duty or something totally unrelated to the true circumstances which were likely to be innocuous without any blame attaching to the beat Constable. Keyholder had possibly called back for something and failed to put the latch on the door before leaving. No need to cause a fuss by calling him out at four o'clock in the morning.

Rimp decided that everybody's interests would be best served, particularly his own, by releasing the lock and slamming the door. No one

*Intent on a quick retreat from the night air*

would be any the wiser and the premises, which had clearly survived the period of insecurity, would be secure—it wasn't much of an office anyway, nothing worth stealing or likely to attract burglars.

Rimp slammed the door, turned the handle to check it was truly locked, and moved to leave the yard. He immediately became aware of a noise unrelated to his movements—a flushing toilet. A door opened from one of the minor outbuildings and a pyjama clad figure stepped into the yard and headed briskly towards the main building intent on a quick retreat from the night air. He failed to make it, finding, to his evident surprise, a locked door and a policeman standing nearby wishing he was somewhere else. The discussion that followed related to keyholders who lived above premises without telling the police; it also covered outside toilets, building access, interfering policemen and how cold it was at night. Rimp left; well, the building was secure.

When is a building secure but insecure? A conundrum that tested a few officers when balanced window displays became unbalanced, sometimes with a considerable knock-on effect. The phenomena of rogue window displays was arrived at through internal strain or outside vibration—traffic or human inspired. Large windows and pyramid displays of tins, notable in grocery shops, attracted youths who found that consistently bouncing their bodies, mainly the posterior, against the window could flex the glass and reverberate it into the carefully mounted display. The resulting movement of three hundred tins of baked beans, running wild in a balanced display of varying grocery products, gave much joy to the window bangers and acute displeasure to the shopkeeper who had engineered the original construction.

On rare occasions the insecure found the Constable, or the creator did. Put another way, the burglar appeared without detecting the presence of the very one he should have been looking out for.

The Two Beat man was taking time off to rest in Old Post Office Yard, which was even darker than the adjoining Bedford Street, and was contemplating all manner of things far removed from police work when his thoughts were forced to return to his employment by a pair of legs carefully negotiating their way down the drainpipe alongside him.

When leaving premises you have broken into it is all very well looking up and down the road, or yard, but you are strongly advised to look immediately below, especially if that is where you are going to land. Next stop Bethel Street.

Visible and noisy scheduled working rarely achieved the element of surprise but, go to ground for a rest or a smoke and anything can happen. The Constable tucked into a doorway in Swan Lane (Two Beat again) in the middle of the night was most interested to observe the shop door immediately opposite open and a man sidle out casting anxious looks up and down the lane. The chase that followed took in a fair proportion of the city centre but the conclusion was the right one. Bethel Street again.

The problems that attended insecure property came in many forms and often arose because of the need to search the interior—the unknown.

The Sergeant visiting two Constables (one was a probationer being shown round) at Twenty Eight Pillarphone, situated at the murky junction of St. Mary's Plain and Duke Street, instigated a three way discussion (more likely two way, probationers only spoke when spoken to) which held the attention of all until it was noticed that the door of the corner shop opposite was ajar. This discovery was enhanced by a scuffling noise from inside. The order of squeezing past the door, which seemed to be wedged, was Constable, probationer, Sergeant. The order was instantly reversed as the scuffler appeared as a large dog bounding forward in a mood of unbridled ferocity. The Constable only just made it.

To return to Two Beat which was, apparently, full of incident and insecurity. The Bridewell Museum was, and is, a significant building and finding the side door open was an invitation to the unknown. The discovering Constable, who did not regard himself as fortunate in his discovery, was at least in possession of a new Ever Ready torch. Plumbing the uninviting blackness with a Wootton lamp would have been an exercise in blindness.

The interior was quiet, but pitch black, with only the vague shape of old looms accompanied by a musty smell of old clothes. Suddenly, movement from behind the Constable as he crept forward. He swivelled and the beam of the torch caught two ghostly green eyes. Then, a flurry of movement and something landed alongside him. He dropped the torch and found himself in total darkness as the single beam disappeared. Cursing at the much publicised heavy duty qualities of the torch he groped around for a light switch only to find that a mains switch had obviously been employed.

The Two Beat man trapped in the museum had two objectives. Find his torch and get out of the place. After tangoing with a dummy that he had not expected to find he came into contact with something furry and warm. A purring and "Miaow" told him who to blame for the loss of the torch. Eventually, he found the door and exchanged inside darkness for the outside variety. How to get his torch? The keyholder was the answer. Off to Twenty Two Pillarphone, opposite Exchange Street, and a report of an insecure.

"Wait until we contact the keyholder" was the instruction.

The light then flashed with a reply, one that the Constable did not like. "If everything is all right, pull the door. It will lock on the Yale".

No way was the Constable going to lock his torch in the museum. Inspiration followed desperation. "Tell the keyholder I heard something. May have been an entry. Will require him to check".

"OK. Return to scene. Await keyholder". That was better. The Constable returns to museum, cat and, hopefully, torch.

Eventually, the reluctant keyholder arrives on a cycle only to wonder at the keenness of a Constable who insists on turning on all available lights and searching the floor space. The end result was a secured museum, more relaxed cat and a Constable in the station explaining that his "bulb had blown". He also got a cup of tea for his nerves.

Two Beat again, and Terry was the Constable exploring its mysteries. He was working B schedule and on course for an uneventful full check of his property as he approached the Maddermarket Theatre at ten past one in the morning. Another twenty minutes and he should be finished, then, ten past two it was refreshments.

It happened; an insecure. The side door of the Maddermarket was unlocked; a box lock with the key inside. A search of the premises was necessary and Terry began to explore with the aid, if that is the right word, of his feeble Wootton lamp.

Terry was level headed and uncomplicated in his view of life's mysteries and human frailties, not impressionable or given to wild flights of fancy. He knew the Maddermarket Theatre was a centuries old building with a distinguished history, but it was as an enquiring policeman doing his duty that he entered and ferreted around the building rather than a patron of the arts overwhelmed with a sense of history. He had no reason to change his attitude after an uneventful search of what was, admittedly, a very interesting place. Racks of period costumes showed the wide range of performances that were conducted in the compact theatre. However, it had to be the keyholder. The station was duly informed, but it seemed that Two Beat keyholders were a retiring lot. The instructions were to conduct a thorough search, lock the door and deposit the key at the Police Station.

Terry began to check the theatre again and found himself in the costume room, which was long and narrow with a sturdy metal rack running the full length. It was crammed with clothes of all descriptions, from full dresses to blouses and evening capes. At the far side was a sash window and he wandered in that direction to make sure that it was fully secured. To this day he cannot explain the sudden chill that ran through his body accompanied by the feeling of hair standing up on the back of his neck. The whole room had become very cold.

He called out "Anyone about?", at the same time casting the impoverished Wootton lamp in different directions. The light made for shadows but he was then aware it was not all related to his lamp. The costumes on the rail were moving, individually, from the window onwards, and towards him. The impression was that an invisible person was walking slowly towards him pushing each costume as it passed.

Terry was now seized by an uncontrollable urge to leave. He fled, closing the door behind him, and such was his speed that he ran into two other Constables walking up Gaol Hill towards Bethel Street for refreshments. They remarked that he looked as if he had seen a ghost, which did not go down very well. When they were invited to return with him to the Maddermarket they declined on the grounds they would be late for refreshments. A white faced Terry then went off to make a considerable impression on his Sergeant.

Ancient buildings, and their areas, were forbidding at night. The Thirteen Beat man's discovery of a complete circle of footprints in the snow in the Cathedral Close, no entry or exit marks, was never solved.

A small office equipment shop in Pitt Street was far removed from the mystique of the Maddermarket or Cathedral, but it was found insecure by the early turn beat Constable and this raised a number of questions, the first being what was the early man doing in contact with door handles? Usually this could be answered by the identity of the officer concerned.

Peter, the discoverer of the unlocked door, was known for his quiet manner and conscientious duty which would have caused him to wring a few door handles as he passed along the street; either that or it was subconscious, not entirely unknown in an employment that spent a lot of time reaching out to door handles. Having found the insecure he now had the problem that has been discussed before. Had the night man missed it or had something happened that now required police attention?

A check of the premises and its upstairs flat seemed to be required. That looked straightforward enough, for the shop belonged firmly in the pokey group; forming part of a building that had seen much poverty, if not actually contributing to it. It was the sort of place you could search without moving very far. Nevertheless, Peter was to have assistance in the person of his Sergeant, Johnnie, who has previously turned up when he was not wanted.

The equation of small shop and large policemen, although Peter was not in the same area of size as Johnnie, did not lead to a comfortable passage from one point to another. This was amply demonstrated as Johnnie moved purposefully through the shop intending to access the stairs to the upstairs flat. His shoulder caught a shelf which became dislocated from its bearings and crashed onto a lower shelf, which in turn refused to accept the extra responsibility. Stationery and office equipment of varying descriptions scattered across the shop, creating in the confined space a scene that could only have been equalled by the proverbial china shop bull or a quantity of dynamite.

The occupier was roused from his flat by two anxious policemen wondering how he had slept through the resounding succession of crashes on the lower floor. It did not remain a mystery as he explained that he had entertained friends the previous night in what he called a "drinking party". He presumed they had left the door unlocked when they left in the early hours; he also presumed they had been extremely disorderly in the manner of their going.

It was not necessary to be in uniform to find premises insecure. Late one Christmas night, the plain clothes patrol (two Constables extracted from the night shift) wandered along Waggon and Horses Lane and noticed a window open at the side of the Samson and Hercules ballroom. The building was closed, or should have been, and it was suspicious.

Roy and Basil (the dog lover) were keen to justify the mantle of plain clothes and decided to investigate further. They were in the process of struggling through the window when an elderly couple walked past looking rather dubious about the less than normal method of entry to the ballroom. Explanations and warrant cards followed: Christmas greetings were exchanged and the public spirited citizens went on their way. If only

49

Roy and Basil had known how public spirited these good citizens were!

Entry was completed and the inside of the ballroom appeared to be in order. The open window was apparently a lapse on the keyholders' or an employee's part. No need to hang around; but a large empty ballroom is an impressive place and the sight of the trappings of a full orchestra on the bandstand was too much for the curiosity of the plain clothes men. They moved into various seating positions behind the musical instruments, Roy on wind and Basil on drums, and began to explore individual, and apparently doubtful, talents; resulting in a cacophony of noise considerably removed from anything that might be called music.

How long this distorted orchestral rendering would have lasted is not known because the ballroom was suddenly full of uniforms and Roy and Basil were very quickly arrested. They were just as quickly identified as the plain clothes patrol and released with critical comment from the Sergeant covering their actions, both on and off stage.

An Englishman's home is his castle and if he left it for a significant period it was not a case of pull up the drawbridge and hope for the best; the best attentions of the Norwich City Police were available through hands and eyes that had clutched handles and peered through windows of innumerable commercial premises. The Unoccupied House Register was carefully maintained, with suburban lists ever growing in response to open advertisement to let your friendly policeman know when you were away. It did not escape the notice of some people that the less than friendly criminal could identify unoccupied houses by watching the beat Constable working his way down the road.

In July and August the beat men working outer areas of the city would have a considerable amount of individual property to check, something that was not easily avoided because Sergeants and Inspectors were always asking about "unoccupieds"; not that it was regarded as a tiresome task in certain areas where curiosity as to how the other half lived could be fulfilled in an official capacity, at the same time enjoying the pleasures of secluded tranquility and garden furniture.

A certain bored and weary early turn Constable was only too pleased to explore a splendid suburban garden endowed with an enticing orchard and even more tempting hammock. On a lovely summer's day it was more than flesh and blood could stand. Placing his cycle in a discreet position he selected the best Cox's, removed his helmet, undid his tunic and slumped into the hammock to enjoy the sun's warming rays. At peace with the world, soaking up warmth and nourishing juices, he was faintly aware of a voice. Through half closed eyes he tracked its origin to the upper part of the house where he focused upon a head and shoulders framed in an open window. By process of delayed action he was aware that the voice was inquiring whether he was comfortable and was also concerned over the quality of the apples. Sitting bolt upright he knew he was about to receive confirmation that a certain holidaymaker had returned home early.

The Constable who examined the house listed as unoccupied and

50

found a rear patio door insecure could find no marks or sign of forcible entry. Everything inside the well appointed lounge appeared to be in order, including a fine drinks cabinet which showed that the householder was far removed from a teetotal or poverty stricken existence. The Constable, who had done his duty in finding the house insecure, decided to reward himself with a sherry before setting off to ring in for a keyholder. He poured a generous measure of the glowing nectar and occupied an easy chair to reflect upon the unexpected pleasures of police work. The opening of an inner door, and the appearance of a puzzled looking householder, interrupted his meditation. Another one home early. Holidays must be lacking in appeal.

Policemen were human beings, despite some assertions to the contrary, and they did not like falling through doors, being impaled on fences, locking out incontinent flat dwellers, upsetting ghosts and wrecking shops; neither did they wish to purloin apples and sherry from householders recovering from a miserable holiday. They desired the simple life of secure property on a beat. Boredom was better than insecure and into trouble.

# From A to B and Vice Versa

MOVING FROM one location to another within the confines of the Norwich City Police area usually presented few problems. One foot in front of the other achieved the objective; a sedentary movement which proved advantageous to those senior officers who moved at a more rapid pace with the assistance of a cycle or car. However, there were opportunities for speed, exploration and disappearance over large territories through the official issue of two wheels.

Police cycles were heavyweight machines without gears and they had to be approached with care. Smaller Constables could be seriously disadvantaged by grabbing a machine from the station racks without appreciating that the previous user was significantly taller. The inevitable result was the unedifying spectacle of a representative of the law frantically trying to hit the pedals on the up stroke in order to maintain momentum. This puppet like progress on the tank like machine was doomed and the rider would topple into the kerb before trudging back to the station in search of a spanner or replacement cycle.

Normally, the majestic approach of the law upon a cycle was a little like watching a slow motion film. The scene could be one of utter confusion with distressed and disorderly persons participating in a miscellaneous medley of opposing action, yet the arrival of the uniform on a cycle would be a symphony of unhurried smoothness. Keep the dignity even if you don't know where to start.

Dignity, and the myth of indestructibility, collapsed when a Constable cycling in Dereham Road changed from an astride position to a one pedal scoot preparatory to dismounting. The one pedal snapped and a bored bus queue was enlivened by the sight of a somersaulting Constable and cartwheeling cycle.

Some officers were more disposed to cycles than others. 'Flash' was a cheerful and vigorous Sergeant who seemed welded to a cycle and was aptly nicknamed because of his speed on the machine. He epitomised cycling and would have given the Milk Race a run for its money.

You could guarantee at least two visits from Flash during a tour of duty but such was the speed of arrival and departure discussion should have been previously anticipated, if not rehearsed. When Flash was moving he was not easily diverted, as a drunk lying in Westwick Street found to his cost one night. He had the tyre marks to prove it.

Flash's affinity for the cycle was demonstrated one evening when he visited the beat Constable outside the Samson and Hercules ballroom. He chose to remain seated on the cycle, with his foot against the kerb, awaiting the Constable's pocket book. (A not unusual state of affairs for it was always difficult to part Flash from his beloved cycle). The Constable removed the pocket book from his tunic pocket with the intention of recording the time and visiting supervisor. Flash waited to sign this important record, and various members of the public walked or staggered past. The staggering types were emerging from the ballroom having been satiated with liquor, foxtrots and girls, but there must have been an excess of one or the other because a scuffle developed and the Constable felt compelled to take some restraining action. This provided some conflict of interest, for one hand was clutching a pocket book that Flash was patiently waiting to receive and the other was firmly gripping a member of the public who wished to fight the world; starting with the policemen who was choking him.

The Constable became intent on calming the excitable one to the exclusion of Flash who merely wished to sign the pocket book and found the whole business rather inconvenient. Different objectives and they had difficulty in coming together. The Constable danced back and forth along the pavement maintaining his grip on what he considered the more immediate problem—at the same time managing to release a hand waving a pocket book. Flash remained firmly on his cycle and made a series of unsuccessful clutches before his timing coincided with a passing movement of the pavement strugglers. He signed the book and, with improved timing, managed to return it as the Constable and his struggling subject passed yet again. The strict order of Flash leaving and the Constable subduing the now exhausted reveller is slightly unclear; but the visit was recorded, that was the main thing.

Flash did come unstuck on one occasion, literally. In the early hours of a cold frosty morning he approached the beat man at Twenty Nine Pillarphone in Fye Bridge Street by accelerating downhill from Wensum Street, preparatory to the short rise onto Fye Bridge and then the usual swerving flourish into the kerb where he would sit back on the saddle waiting for the Constable's declaration as to the state of the beat. It was the usual approach which, despite the speed, would be judged to the very inch of its juddering arrival before the target who would be reaching for his pocket book in a detached and unimpressed manner—he had seen. it all before.

Speed on a frosty morning, on an unused road, over changing levels with sudden braking and movement to one side, can, and did, produce a very definite result, namely, the loss of adhesion. Flash was on his final approach on the down side of the bridge, engaged in rapid deacceleration as he moved to the nearside, when his rear wheel found a new direction causing the cycle to lay down in the road and shoot off at a tangent. Flash did not go with it but continued along the road in a semi-sitting position in his original direction, passing an interested Constable holding a pocket book.

A Constable, whose tour of duty had brightened up somewhat, assisted in the reunification of rider and cycle at the same time making solicitous enquiries as to the state of health of both. No undue damage, visibly that is, and the main thing was that Flash signed the pocket book before riding off at a reduced, and slightly unsteady, pace.

Albert was a Sergeant (later Inspector) partial to the occasional use of a cycle, and welcomed as a kindly and sociable visitor to the beat Constable; but he caused problems by parking his cycle, initiating an amiable conversation, and then retreating on foot. If the Constable did not call him back it was an abandoned police cycle, until found by another, or memory and Albert returned.

There was an almost unique occasion when an Inspector was seen riding a cycle. This had to be and was 'Crackers', sometimes known as 'Crackerjack'. A nickname bestowed upon an Inspector of short stature but fierce temperament. The nickname had obscure origins but related more to fireworks than Christmas.

One night, somewhere around the hour of midnight, he was seen, quite inexplicably, weaving his way through the silent, gloomy and relatively unused thoroughfare of Peacock Street on a cycle. His intention was to see the Fourteen Beat Constable, which he duly did; but not before the Constable had seen him. A meeting was recorded without comment— the Constable could not think of anything that would cover this Columbus like occasion.

That Crackers should next be discovered cycling through the narrow and confining blackness of St. Faiths Lane on Thirteen Beat can only reflect a certain determination on his part. The beat Constable in St. Faiths Lane retained his composure and reported the state of his beat to a breathless Crackers who triumphantly replied, "Bet you didn't expect to see me on this", indicating the record breaking cycle.

The Constable studied the unusual sight and carefully replied, "Sir, nothing that you do will surprise me".

Crackers thought about that reply and then returned the cycle to the station.

Motor cycles also provided a means of A to B, or B to A, mixing metaphors and Divisions. Allocated to a large suburban area they could be found just about anywhere, often calling at a Police Station because their usefulness was such that they were much used for messenger duties; also for a faster response to incidents that had failed to attract the beat man via the flashing pillarphone. Our conscientious ratepayer was not always on hand.

After an early flirtation with BSA machines the famous whispering Velocettes became the regular steeds. The later versions were labelled 'Police', just in case there was any doubt as to the identity of the rider.

They were not very popular with criminals because they could not hear them coming. Senior ranks found them awkward because they could not always track them down; they moved too quickly and their convenience attracted extra work which was often an excuse for missing a ringing-in point—much to the chagrin of the waiting senior rank.

A fair proportion of Constables liked the motor cycle and sought after the role. It provided variety and rested the feet. An extra two weeks of days on the beats rota was also welcome. Unfortunately, a motor cycle policeman wore out his right boot at twice the normal rate and inclement weather was further aggravated upon a set of wheels, especially when the consistent use previously mentioned meant there was little chance of seeking dry and undisturbed shelter. During very bad winters the Velocette man wore so many clothes that if he fell down he was in danger of imitating a large beetle on its back, incapable of rising unassisted. He certainly eroded his refreshment period by the time taken to divest outer clothing.

Riding a motor cycle meant that lock-up property could be scanned at a fast and inefficient rate. The Ring Road premises of an oil company conveniently left a boundary chain on the ground which allowed the motor cyclist to sweep in off the main road, circle the premises, try a door handle without getting off the machine, and ride out onto the road again. Very convenient and much appreciated until the night the chain was left in the up position. The police motor cyclist failed to detect this unusual state of affairs and consequently the motor cycle went into the premises without him. He remained at the chain.

The motor cycle could be an asset or handicap when catching criminals. The Mile Cross motor cyclist was shooting through Hellesdon Hall Road, very rural and badly lighted, when he saw two bag carrying figures walking quickly in the opposite direction. A smart about turn and he was upon them before they had time to flee. He was actually upon them too quickly because the motor cycle did not stop in time and pinned them against a convenient wall, then, from the jaws of victory came defeat. The motor cycle, having exhausted its impetus, slowly toppled sideways, leaving its rider pinned beneath it and the bag carriers free to disappear into the night. The motor cyclist picked himself up and the C.I.D. picked up the bag carriers the next day.

Exciting new areas were speedily accessed by the Velocette; including Mousehold Heath in the early hours when the ability of the rider could be tested through narrow tracks, up and down hills, along ravines and gullys, all in unspoilt heathland away from the potentially horrified gaze of the public. (Whatever happened to the byelaws learnt at the Lads Club?).

Occasionally, the public appeared in the form of a courting couple. They would be taken by surprise and then ardour dampened by the sudden appearance of a motor cycle charging ghost like through the grass in an area believed to be restricted from the view of others. Was that really a policeman on that motor cycle? Was it a motor cycle? It was upon them and gone before the engine was heard. Whatever it was, love's dream would not be the same again. It should also be said that the police motor cyclist did not like the sudden swerves necessary to avoid the bodies. It spoiled his concentration.

The Velocette was also a goods vehicle on an internal ferry system, carrying in its panniers briefing documents for outlying stations and the refreshments of men parading for duty at one station but scheduled to obtain sustenance at another. Unhappy was the officer who found his delicate egg sandwiches had been crushed during their confinement in the pannier. Even more unhappy was the owner of refreshments discharged from an overloaded container into a following stream of traffic.

Motor cycles and cycles sometimes came together with advantages for the cyclist. Aylsham Road was the scene. A long, fairly straight stretch of road from Mile Cross Section Box at Woodcock Road to St. Augustines Gates where Thirty Seven Pillarphone awaited the early morning visits of the cycle beat man (Aylsham Road to Sprowston—Twenty Three and Twenty Four Beats), and the motor cycle beat man (Aylsham Road to Dereham Road—Twenty and Twenty One Beats). Two fifty a.m. for the motor cycle and three five a.m. for the cyclist. The latter should have long cleared his refreshment period but he was disposed to hang about and move down the Aylsham Road in the company of the motor cyclist.

At this time in the morning the cyclist's hand on the motor cyclist's shoulder provided an effective and unobserved tow. It had to be unobserved for the obvious reasons of legality and a lack of understanding from outside sources. No problem really, nothing much moved at that time in the morning and, if it did, it was liable to be animal, criminal or behind a Wolseley engine. The Sergeant would be waiting at the pillarphone or approaching it form the direction of snooker and sandwiches. More likely the latter.

Came the morning a small motor cycle containing a bleary eyed civilian defied the normal reasoning and appeared from Berners Street into Aylsham Road, accelerating smartly towards St. Augustine's Gates. The rider did not see the police twosome in the distance, and failed to hear the whispering Velocette above his own engine. Neither did he see it later, because the police motor cycle turned off before reaching him. What he did see was a pedal cycle rocket past him with a Constable freewheeling and calmly looking around as if 40mph was his normal speed on a cycle.

The civilian motor cyclist definitely noticed. His erratic progress onto the pavement and back to the road showed that the rapidly disappearing cyclist had made a nerve shattering impression. He had, however, recovered control as he approached the traffic lights at St. Augustine's Gates, but his nerve had clearly gone. The sight of the Constable standing by the pillarphone with a perfectly ordinary cycle was too much and he missed the red light pointing in his direction, swerving violently to go round a milk float that was trundling across his path following its own green light.

From two wheels to three. The first patrol cars were BSA three wheelers. These were later replaced with Austin 10's with a folding dickey seat and the sensible allocation of a wheel at each corner. One of these in a hurry with two burly policemen in the back holding on to helmets was real Keystone Cops progress. By the forties the more impressive and substantial Wolseleys were in being.

Although the Wolseleys were imposing vehicles, and gave little trouble, a very senior rank complained that the new model was giving out a regular thumping noise from underneath. Detailed examination by the mechanic revealed nothing until it was mentioned that Newmarket Road was the best place to hear the offending noise. All was then revealed—a new device called 'cat's eyes' had just been fitted along this road. No further comment from very senior rank.

An even more substantial four wheeled transport was available—a bus; the fact they were not owned by the police was a mere detail. Firstly, there was the convenience of a large red (or any other colour) double decker bus. (Single deckers were awkward to hop onto with any vestige of accuracy or dignity). Obviously a daytime advantage, but one which had a ready availability. Just step to the edge of the pavement and look the approaching driver in the eye at the same time inclining the left hand outwards. Not a proper stop signal, but a request. The driver understood and responded by slowing down. There followed the art of timing the handrail on the running board. Usually no problem, but if the grab was too vigorous and the bus speed too great it was possible to arrive alongside the conductor in an ignominious heap. Worse still, the impetus of clutching the handrail could promote a complete revolution giving pedestrians and following traffic the riveting sight of a double decker bus with the accessory of a spinning policeman.

Buses were reliable and you knew where they were going. Very handy when heading towards the main station at Bethel Street for that most important appointment with refreshments—provided of course your Velocette man had not inadvertently deposited them under another bus. One such Constable, who began his Bethel Street journey from the upper reaches of Magdalen Street, was prompted to leap nimbly aboard a convenient bus by the first drops of heavy rain. Perfectly reasonable when you appreciate that his top coat was at Magdalen Gates Police Station, he was hungry, and rain had not been forecast. Only one problem. The Inspector was afoot (it must have originally been a nice day), heading up Magdalen Street intending to make a significant visit to the Constable.

That the Inspector was on a collision course was, of course, unknown to our young Constable now leaning casually upon the bus platform chatting to the conductor. The sudden driving rain was emptying the pavements, and there was still the distance form the bus stop to the Police Station to be negotiated. Future plans were, however, temporarily forgotten as the bus slowed in traffic, and the Constable gazed directly into a very familiar face. A face peering from a shop doorway and wiping an Inspector's cap.

The misfortune was compounded by the fact that the Inspector happened to be Crackers and his temper was obviously not improved by his misjudgement of the weather. Further aggravation was the phenomena of a wet Inspector and dry Constable. The final blood vessel bursting act was the action of the Constable. As the bus passed the trapped Inspector the Constable stood on the running board with one hand on the handrail and the other alongside his helmet in the most respectful of salutes.

Crackers actually made very good time to the Police Station to discuss the matter with a dry and refreshed Constable. The discussion was a bit one sided, they usually were with Crackers, and centred around the use of public transport to the consequent neglect of the public. A counter view that as the public were on the transport in question they were not being neglected was not well received. At no time was the weather mentioned.

Policemen were great improvisers. The Constable at Foundry Bridge who wished to catch the boy who had set all the boats adrift from the yacht station had a problem inasmuch the juvenile delinquent was sitting astride a cycle, several hundred yards into Riverside Road, cheerfully watching the fruits of his labours. An undetected approach and capture was apparently impossible with the getaway cycle at the ready.

One young anti-social youngster was considerably surprised when a passing milk float revealed a large policemen who made the most of the element of surprise.

A beat Constable did not usually contemplate thirty years on the pavements. He rather hoped to be chosen for something special or different before rheumatism and flat feet took their toll. That something special could be promotion or a transfer to the C.I.D., or 'the mobile'. This latter term was the recognised reference to the Traffic Department, or at least that part of the Traffic Department that glided around the city in sleek Wolseley limousines.

The mobile was the most coveted piece of elitism and it had built in comforts. With nearly every officer using foot or cycle to get to work it was very nice to climb into a status symbol and be cosseted in sumptuous leather to the exclusion of bad weather and prowling senior ranks. Sometimes, you could ring the bell and scythe through the traffic with that superior air reserved for rescuers, dragon slaying knights and other like folk. You also got to wear a peaked cap and black leather gloves.

The C.I.D. had a car which, to the disgust of the mobile drivers, was often driven at furious speed without consideration for those inside or outside the vehicle. They also had two bus passes which were rarely seen because the Detective Inspector always had a prior use.

A transfer to the C.I.D., or the mobile, did require some adoption of new habits and the understanding of a new language. C.I.D. officers spoke of 'coughing' and 'singing' when they meant the same thing. A person who 'croaked' had a terminal condition rather than a throat complaint, and a 'snout' was someone who talked as opposed to something that sniffed.

Mobile officers talked about tenths of a mile and abnormal loads. Abnormal did not just mean weighty and awkward—they could behave in an abnormal way. The escorted tank was an example; it was not as if it was armed or tearing along on its tracks; it was inert and harmless, loaded onto a low loader lorry and escorted by a shiny black Wolseley with two flat capped, leather gloved, proud occupants.

The objective of a tank in the city centre was an Army recruiting campaign to be staged on open ground near the 'Woolpack' public house in Golden Ball Street. Logically the tank could not proceed under its own power for fear of alarming the populace and creating roadworks for a long time afterwards, but neither could it be deposited exactly on the display site from the carrying lorry. It was, therefore, decided to escort it to a narrow lane at the rear of the prearranged spot. There it would be unloaded and driven a short distance to the position where it could be admired and encourage the young men of the day to throw their lot in with the Army.

Escorting police cars must, of necessity, lead and clear the way, which meant that the pride and joy of the Traffic Department rolled into the approach lane and drove to the display site to turn round, preparatory to an exit and self congratulation on a job well done. The tank carrying lorry stopped at the beginning of the lane and the tank was unloaded.

It is not clear why the Wolseley was still at the other end of the lane when the tank moved off towards the display site. Unloading a tank is not a few seconds operation and it must be assumed that the unloading was extra efficient and the Wolseley's crew dallied at the display site with the natural curiosity that has both helped and hindered policemen through the ages. In this case it should not have been a problem. The Wolseley crew driving down the lane could clearly see the tank churning uphill towards them, its engine revving noisily and tracks grinding into hard ground. Presumably, the eyes peering from the aperture at the front of the armoured juggernaut meant that the tank driver could see the Wolseley and would stop to allow the car to pass. The narrowing lane meant that if he didn't quickly apply his brakes there would be no room and someone would have to reverse. The Wolseley stopped and the crew waited. The tank kept going and the eyes in the aperture now had a frantic gleam, which was nothing to the alarm that might have been experienced in the Wolseley if the occupants had known that the person at the helm of forty tons heading in their direction knew very little about driving tanks.

Just move it up the lane they had said. That was all he had to do. No one had explained the relation of hydraulic pressure to braking efficiency. Start it, steer it and stop it at the right place seemed simple enough; but life had become complicated by a police car that was sitting in the lane ahead with expectant faces gazing through the windscreen.

The expectancy changed to anxiety, and then to alarm, as the tank continued with the panic stricken eyes in the aperture giving a clue to the inadequate fumbling of limbs behind the metal casing. The tank was not going to stop and the policemen's contrary expectancy had left them little time to find reverse gear in the Wolseley. They left, quickly. Two doors flew open and two mobile officers scampered rearwards as the iron

*Just move it, they said*

monster climbed over the bonnet and stopped at the windscreen.

The eyes in the aperture surveyed the Wolseley roof and then disappeared to seek instruction on how to reverse a tank. The Wolseley crew inspected the damage and decided that it was beyond the scope of any panel beater and there was going to be a lot of writing.

The Station Sergeant, on receiving the news, ignored an element of merriment from other officers in the station and queried how an escort could have a head-on collision with the escorted. The Traffic Department contented itself with references to the British Army which were unlikely to have helped the recruiting campaign.

The march of progress, and wonders of modern technology, did not entirely escape the Police Force. Radios in cars was a great step forward, but the provision of public address equipment in the Wolseleys was altogether irresistible. The flick of a dashboard switch could carry other than the spoken word. One of the mobile drivers was fascinated with this new toy and held a large 'turnip' watch to the microphone causing pedestrians in the street to glance round in alarm to ascertain the origin of the heavy ticking that had suddenly filled the air. There was no reason to connect it with the slowly moving police car and a crew that seemed more cheerful than usual.

Passing, or slumbering, dogs were a target for another driver whose switch down, imitation bark, switch up sequence, brought many an innocent animal to the point of abject bewilderment or instant flight.

What did a mobile crew do over eight hours? They could not drive all the time; perpetual movement over the shift would cover enough mileage to seriously threaten the existence of the member producing the excess. Wolseley crews, having arrived, were not going to prejudice their appointment. Therefore, a number of sitting up periods were necessary, either on a main road—causing rapid deacceleration of passing traffic, or in a car type hiding place—where things could be smoked, eaten and discussed away from the prying eyes of the public. Even then they were not safe.

Kenny (not the horse chasing Kenny), was working Ten and Eleven cycle beats at Tuckswood on nights. He was a diligent officer quick to use his initiative and speak his mind, which had previously proved embarrassing to both law breakers and senior officers. Entering the complex of old ARP buildings next to Tuckswood Police Station Kenny was startled by the sudden illumination of car headlights directly in front of him. Had he disturbed villains about to make a getaway? Wyatt Earp would have been proud of the quickness of draw for within a split second the truncheon had left the trouser pocket and was speeding dead centre towards the lights in front of him.

If the car behind the headlights had been a getaway vehicle, packed with desperadoes intent upon escaping with their ill gotten gains, Kenny would have been a hero because the truncheon crashed onto the roof line above the windscreen completely unnerving the occupants. They left the vehicle very quickly, but, instead of fleeing into the night, they commenced an anxious and detailed examination of a police Wolseley which now sported a noticeable dent. They then undertook a detailed examination and appraisal of the truncheon thrower.

Kenny was philosophical. He recovered his truncheon and listened patiently to two mobile officers debating various avenues of escape from an all too obvious predicament. A plan was evolved.

It just so happened that the ARP buildings housed a motor engineer who was friendly and supportive of his local police force. Very friendly and very supportive he was about to become. The conspirators made a telephone call and awaited the arrival of their saviour. A garage was unlocked and a black Wolseley disappeared inside. Lights burned late that night and there was much banging, whirring, grinding and hissing of equipment. Eventually, the Wolseley reappeared with a smooth and shinier roof and faded into the early hours darkness of Hall Road. In those days Mr. Ford's words had real meaning. "You can have any colour you like as long as it's black".

There may have been problems on wheels but at least you could move smartly to avoid some of life's misfortunes.

# Excuse Me Officer

POLICE WORK traverses the encyclopaedia of life, no more so than when the public are having their input. After all, it is a public service; even though some of them do not want it. Suitable training and experience can make the service quite comprehensive and, therefore, training for eventualities appears at intervals in an officer's career. Some of it is speculative, and will, hopefully, never be required. Cometh the hour, cometh the man—or police officer.

It was not so much the hour that featured in higher thinking for an important course of 1950's training as four minutes. This was the time permitted for counter measures when obliteration of the United Kingdom was imminent, there being every reason to believe that the Norwich City Police area would not be exempt.

The training to combat this awesome prospect consisted mainly of lectures, and the presentation of daunting instruments with even more daunting names. The dosimeter was a prophet of doom for it was designed to measure radiation on the beat.

The early warning system was explained with instructions as to procedures that should follow the siren's warning, but these instructions never quite covered the inadequacy of the beat man in such circumstances. It was wryly remarked that if the Inspector had not signed the relevant report within the four minutes the whole event would have to be postponed.

The matter was put in perspective by Ted, a Constable with certain fishing and knife grinding abilities who was also renowned for his matter of fact views. Having sat through a detailed lecture covering his required movements within the relevant four minutes he dryly informed the lecturer that his own four minutes, and any extra that might be forthcoming, would be spent heading towards his own family. This point of view received much sympathy and effectively closed the lecture as far as it concerned a co-ordinated police response.

Public contact and organisation was vital and, thankfully, it was not tested by the ultimate threat being realised, an obvious statement in the light of the present ability to recount the facts. Defensive measures did, however, come very close one particular night when a Constable working the switchboard at Bethel Street Police Station decided, in agreement with a colleague, that too many lights were on in the station. Various switches were then employed to reduce the illumination, some obvious, some not so obvious. During the course of this switch throwing exercise the public siren was heard wailing. Obviously war had broken out, or a switch too many had been thrown.

The sequel was a replay of switches which included an unmarked specimen under the switchboard. End of noise from siren, but beginning of noise from other sources. It was two thirty a.m. and the Superintendent, who lived in a flat above the Police Station, had been awakened. His relief at discovering that he had not been targeted for early obliteration was replaced by anger at the interruption of his sleep; and concern at the possible reaction of the local population who would be unaware of the falseness of the alarm. That the Civil Defence and the Territorial Army were not massing outside the City Hall provided some relief, but raised the question whether anyone would notice if the siren went off for real.

A further problem for the unhappy switch thrower was that the Night Duty Inspector was Crackers, who had been in the process of inspecting his troops in the field (alias beat Constables) when the alarm went off. His return to the station to organise resistance was extremely fast, as was his speech when he discovered the true nature of the alarm. He advised the switch thrower of his future, or lack of it.

In addition to war training there was, of course, the need to qualify as a first aider. These sessions appeared at intervals during an officer's career and he usually found that knowledge gained from earlier courses was ruled invalid because someone had rewritten the book and what was anathema before was now recommended.

Policemen's abilities with slings and bandages was questionable, the victim tending to become restricted and tied up in a life threatening manner. Applying tourniquets was efficiently done, but often forgotten in a class situation where several practice roles were happening at once. The colour of the 'patient' and some unsuitable language would attract the instructor's attention and save the constricted limb, the zealous applier of the knot having lost interest and moved on to collarbones elsewhere in the room.

One highlight, savoured for some time afterwards, was the occasion when a Constable was selected to demonstrate in front of the class the circulation of blood using a diagram on a blackboard. He got so carried away with the description and graphics that he fainted and fell over the blackboard.

Having dismissed the possibility of the beats being restructured by some far off unfriendly power, and demonstrated the capability to sustain the public through unforeseen injury, it was a case of more immediate problems which conditioned a policeman's lot. Namely the public at large.

The beat Constable standing on a street corner, peaceably watching the world go by, was easily accessible to the public who tended to subdivide into "Excuse me officer, can you tell me" or "Excuse me officer, did you know?"

The first group was easy and innocuous. On a fine summer's day a queue of culture seeking tourists would form on the pavement, each requiring guidance to a notable place. The Cathedral, Castle and Elm Hill were favourites, with the predominance of first two upon the skyline having escaped the attention of most searchers. Commercial travellers and lorry drivers could be consigned in a rough compass direction of their required destination with an air of authority and, generally, everyone was happy.

In the late nineteen forties a stranger approached a uniformed Constable at Guildhall Hill and asked the way to Bethel Street. Quite incredibly it was the officer's first morning on the streets having arrived post haste on transfer from the Metropolitan Police the previous day. (His guiding Constable was no help for he was directing traffic at London Street crossroads). He apologised for not knowing the location required, and the stranger moved on to seek a more fruitful source of information. The new Constable did not move too far, mainly because he did not know where he was, and within a very short time the stranger reappeared. Fixing the Constable with an accusing glance he coldly asked if he had been taking the 'mickey' when failing to direct him to Bethel Street. More apologies and explanations before the stranger left with the parting shot, "Well I hope you find it soon because your Police Station is there."

Not all enquiries were straightforward; differing accents and pronounciations could cause difficulties. The officer who dealt with a request from an American airman for Sine-a-go-gee Street triumphed by directing him to Synagogue Street.

When dealing with the enquiring public it was necessary for the policeman to keep his wits about him in more ways than one. He could not expect support from even the most law abiding and fervent supporters of the police, as Ted, the disposer of the Civil Defence lecturer, found out. Now Ted was a taciturn individual not given to over elaboration and time wasting. He was also broad in stature and, therefore, not easily missed. These qualities were, however, insufficient to save him from an enquiring but slow witted member of the public whose lack of initiative was compounded by the narrowness of Charing Cross crossroads.

A middle aged Northern couple approached Ted at Charing Cross and courteously asked the way to the Cathedral. Very easy this one because it was not far and in a straight line as the crow flies. Fully conscious that he was not dealing with crows Ted very conscientiously turned in the Cathedral direction and was at pains to explain the slight deviation necessary to those heading there via the streets. Ted is, therefore, pointing, and the man is listening and looking in the appropriate direction. His wife is ancillary to the conversation and content with the view of A47 traffic fighting its way into the city through the narrow crossroads.

Ted's careful instructions are cut off in mid flow by a blow to his back which propels him forward and leaves the attentive listener without speech and speaker. What was routine and straightforward is no longer. Ted is grounded at the feet of the enquiring couple who immediately respond by helping him to his feet and dusting him down. The lady retrieves his helmet, which had taken off with a greater impetus than its more substantial owner, whilst the cause of the catastrophe, an open backed coal lorry, is observed proceeding blithely on into St. Andrews Street , its driver happily unaware that one of his overhanging sacks of nutty slack has just bowled over the law in all its majesty.

Ted is less than majestic as he re-orientates himself, adjusts his uniform and receives the helmet proffered by the lady. The likely follow-up would be consoling messages of sympathy from the Northern couple, and a renewal of Cathedral directions. However, this anticipated pattern is short circuited by the lady informing Ted that she had seen the coal lorry approaching and had noted that the overhanging sacks were on course to connect with him. Taken aback by this information Ted is rendered speechless by the final observation from the dear lady that she had not imparted information of the forthcoming collision because "I could see that you were busy talking and I did not like to interrupt". At this point an embarrassed husband decides that either he knows the way to the Cathedral or he does not really want to go there. Muttering thanks

*Careful instructions are cut off in mid flow*

65

and other apologetic phrases he hustles his lady away from Charing Cross and a bemused policeman.

The "Excuse me officer, did you know?" approach was potentially dangerous and often a prelude to embarrassment or work, or both. It included conversationalists who knew someone whose second uncle twice removed used to, or still did, serve on the force. Maybe they knew a serving Inspector or Sergeant, in which case they should be treated very carefully indeed. Quite often they were friends of the Chief Constable, although this type usually appeared behind the wheel of a car after some violation of the traffic laws. The Chief Constable had an amazing number of friends.

The street corner chatters occasionally wanted legal advice for a 'friend', although sometimes it was emphatically stated that they themselves were the victim of a horrible miscarriage of justice and what did the officer think of it. Usually, after recitation of the tale of woe, the officer thought that the complainant had got only just desserts, but diplomacy made for a quieter life. Very tricky this one. Solicitors charged twenty guineas for advice. The policeman in the street was free. Both could be quoted, but you could not embarrass a solicitor.

"Did you know" was often the opening shot of a public spirited citizen eager to impart information of an event which he had observed, but with luck and a speedy retreat would not involve him as a witness. It usually signified that the Constable did not know, but would soon have to find out.

There was a more pointed variation of this freedom of information theme, namely, "I think you are wanted down there". The messenger would then depart at a rapid rate leaving the recipient of the information wondering whether his peaceful tour of duty is about to be broken by recalcitrant motorists arguing over buckled metalwork or a drunk arguing over his right to stand in the road and direct traffic with a whisky bottle.

Rarely was the person providing the information an expert—a genuine expert. The man who knew about swans was, although he did not have to tell the Constable that one of these fine birds had landed in Tombland. He could see it. Why it should have chosen the tarmac and cobbles of Tombland to the River Wensum is a matter for the ornithologists; all the beat man knew was that a discomfited bird of awesome proportions had interrupted his late turn shift and was defying human interference. But there was the expert. This passing member of the public (who happened to be a well known television personality) stopped and picked up the aimless bird by folding its neck into its body. He then handed the now rounded package to the Constable advising him to keep a firm grip on the neck. Further instructions referred to the necessity for water before our expert departed the scene leaving a landlocked Constable tightly gripping a neck submerged in a large bundle of hissing feathers.

The Constable's journey to Fye Bridge was not without some strain brought about by sounds of swan type displeasure, but increased by the realisation that the river banks were unapproachable from that area.

66

Standing on Fye Bridge he was in the position of a man holding a grenade with the pin out. Passers-by waited for the next move with interest. Only one solution—the swan was unceremoniously launched from the bridge, plummeting into the river before its suddenly freed neck could obtain its bearings. Only dignity suffered; for both parties. The swan scuttled away up river leaving a Constable in stained uniform peering over the parapet reflecting upon his new found knowledge. It was, however, never to be required again. Disoriented swans missed the rest of his service.

Occasionally, the harbinger of news or advice would be thwarted by the absence of a uniform in the streets and would take time off to track one down in the most obvious place: a Police Station. Not just the main station at Bethel Street, but the smaller variety; Section Boxes and Magdalen Gates would yield an officer during the day. Clerking and public reception in these stations was a much prized duty, for it was warm, dry and restful with only a few Police Gazettes to index. It made a welcome change to working the beat, unless, of course, our fateful messenger landed in the office eager to provide news of a great disaster, and even more eager to observe the response.

Phil was the regular Constable Clerk at Magdalen Gates Police Station and he jealously guarded his domain, being particularly severe upon officers who performed evening or other stand-in duties without satisfactorily maintaining the high standards he set for the smooth running of 'his' Police Station. He was known to both colleagues and public for his great cordiality when dispensing advice and information to all who sought his counsel, and sometimes to those who did not seek it. He also made tea for the visiting beat man who was prepared to risk discovery by a visiting senior rank. His anxiety over the potential discovery of that beat man was only partly allayed by the word 'toilet' in the booking-in book. Some officers had a theme of incontinence and Phil worried for them.

The young Constable, not far removed from probation, who found himself as B Division Clerk at Magdalen Gates one evening could not believe his luck. Some senior rank had made a mistake on the duty sheet, or perhaps he had a friend in high places—he quickly ruled out this option. Whatever the reason, he was there. A comfortable evening in prospect. Make some tea, index a few gazettes, type a few reports (but more likely leave them for Phil the next day; he would not like the typing), answer a few routine callers before refreshments at ten p.m. followed by a cycle beat. Things were looking up for this Constable who should have remembered that luck has a habit of changing, and the beauty, or otherwise, of police work is that no one knows what is around the corner.

The young Constable Clerk had hardly made himself at home before the small station was full of people talking about a man with a gun. Realising that the expectant looks on the faces of the informants meant an end of clerking duty he duly locked the station and set off, at what he thought was a brisk pace, in the indicated direction.

Stump Cross was apparently the area where the gunman was disporting himself, although there was a paucity of detail which allowed a racing imagination to top up with all sorts of unsavoury circumstances that could effect the well being of this particular emissary of the law. Training School had provided a mass of complicated information concerning firearms, but the objective must be simplicity itself—ascertain which way the weapon is pointing before embarking on any dialogue.

Approaching the danger zone the Constable was aware that the informants had disappeared, but Stump Cross, a wide section of the road created by the divergence of Magdalen Street and Botolph Street, with bus stops on both sides, appeared normal—no crowd in evidence.

A double decker bus was stationary in Stump Cross at its appropriate stop, obviously heading out of the city taking the nine to fives and similar workers to their well earned evening meal and rest. Near the stationary bus a small group of people were staring at the vehicle in an intent state of fascination. They had the appearance of a bus queue, but they seemed loth to climb aboard. This was possibly connected with the absence of the driver and the movements of those already on the bus.

As the Constable approached he became aware of a strange ritual within the bus. On the lower deck it appeared empty, and then crowded as faces alternately rose and subsided from view beneath the window line. There also seemed to be some amount of scrambling from one side to the other, giving rise to the thought that if it had been a boat there would have been a danger of a capsize. It was both a moving and stationary bus. Although the up and down heads retained some stability they were

*A gunman disporting himself allowed a racing imagination*

obviously fighting for space with the side to side heads.

The cause of the moving heads phenomena was not difficult to find. It was a small inoffensive looking man who could be described as middle aged or elderly, depending on the age of the viewer. He was wearing a raincoat and carrying a paper bag. Positioned alternately in the road and on the pavement, he was circling the bus peering through the windows thereby producing a startling effect of an empty space where previously there had been a succession of faces pressed against the glass. The revolving, jostling mass of humanity inside the bus followed his outer progress, but evaporated as he stopped to look through a particular window. As he passed on to the next window faces gradually crept back into view. This mesmeric routine could have entertained non-participants for a considerable time, but the police uniform had been spotted by the audience. A conclusion was obviously expected.

The Constable went to the running board as the object of attention moved into another orbit at the front end of the bus—causing an evacuation of seats behind the driver's cabin. Both driver and conductor were on the running board and they quickly explained that they were letting no one on or off. The reason for this impasse was the circling bag carrier who was now approaching along the pavement side of the bus and was believed to be in possession of a gun, although details of the weapon and who had actually seen it were somewhat indistinct.

The Constable could not help but notice that as the small inoffensive looking man, alias gunman, approached, the bus queue showed a similar fluidity of movement to the bus passengers, visibly shrinking backwards into the deep recesses of Attoes furniture store and beginning an earnest study of G Plan exhibits which abated as the man of the moment passed.

It did not require any outstanding detective ability to see that the small inoffensive man was the catalyst for the whole series of bizarre actions, on and off the bus, and as he approached, the Constable prepared to speak to him.

"He's got a gun" a helpful voice cried.

The voice had taken away the Constable's opening line leaving him with the corollary question, "Have you?"

"Oh yes" replies the small man dipping into his carrier bag.

"Look out" cries the interfering voice.

People who had started to move forward, anxious not to miss out on the final spectacle, immediately went into reverse, and a crowded running board dissolved into an empty space. Heads that had risen above the window line vanished, and Attoes G Plan received a concentrated study from ground level.

Those who had expected a dramatic confrontation were about to be disappointed. Inoffensive looking man behaves inoffensively by handing the Constable a sawn off shotgun, explaining that he wished to impress the love of his life who is on the bus but is disinclined to talk to him. Apparently, she had become even more disinclined when he showed her the gun and her panic and consternation was shared by other passengers.

The conductor also did not approve, resulting in the gun toting suitor being ordered off the bus. Since then he had been prowling the outside of the vehicle hoping to spot his lady and renew his advances.

The lovelorn gunman explains that the gun was sawn down for convenience of carrying and its presence bears no relation to his intentions which are extremely honourable. He appears concerned over the fuss he has caused, admitting that his aggressive courting routine may have been unwise. He further agrees that a prompt visit to the Police Station is advisable. It has not escaped his notice that the crowd, consisting of passengers, prospective passengers and busybodies, have noted the gun in the hands of a uniform and are displaying a much closer and hardening attitude. The bus crew are particularly upset over the interruption to their schedule.

The lady love is identified and winkled out of the bus bemoaning her misfortune. She rues the day she first made contact with her admirer, who is, apparently, quite content now that he has her complete attention. The fact that he has the complete attention of many others is of little concern compared with the realisation of his objective.

The bus continues on its designated route and the man of the hour accompanies the Constable to Magdalen Gates Police Station. Barely has the station been unlocked when the Sergeant appears having heard all manner of tales, most of them wildly exaggerated. Explanations and questions are struggling for supremacy, with the ex-gunman appearing to be the most unconcerned man in the room. Cross questioning is suddenly interrupted by the discovery of a number of faces pressed against the the station window. Two of these appear vaguely familiar and when they appear in the doorway they are identified as C.I.D. officers.

The C.I.D. are very interested and ask if help is required. The Sergeant surprises the Constable, who thought criminal investigation was within the terms of reference of the department, by politely declining the offer and then ignoring their reluctance to leave the doorway. The star capture, because that apparently is what the small inoffensive ex-gunman now qualifies as, is moved to the back room where he shows a complete willingness to assist the Sergeant in his enquiries.

A simple clerking duty. Is nothing sacred? It all finishes at Quarter Sessions, but not before the small inoffensive ex-gunman, alias star capture, has revealed an unsuspected degree of cunning by giving vague directions concerning the burial of the sawn off barrel in his garden. This not only results in failure to trace this desirable exhibit but produces a completely dug garden ready for the next potato crop should the Recorder be minded to allow the owner access in the near future. He did.

The Courts provided an arena for examination of police, public and the high ideals of the much vaunted English judicial system. In theory the process dispensed truth, wisdom and, sometimes, justice to all parties. In practice it was a test of memory, temperament and mental stamina within a set of rules understood by few and feared by many.

Policemen were not exempt from the embarrassment of ineptitude, error and misjudgment, brought about by the sense of occasion, overpowering atmosphere and a right 'smart aleck" asking awkward questions; indeed, the formality of the proceedings, combined with the greater expectation of their official position, made them more prone to nervousness. Why is it that a brain that races in normal circumstances seizes completely because an assembly of wigs and gowns are framed within a room of historical furniture, and questions are being asked in stilted, cultured tones by an overdressed man who seems to be doubting the witnesses' qualifications to the human race?

The Constable who gave evidence of a wartime lighting offence said, "I saw a sea of light shining through an opaque glass window in offices in Bank Plain". Some may have wished to blame the occasion, atmosphere and hostility of the questioner, but it was simply that he was a poor judge of adjectives; after persistence from the Court Clerk he decided that the window was transparent—anyway, he could see through it.

Young officers were required to attend the Courts to gain experience of the rituals practised by those inside. The Magistrates Court was a useful starting place for there the officer would be called a liar by plain speaking men in plain suits. The condemnation of his evidence was through well worn phraseology—"I put it to you that you are mistaken officer".

The plain suits were recognisable by their frequent and devoted attendance at the Police Station in their never ending search for clients, truth and money: the theory was that all three went together. They were solicitors and, invariably, they were required to call into question the slings and arrows of outrageous fortune or the unscrupulous police behaviour in the case. Some were better at the latter type of speech than the former.

The rapport that existed between some solicitors and policemen was evidenced when a well known, semi-respected, member of the local legal profession presented himself at the Station Office late one evening on a busy weekday. He wanted to see one of his clients who was incarcerated in the cells and, yes, he fully understood that the station staff were too busy to remain in the vicinity during the course of the interview. He would be happy to be locked in the cell with his client. The interests of justice were duly served and the solicitor was locked up.

A busy night got busier until, at a quarter to two in the morning, the Station Sergeant relaxed and conversationally asked what time the solicitor had left. There followed what can only be called a pregnant pause as a Station Office Constable searched for an answer that he was increasingly aware did not exist. The solicitor had not left. The stampede to the cells revealed a prisoner sitting on his bed, elbows on knees and his head between his hands. His legal adviser lay full length on the bed fast asleep. He was roused and led, in a confused manner, to the upper floor where he looked at his watch and said, "H'm, time I was getting back to the office". He then tottered out into the stillness of the night.

An important part of solicitor's work was the briefing of barristers, who were also lawyers but operated in a more theatrical fashion in the rarefied atmosphere of Quarter Sessions and Assizes. These were similar institutions with Assizes being accorded more pomp and ceremony in keeping with the higher authority of the Judge. He sat in a Father Christmas like outfit before a cringing, servile group of lesser bewigged gentlemen who sought to impress him, and the twelve intent faces nearby, that what appeared to be so was not, or if it was, it was a mistake and he didn't mean it. The person who did not mean it sat directly opposite trying to look like someone who was the victim of misfortune. To equalise the position a learned friend (the ritual of addressing each other) would be insisting that it was indeed so, and what is more—he meant it.

Cross examinations of witnesses had a greater mystique in the higher courts and it was nothing to do with the ancient furniture and serious faces glowering under historic architraves and lead framed windows. The Guildhall, scene of Magistrates Courts, was beautifully equipped as a period piece that would qualify for any antiques show. The Shirehall, scene of Quarter Sessions and Assizes, was similarly adorned but it was a stage that had the players with wigs, robes and gestures, not to mention a script of phrases designed to impress and confuse. It was not so much the question, it was the way it was asked with two hands gripping the upper folds of a black robe, an intent gaze upon the lofty ceiling, accompanied by a settling back on the heels, then, and only then, in the most scornful tones, "Are you suggesting officer?" There follows a repeat of the part of the officer's evidence that was particularly disliked. At some point in the repetition the words "So you say" will appear. At the conclusion of this distant address to the ceiling the officer receives a look of pity as one would bestow upon a naughty child.

After the officer has provided a few guarded answers to statements masquerading as questions he receives the next phase which is the "Well really officer" approach. This leads into "Would it surprise you to learn" and then the familiar, "Come, come officer" which is not an invitation but the penultimate condemnatory analysis of his evidence. The ultimate? That is familiar ground. "I put it to you officer" arrives with the aid of a swishing gown and an expansive gesture of Shakespearian effect. There were variations. The gesture and swishing gown could come at an earlier stage, preceding the final critical dissemination of the evidence which would be accompanied by a slowly subsiding figure that would, suddenly, and very emphatically, but beautifully timed with the final dramatic sentence, hitch up a black gown and drop into a chair, rather like a collapsing Dracula.

The young Constable would later meet his articulate accuser in the corridor and discover that he was an ordinary human being, cordial in manner and knowledgeable in police methods. He was just a man doing his job. Some barristers got more job satisfaction than others.

The officer in charge of a case was required to follow a conviction by giving the offender's antecedent history preparatory to sentencing. Always a minefield because Judges and barristers were in the habit of asking questions concerning the defendant's past life to which the officer did not know the answers, giving rise to tut-tutting and muttered asides about inadequate enquiries. One safe question was a request for the officer's opinion concerning the various culpability of those concerned in a criminal enterprise. Well, usually safe.

A Recorder at Quarter Sessions leaned forward from his lofty perch to question a seasoned detective following the conviction of three out of four men on trial for receiving stolen goods.

"Tell me officer, who in your view was the ringleader in this matter?"

"The jury have found him not guilty Sir" came the courageous reply.

He got away with it on the grounds that the Recorder had asked for an opinion and got it.

Policemen's opinions did not always matter but they were generally available, along with all the other services.

# Traffic—Left, Right and Centre

TRAFFIC WAS fairly well defined by the Norwich City Police. It meant moving vehicles. If they were not moving then somebody wanted to know why, and somebody else was expected to do something about it.

The first somebody would be a Sergeant or Inspector, or the Superintendent on his occasional foray into the outside world. The do something about it group comprised the beat Constables.

For those that believe that traffic jams are a modern problem it is a matter of public record that the Superintendent announced in 1946 that the traffic in Norwich was chaotic. He was not revealing any deep secret to the locals, who were not so much interested in his statement of the obvious, but more as to what he, in the form of the police, was doing about it. That is where the Constable on the street came in: he was not allowed chaos on his patch.

A stationary vehicle was potential trouble for the man on the beat, though to be fair, it was also viewed with seriousness by those above who allocated assistance in the form of a superimposed patrol in certain streets. These patrols operated between ten in the morning and six in the evening and offered the heady prospect of contemplating the whole 100 yards of Rampant Horse Street for that period of time, or perhaps the extra 50 yards that was offered by Westlegate which had the excitement of a bend in the road. Bends and curves had advantages in that Sergeants and Inspectors could not detect the Constable's absence in a single glance. However, even a bend in the road could not compensate for eight hours in the restrictive, medieval confines of Colegate.

Luxurious roads, such as Gentleman's Walk, offered time restricted parking. This prompted mental calculations in respect of different vehicles with the attendant need to make sure that they were absolutely right, otherwise a returning driver would provide ample evidence that this particular street was not so aptly named.

George was a beat Constable of War Reserve vintage and was extremely meticulous in assessing the times and positions of parked vehicles. He was also very thorough in his application of the parking laws. Known as 'Honest George', he would be onto a parked car before the

74

engine revolutions had completely died, and it was no use the driver returning to claim the vehicle had moved during the whole illegal period. George chalked the wheels when he first timed it.

The other problem was the returning driver who settled in his vehicle only to find a helmet rising above the bonnet as George carefully surfaced from a crouched chalking position. When he gave evidence against a driver it was a foregone conclusion. Never was a murder scene more rigorously examined and recorded than a car parked on George's beat.

Vehicles that had involuntarily stopped had to be investigated, or rather the cause of the stoppage had to be found. The answer was usually very simple. The vehicle in front had stopped, and the one in front of that, and so on. This chain reaction had to be followed until the obstruction was revealed. A process of cause and effect with the effect being obvious and detrimental to the equanimity of the Constable. He had to find the cause and remove it before his beat, or patrol area, received unwelcome publicity and attention.

Traffic jams prompted questions and, sometimes, the questions were asked before discovery of the offending congestion by the patrolling Constable.

"I suppose you know that the street is jammed up round the corner?"

An unhappy state of affairs for the Constable who obviously does not know any such thing because no person has previously imparted the information and he does not have the benefit of round corner eyesight. If he had known, several options were open and one was not to be in the vicinity of the problem in a state of inaction.

Certain junctions leant themselves to congestion because of the volume of opposing forces. This was anticipated by the powers-that-be by the allocation of an officer at certain times when the opposition was deemed to be unacceptable. Such allocation, usually at peak traffic times, involved the donning of long white armlets, in recognition of the importance of the junction and as an aid to self preservation.

At the appointed hour the suitably garbed Constable would stride into the middle of the road, nimbly avoiding frantic last second surges by drivers prompted to clear the area before submitting to human control. He would wave his arms around for the stipulated period, escaping to the pavement at the laid down time of conclusion. At this time, according to the book, the traffic flow had lessened. The Constable had read the book, but the drivers suddenly deprived of uniformed guidance had not. They were still sparring in the road and wondering over the sudden absence of the policeman.

Further complications arose when the Sergeant decided to visit during this traffic point duty—usually five minutes after the official starting time to see if the Constable had set a new starting time.

Now a visit was too important to go unrecorded. After a few minutes of studied admiration of the performing Constable, or it may have been contempt, the Sergeant would call out "All right?"

In police speak it was only "All right" if there was nothing to report.

In the Police Force the negative was usually all right. But what if there was something to report, or a query to make? The Constable may have required some counsel or guidance from his senior and more experienced colleague. Standing in the middle of St. Benedicts Gates with a double decker ruffling his backside, a thirty tonner attempting to burnish his tunic buttons, and forty cyclists hunched over machines glaring in his direction impatiently waiting for a signal because they were already late at the shoe factory, then everything was going to be "All right Sarge".

"Put me down at nine five".

This was not an invitation in the veterinary sense. It merely indicated that the Constable had to remember to write the visit in his pocket book when he had finished his point duty. Trying to record it during a lull in the traffic was a recipe for disaster. The mere obtaining of the pocket book from the tunic pocket might re-schedule a bus route, and the mind could not contemplate the diversions that could result from the flourish of a pen.

"Sign it later" as a parting remark was only too obvious. No Sergeant was going to enter the melee in the centre of the road just to sign a book. If he did not get caught by a vehicle whose driver was concentrating on the white armlets, he was risking a straight right to the head as a line of traffic was waved on.

St. Benedict's Gates was a designated traffic point at certain times, although it was not a real converging crossroads in the traffic sense. Barn Road and Grapes Hill, on either side of the A47, did not provide too much crossover traffic, except at certain peak times which were considerably exaggerated in the beat book. The problem with this traffic point was the speed of main road traffic into the city. If they did not get an early signal they could decorate the road with rubber and collect a new mascot on the bonnet. The potential mascot was only too well aware of this possible end to a promising career and he did not offer himself as a victim if the main road was running smoothly without a contestant form a side road; in other words he stood on the pavement and watched.

Early one morning, just after the official traffic point of seven twenty five a.m. the designated Constable stood on the pavement admiring the even running traffic believing, quite rightly, that no complications were required from himself. The Inspector's car stopped in Barn Road and a counter view was expressed. The beat book said the Twenty Two Beat Constable should be in the middle of the road and that is where the Inspector wanted him to be.

The Constable made an error. He applied logic to the situation.

"Nothing to do. All through traffic". Adding the obligatory "Sir".

A simple and obvious answer which was immediately rebuffed by a senior rank unmoved by logic or common sense. He ordered the Constable into the road and declined to drive the Wolseley over the crossroads, irrespective of the opportunities presented, until the Constable was adorned with white armlets and in position to give him a signal. The signal he would liked to have given was entirely different to one he did give.

Directing traffic at road level provided senses of power, but also vulnerability. No more so than at Charing Cross where traffic light failure was an overture to chaos and an invitation to perform actions above and beyond the normal course of duty. It was a real George Medal junction.

The problem was not speed, anything but, it was width, or lack of it. One line of traffic at a time, or two converging lines if buses, lorries and similarly sized vehicles did not meet in the centre of the crossroads. If this happened there was room only for a slimline policeman, and he had to breathe in.

The more judicious Constable would observe the impending crossover of the heavies and halt one of the approaching lines. Others thought discretion was the better part of valour and were known to bolt into the doorway of Lamberts the tobacconists, reappearing with a jack in the box effect as soon as reasonable sized traffic had resumed.

Even if the Charing Cross traffic lights worked normally, the Constable could be forced into the road by the presence of a nearby warehouse and its reception of large unloading lorries. The day a struggling Constable sought to regulate a single file past a goods vehicle being unloaded by a driver and warehousemen, who apparently had cement in their shoes, was another auspicious day for Crackers. He stopped and offered to help. Most Inspectors would have taken a detour. The Constable was grateful and concentrated on the unloading vehicle as

*The routine of traffic—a sense of vulnerability*

77

Crackers stepped into the crossroads to prove that democracy went further than riding cycles and getting wet. Traffic flowed evenly and unloading continued until, suddenly, everything was at a standstill. Two lorries contesting for space in the centre of the crossroads were jammed alongside each other with much shouting and wheel twirling from their respective cabins.

The Constable's search for Crackers was unproductive, and reassuring inasmuch he was not in between or under the lorries. He was in Bethel Street enjoying refreshments and possibly wondering on the ineffectiveness of a peaked cap compared with a helmet in certain situations; may have been mistaken for a Park Keeper, or Water Board official, or had he become hungry and left before the coming together of the heavies? The Constable later thanked him. Crackers elected the right of silence.

The reliability of the Charing Cross traffic lights, and the incidence of unloading lorries, was very important to the beat Constable who could, suddenly, find himself plunged into a restricted area challenging the traffic for the limited space available. Compare this with the G.P.O. plain where the officer actually directed the traffic from a refuge; an island which contained the traffic lights control box. This practice was frequently used in the 1950's to speed up the evening rush hour and involved switching the controls from automatic to manual, but there were those, from a pre-war era, who remembered when they stood in the centre in a white coat.

There was an occasion when this island sanctuary was breached by a vehicle, or to be more precise— part of a vehicle. A car clipped a slower moving car, detaching the bumper of the assaulted vehicle and hurling it onto the island at the feet of the Sergeant who was watching the Constable's button pushing routine. The Sergeant was Flash, and he was not given to demonstrative behaviour. Viewing the distorted bumper with mild interest he stepped over the offending piece of metal, announcing to the Constable "I think you are wanted over there", before collecting his cycle (never far away) and departing for more tranquil surroundings. The Constable was left with his buttons, bumper, and two drivers engaged in a very lively conversation. No such thing as a safe traffic point.

Problems did not always arise through vehicular traffic: pedestrians could, and did, provide headaches to a white armletted overseer in the road. They mainly occurred on Saturdays when relief from the weekday points was tempered by a stipulated tour of duty on a pedestrian crossing. The precedence and regular flow of pedestrian traffic on these days meant that certain roads would have been permanently bisected unless a Constable was present to give vehicles a chance of progress. Unfortunately, this simple attempt at justice and fair play escaped a number of jaywalkers who regarded a pedestrian crossing as simply—a crossing for pedestrians, totally oblivious of the uniformed presence in the centre. It was not unknown for such single minded persons to duck under the policeman's arm to gain the other side. If the officer was quick enough he could grab the offender, and after a little dance in the centre of the crossing—much enjoyed by the throbbing mass poised on the pavement waiting for a signal, he could successfully remonstrate and feel honour was satisfied. If he missed with his grab, it was a choice of bawling suitable phrases of admonishment or pursuing the fleeing figure and thereby abandoning the crossing. Whatever the procedure, officialdom had to be seen to make its point—or put another way, no one should be seen to get away with anything.

St. Stephens traffic point, at the confluence of Westlegate, Red Lion, Rampant Horse and St. Stephens Streets, was the Piccadilly Circus of Norwich. Constables standing in an elevated position, in a prominent black and white striped box, lorded it over the opposing traffic and the passing populace of the city. "The Point", as it was known, was an experience to policemen and public alike. It was absorbing, compelling and, at times, embarrassing. It produced characters, styles and incidents. It also had its own brand of vulnerability.

The squareness of the box provided corners and there were occasions when these corners came into conflict with passing traffic. The result was simple, dramatic and disconcerting. It varied only in degree. A sudden turning of the box and the signal aimed at one line of traffic is received by another, accompanied by some perceived unsteadiness on the part of the signaller. If it was a severe glancing blow the occupant would disappear into the depths of the box leaving the astonished audience with a Punch and Judy effect.

Different policemen revealed a variety of mannerisms and movements, and whilst some would have qualified for a Swan Lake audition others were more reminiscent of a demented tic-tac man at a racecourse. Some had the appearance, the dominance and what can be called the presence, to sweep all before them. This was very helpful in dismissing drivers of gigantic lorries who chose to pull up alongside the box with a request for instructions to a most obscure, and previously unheard of, firm somewhere in the remote outskirts of the city. This sudden disappearance of the policemen and box behind the lorry was an irritant to drivers who were impatiently waiting a signal to continue a journey. It also did not help other drivers who could see the policeman but had lost his interest through this complete absorption with a confused lorry driver. (In those days a policeman never admitted that he did not know the whereabouts of a particular address; the tactic was to promote a discussion and leave the enquirer with some sense of useful investigation, if not the answer to the original query).

Getting into the swing of things after the departure of a now even more confused lorry driver created more problems because someone was sure to have missed a turn. The sequence of come-on signals was restored only with a sense of injustice to some of the waiting drivers who had for several long minutes been patiently examining an eight wheeled truck at close quarters. With a suitable batting order resumed, the return of a scowling lorry driver does little to help the proceedings. His temper and confidence in the local police force will not have been improved by a brief and awkward examination of back streets that he had no desire to visit.

Sometimes, drivers did not know here to go, but did not get around to asking, well not immediately. The tale of the flying Austin Seven has passed into folklore, as must have its occupants who were rather elderly at the time. They prematurely aged the St. Stephens traffic point man on a fine day in the 1950's when they approached him from Red Lion Street seeking to turn right, or was it left, or did they know something he didn't? It had to be right or left because entry into St. Stephens Street was not possible; not lawfully anyway.

Ted was the Constable and he did not immediately suspect trouble when the Austin changed a semaphore left signal to a right one, but he did become alarmed when both indicators stuck out from the car giving the impression that take off was imminent. Alarm increased when he noticed that both driver and passenger were elderly ladies who looked as confused as the car.

With the car coming ever nearer, Ted offered signals to Westlegate or Rampant Horse Street and ensured that other traffic was not going to conflict with either choice. No response from the advancing Austin, other than a change in the occupants from confusion to what appeared to be panic. The whole crossroads was now abandoned to them for Ted had no other solutions other than a last minute stop signal, or flight from the box. He chose the former and it had the same amount of success as the other signals, the evidence of which was the Austin hitting the box and pushing it, and occupant, several feet towards St. Stephens Street.

Ted steadied himself and peered from his now stationary box through the open roof of the Austin upon two embarrassed elderly ladies dressed in very smart summer finery. They twittered and smiled and completely disarmed a Constable who would have given anything to have found himself dealing with adult males who would have understood the depths of comprehensive language he was now bottling up inside him.

Whilst Ted searched for appropriate words, and wondered if they were any relation to a certain coal lorry driver, the ladies offered apologies and sweetly asked if they could be directed to the garden party being held at Bonds in All Saints Green. They were directed with a fervent prayer that they should not return within the tour of duty, or better still, take another route home.

Strong and imposing characters asserted themselves from the box and it was not always with hand signals alone. 'Gillie' was an exponent of all round traffic control. Ex-guardsman, and he looked it, this jovial and popular Constable could insert considerable menace into his visual and verbal instructions. The public not only watched with some awe the imperious and commanding movements of Gillie and others, when Gillie was in form they listened as well.

If Gillie signalled a driver to turn right, he turned right. The fact he wished to go to the left was immaterial. Arguments and contradictions with the central figure was something to be avoided.

There were, however, the unfortunates who made a mistake. Tales of their experiences are legion. Gillie had a definite and unforgettable way of drawing a motorist's attention to a problem; so much so that people flocked to the junction when Gillie was addressing an erring motorist. Persons who had not intended to be passers-by became so, specifically for the privilege of watching the event that was unfolding.

The error or indiscretion in question could be of a minor nature, such as slow start following a come-on signal, or it could be much more serious and this included the offence of not stopping, either at the indicated point or not at all. The first might receive a glare and/or comment, but the second was a capital offence liable to immediate retribution.

Motorists who overshot the stop signal could be sub-divided again. Those whom Gillie could reach and those he could not reach. This was very important as the driver who went too far and stopped close to the box would find out. Gillie would abandon his interest in all other traffic and home in on the luckless driver, now positioned neatly alongside and under his unfuriated gaze. Winding the window down and apologising for failing to grasp the stop signal at the earliest opportunity was of little use. The full gravity of the misdemeanour was defined in stentorian tones, emphasised at regular intervals by Gillie's fist upon the roof the car so conveniently placed next to him.

Gillie was a big man with a big fist and a penchant to emphasis. The result was a reverberating car, dazed driver and full circle of fascinated drivers and pedestrians.

After the monologue the driver would be summarily dismissed with some parting comment concerning his eyesight and the need for attention in the future. Life at the junction then returns to the steady normality of passing and re-passing traffic.

Came the day the driver failed to see the stop signal and drove happily under Gillie's arm, from St. Stephens Street intending to make a safe haven in Red Lion Street. The "Oi" that accompanied his passing of the box could well have brought all of Norwich's traffic to a standstill. It was in fact a standard greeting from a police officer who has espied something that required an explanation and someone who could provide it. In some cases it was followed by a "What's going on here?", but in this case it was perfectly apparent what was going on—a motorist who should not have gone on.

There can be doubt that the offence was innocent and without malice aforethought, absent minded and, perhaps, driving with other thoughts crowding for attention; but whatever the mitigation the trial was about to begin. The defence had no chance. The fact the car was beyond the box and out of reach was not to be salvation from a closer contact with Gillie.

The only thing that moved at St. Stephens crossroads after the "Oi" was Gillie. He unlatched the door of the box and stepped into the road with the air of a man about to do his duty, however unpleasant. With measured tread he approached the transfixed driver who was wondering if he had mistaken the sound of thunder or was it related to that ferocious looking policeman who was menacingly filling his rear view mirror.

*The full gravity of the misdemeanour was defined*

Gillie's expression indicated that he was not about to engage in light conversation. The crowd gathered and waited. Nearby shop assistants stopped serving. The victim, an honest looking and fairly respectable example of a middle aged male, wound the window down. Some considered this his second mistake. Gillie put his face into the open space thus created and delivered an assessment of the character and driving ability, or lack of it, of the citizen now tightly holding the steering wheel, using verbal force and an extensive vocabulary nurtured through several years of worldly wise policing. The occasional thump upon the car roof drove home the points that particularly needed some extra emphasis. If the besieged driver did not remember the words he would definitely recall the manner in which they were delivered.

Nobody timed the verbal execution and not one person waiting in the ever lengthening traffic queues, or growing crowd on the pavements—they had suddenly become quite crowded, sought to show impatience, sympathy or any other emotion.

Now for the finale. The ordeal was not over for the unhappy driver whose contribution to the verbal encounter was a form of spluttering in which the word "sorry" definitely appeared. Gillie ordered his return to the point of unlawful departure. With a gesture similar to that of King Richard offering his kingdom for a horse, Gillie pointed to the far off spot in St. Stephens Street and sounded the retreat. A slight problem was revealed by its obvious occupation by traffic that had dutifully stopped and was now being entertained by the unfortunate who had not.

Gillie advanced upon the St. Stephens traffic queue with a shooing motion last seen when cattle were driven through the streets. Drivers, who were suddenly transformed from witnesses to participants, leaned out of windows gesticulating to those immediately behind who repeated the process thereby gradually shuffling backwards a queue of at least twelve vehicles.

Under the threatening gaze of a now silent Gillie the overshooting driver examined his gearbox hampered by his shattered nerve and continuing presence in the public eye. He found the right notch, after several chainsaw like noises which saw Gillie adopt a hands on hips stance that ruined any chance of the driver recovering his composure.

Sufficient space was found in St. Stephens Street to accommodate the returning driver. Under the stern supervisory gaze of the law, and with the amused attention of the local citizenry, the defaulting car inched backwards to occupy a token space. There our victim waited for what seemed like a deliberately prolonged amount of time, incurring further looks of disapproval from those now forced to wait behind him, before he received an exaggerated wave which as a come-on signal would have brought an ocean going liner into port. Happy is the man released from his sentence. Who he was, and whether he ever traversed that route again, is not known. He disappeared into obscurity but who knows, he may have set up the Ramblers Association or started a cycle shop.

Traffic continued to flow in Norwich and policemen continued to wave at it. If it stopped the policeman might have a problem. If it did not stop, the motorist might have a problem.

# All Right Sarge

OF ALL THE supervisory ranks the nearest to some kind of human, civilised and reasonable contact with the Constable was, perhaps unsurprisingly, the next rank up—the Sergeant: a rank which shared the streets, shifts, weather and unscreened public. Sergeants did not warrant a salute, or a "Sir", and they did not take refreshments in isolation. They were, however, front line supervisors and had to be treated with care; in some cases respect.

At Bethel Street Police Station, the Sergeant paraded the Constables, after a token and threatening appearance from the shift Inspector, and marched them onto the street with everyone frantically trying to get into step as the company strode towards St. Peters Street. At Magdalen Gates Police Station, they straggled out as the Sergeant retired to his cupboard.

The patrol Sergeant would usually see his beat Constables once before refreshments and once after, either by looking on the beat, if he had nothing else better to do, or more likely, by appearing at a scheduled ringing-in point. It was not unknown for a Constable to make himself obvious in the street to get the Sergeant's visit out of the way as quickly as possible, however, some Sergeants could be quite sneaky and ruin a good cup of tea by reappearing in totally unforeseen and unwanted circumstances.

On nights, before refreshments, Sergeants could always play the schedule game which simply meant reading the route of the beat man's progress and theoretically being one step ahead. In some cases, when the beat man identified the following shadowy figure as the Sergeant, it was a few steps behind. The tactic of following was obviously intended to check the correct working of the schedule, but it required a certain expertise from the follower. Timing the head round the street corner, or emergence from the doorway to coincide with the Constables rear view, was only part of the art. Transferring the whole body along the pavement, from one recess to another, had to be achieved at double time before the supposedly unsuspecting target reappeared from the yard or alley into which he had pursued his door handle shaking duties. The sudden dive into the shadows as the timing went wrong left the Constable with options of calling out "All right Sarge" or pretending he had not noticed, in which case he would continue on his way murmuring "What a prat". The second option was preferable on the grounds that embarrassing a senior rank could have repercussions at a later date.

The Sergeant who hid in the grounds of the Probate Office in Thorpe Road got more than he bargained for when he decided to test the nerve of the passing beat Constable. The sudden shuffling of feet in the bushes brought an immediate response. The Constable drew his truncheon and charged. The Sergeant survived.

It was possible to turn the tables and the Constable who entered the Cathedral Close at three a.m., on a particularly dark night in the late 1930's, was tipped off by a security man at St. Ethelbert's Gate.

"Your Sergeant has been through here" he was advised.

The Constable was Bert, who had opened his career in 1937 with a drunken driver on Mousehold. He had just completed his probation and was wise to certain supervisory tactics. The Sergeant was obviously lying in wait somewhere in the blackness dominated by the cathedral, relying on the element of surprise to query the working of the beat, possibly hoping to witness a less than efficient attention to the door handles of the many offices within The Close.

Bert worked a steady programme of examination of the property moving carefully from The Close to the Upper Close, then Lower Close, Gooseberry Gardens, but nothing. Life's Green and the Bishop's Palace garden followed and there, beneath the towering spire, standing silently under a tree, was the outline of a man. He had found him. Approaching quietly, and without using a light, Bert circled to the rear of his target. He then crept towards the figure and laid a hand on the shoulder, at the same time shining the Wootton lamp straight into the face. A white faced and speechless Sergeant nearly passed out.

He was still recovering as Bert calmly announced, "Oh, it's you Sergeant. I thought it was someone loitering with intent".

Inconvenient parts of the schedule could be aborted to facilitate progress, but only if the Constable knew his Sergeant. If he was not a follower was he a stake-out man? Was he the devious type, likely to be hidden on that inconvenient part of the route with every intention of proving the major offence of failing to work the beat properly?

The deliberate avoidance of New Mills Yard (a real trap this one) on the grounds that the schedule maker was drunk, or temporarily insane, when he decreed the schedule follower should go only half way and then return, with the other half to follow at a later stage, was a possible prelude to a later conversation which would commence "Go up New Mills Yard tonight?" This sinister opening meant that the Sergeant had detected the missing of the first half, and was not going to be receptive to the plea that common sense had joined it to the other half at a later and more sensible time. Quite simply, if you cut corners on a schedule beware the Sergeant was not around them.

Sergeants liked to visit Constables and receive the traditional greeting of "All right Sarge", sign the pocket book and move off into the next phase of the, hopefully, quiet life that would eventually lead to a pension. They would tolerate circumstances when the greeting was not "All right", provided this meant a non-contentious and uncomplicated report only.

Generally, Sergeants and Constables co-existed with an understanding of the responsibilities of each other; but authority had to be affirmed and some indiscretions of the beat man became intolerable because they were provocative. The motivation for the Sergeant was respect and assertion of his position, whilst that of the hunted Constable, intent upon avoiding supervisory eyes, was anything that was opposite to exposure to freezing cold, aching feet and a grumbling stomach.

Some of the catch me if you can scenarios between Sergeants and Constable imbued the competitive spirit which of course meant winners and losers. Dudley was a Sergeant who had had enough and called up reinforcements determined to be a winner. The projected loser was 'Wimpey', an experienced Constable who happened to be working Eight Beat (Ber Street to Chapelfield) on nights and had punctuated his working routine by going to ground in the second half of the night.

Wimpey was a keen enough Constable who worked his beat well enough before the refreshment period. However, the freezing cold, isolation and silence of the second half of the night prompted him to seek shelter and comfort. This fact prompted his Sergeant to seek Wimpey.

Dudley was a give and take Sergeant who had been through the door handle and weather exposure routine on the beat. His job was now to see that others followed the same path, and, whilst the occasional excursion towards warmth and rest was not going to attract attention, the regular disappearance of the beat officer from public (and more importantly Dudley's) view was just too much.

Every night, after the refreshment period, Wimpey made his ringing-in point and then disappeared, emerging one hour and twenty minutes later for the next scheduled communication. Dudley could not locate him anywhere and he called up reinforcements in the shape of Ray, a Sergeant who also adopted a reasonable approach to the vagaries of police work, but agreed with Dudley that enough was enough. Wimpey's bolt hole had to be found.

Two against one may have seemed disproportionate odds, but it did not immediately reflect in success for the two. Employing various observation points and subterfuges they failed to locate the disappearing Wimpey. When it snowed they failed because Wimpey adopted the ploy of walking backwards.

It was, however, the snow that, eventually, was to lead the plotting and frustrated Sergeants to a boiler house at the rear of the Assembly Rooms in The Chantry. To be more specific it was the tracks in the snow because little attention was paid to which way the feet were pointing.

Finding the boiler house, alias bolt hole, was one thing, finding Wimpey in it was another matter. The Sergeant's triumphant discovery was tempered by the absence of the principal target, despite the tell-tale footprints. It followed that phase two of the operation would have to be a stake out; after all, he could not be far away.

Where Wimpey had gone and why he had so mysteriously disappeared from what was obviously a very comfortable and regular retreat was not immediately clear. It was rather puzzling for Dudley and Ray who conferred earnestly but, in retrospect, might have done better to have sought guidance from above.

The Sergeants took up strategic points to await the inevitable arrival of the doomed Wimpey. They waited and waited. It got colder and colder. No Wimpey. Eventually the watchers had had enough; they retired to the Police Station for warmth, tea and re-assessment. It was there that they learned that the object of their campaign had failed to make his next scheduled ringing-in point. A most serious offence—without a good excuse it would rate higher than being found in a warm boiler house. Further news was that Wimpey had reappeared and was alive and well, if somewhat unhappy at impending disciplinary proceedings for failing to ring in.

A disconsolate Wimpey was later to reveal the manner of the Sergeant's victory, if that is what it was. In any event it was a defeat for Wimpey who had seen the Sergeants tracking towards his refuge and had impulsively decided that if they were looking down, he was going up. He quickly shinned up a very convenient tree and watched as the searchers recoiled from the empty boiler house. To his great dismay the searchers

*He could not be far away*

87

became watchers and he was trapped looking down upon those looking for him. He cursed their persistence, and, because of his elevation and immobility, became even colder than they.

If a criminal had stayed into this little cameo, intent upon burglary in the Assembly Rooms, he would never have believed that a specially formed observation team had not been placed in the area intent upon his capture. If he had sought to commit his burglary before the arrival of the Sergeants, on any one of the occasions that Wimpey was ensconced, the size of his surprise would have been matched by Wimpey's commendation. Indeed, Wimpey may have reflected rather ruefully that when you need a burglar you can never find one.

Sometimes the hunting Sergeant was completely thwarted. 'Duke' was not so named because of any leanings to nobility, but more mundanely, it was an abbreviation of a first name that offered alternatives of misconstruction with marmite or marmalade. He was an extremely well built Sergeant and should have been easily visible on the horizon, especially in broad daylight; therefore, the Constable who dived into the Fifty Shilling Tailors in Orford Place was to some extent the author of his own likely misfortune. Duke was not going to pass up this flagrant act, in which tea was the obvious objective, and he staked out the front of the shop.

The ample proportions of Duke did not lend themselves to a successful observation, and the reckless inhabitant of the price cutting tailors was quickly aware of the ambush. Now came the difference between winning and losing. The Constable knew of a back way from the shop. The Sergeant did not. What he found was the Constable appearing at his side informing him that everything was "All right". Duke accepted the assertion and advised the Constable that he was going to remain outside the shop because he had seen another officer entering via the front door. "Catch him when he comes out" he informed the Constable sagely. The Constable was extremely grateful for superimposed patrols and the occasional straying of other beats. The identity of the tailoring intruder was obviously unknown. The Constable left, wishing his Sergeant well, and resolving to advise him of the true facts later—about one year later.

The Sergeant who approached Three Box at Ber Street Gates in the first hour of the early turn shift was intending to visit Gillie, but was over the five minute waiting time and could, therefore, reasonably have expected to have been unlucky. However, as he approached on his cycle he saw both Gillie and another Constable of notable size and demeanour. 'Bags' was large, expressive, forthright and vigorous. He was usually busy and noticeable. On this occasion he was busy interrogating a lorry driver on the contents of his vehicle. Bags was known to check vehicles and persons with some regularity and keenness, but it was not true that he "would nick his own grandmother"—only if she had stolen something.

Gillie, observing the Sergeant in the distance, and not having a lorry driver to interrogate, cycled off in the opposite direction only to be brought to a halt by a bellowing voice insisting that he held his ground.

The Sergeant had spoken. He spoke again when he reached Gillie, accusing him of attempting to "slide off". Working himself up to administer a severe and critical assessment (for which this tartar of a Sergeant had a reputation) he called for an explanation for the sudden departure in the face of the approaching supervisory officer. Gillie thought carefully before he replied, "Sarge, I thought you were a man riding a bike in a bowler hat". If people were asleep in that area of the city that early morning they soon woke up as a Sergeant climbed several decibels in providing a supervisory reply.

A double production of noise ensued at Ber Street Gates: Gillie faced an irate Sergeant and Bags, never the quietest of interrogators, conducted a side offering by making an accusatory in-depth examination of a lorry driver's character and load. The public liked to see, and possibly hear, policemen on the streets.

Most Sergeants adopted a proper and formal approach whilst maintaining a reasonable level of conversation. Jimmy was a perfect example. Very tall and stern looking, he would gaze carefully into the distance whilst discussing some hilarious event that might have other participants convulsed into uncontrollable heaps. Jimmy would nod, produce a flicker of a smile, and then move on to more serious questions, such as some perceived failure of the Constable to properly carry out his duties. Not easily diverted was Jimmy. As a Constable he had proved that he was not going to be disadvantaged by a rat a second time (recalling his rodent encounter on One Beat). He also was not going to be outsmarted by a Fifteen Beat man with a liking for the cinema.

The Mayfair and Odeon cinemas were two of the few rays of light on Fifteen Beat. The Mayfair was a small affair in Magdalen Street and not known for a presentation of epics. It was, however, better than pounding a dreary beat and in support of this view the beat man placed himself in the back row. No charge of course. Business people were only too glad to see policemen on the premises.

Jimmy favoured the direct approach. Suspecting the presence of his beat man in the cinema he decided he was not going to waste time staking out the place. He went in and achieved immediate success—from his point of view. Back row—one uniformed policeman staring intently at the screen. Now Jimmy was not a man to waste words. The situation spoke for itself; it only required the speech from the defence. Jimmy made himself obvious and waited for the plea of mitigation and mercy.

The Fifteen Beat man eyed his Sergeant and wearily levered himself from his unpaid 1s 9d seat. As he made for the exit he informed the silent accuser that everything was "All right" (debatable from Jimmy's point of view), and then added "I wouldn't go and see that film if I was you Sarge. It's a load of rubbish".

If Jimmy was planning to say anything it did not materialise until they had reached the pavement and he could find words to combat the unasked for assessment of a film that he had no intention of seeing, but about which he was now, admittedly, faintly curious. He contented himself with a concise view of the dereliction of duty that was so painfully obvious, adding a character assassination that was aimed at the officer who had deserted his people to gratify himself with celluloid pleasures.

Sergeants had an affinity with public houses, not because they had a particular liking for their wares, although that may well have been the case, but because they had to maintain a Licensed Premises Register which required regular visits to local hostelries with notes of irregularities. The objective was simple. Ensure strict compliance with the Licensing Acts.

Landlords knew the complications of the Acts, particularly the time restrictions which prevented them from selling to a person who had money and wished to buy; but they were adept at running a business, keeping customers, projecting a friendly profile for the Sergeant's regular visits, and at the same time overcoming the more illogical rules created by the licensing laws: this was most of them—in their view anyway. They also seemed the most popular and generous group of people it was possible to find for they were always entertaining friends at their own expense.

For public house visits the Sergeant would round up the beat Constable and storm around six or seven hostelries before retiring thirstily to the station to make up the register. The visits were not surreptitious; straight through the front door, a lap of the bar, banter with the landlord, the odd jocular remark to the locals caressing their pint glasses, quick dart into the lounge and a chorus of good nights all round. The odd derogatory remark concerning parentage, that followed the closing of the door, was not supposed to have been heard.

It was not unknown for the visiting Sergeant to be offered a drink in the vain hope that he would succumb to the artificial friendship that accompanied it, making it difficult, in the eyes of the landlord, for future transgressions to be properly identified. The evening when a Sergeant responded to the usual banter of "What are you going to have Sergeant?" with a "I'll have a double whisky" caused tremendous interest amongst both audience and landlord, who could not pour it fast enough. The drink was eagerly proffered.

"Thank you, your name Sir".

"Smith" replies an excited landlord.

The Sergeant took the drink and moved over to an elderly lady sitting alone in the corner of the room. Placing the drink before her he said, "Mr. Smith's compliments my dear".

Further visits to that particular establishment were routine and without the banter.

Occasionally, a youngster would be asked his age, and, as the landlord anxiously moved to clean the bar counter in the relevant area, he would instantly become eighteen; but "No!", he could not prove it. The Sergeant knew he could not prove it but the point had been made and the landlord knew it.

Sometimes, arrival through the front door was a signal for sudden activity in the lounge, yet when that door was opened it was either empty or populated by old age pensioners playing dominoes. Again an anxious landlord would be attending to nearby bar duties.

All was not milk and honey, or should it be beer and crisps, and there were times when the gloves had to come off. Drinking after hours was landlord versus the law in the form of the Sergeant, who was responding to the obvious or information received. Winners and losers again. The defences were locked doors, secure windows and tightly closed curtains. The attacking formation, Sergeant and Constable, had to see inside and get inside. Achieve the latter and the former would obviously follow, except that what was seen after the landlord had taken a painfully long time to open the door, in response to prolonged knocking, would not represent evidence of after hours drinking. No money, no glasses—just a few friends in the landlord's private quarters; and if there was a suitable rear exit, not even that.

Make a thorough reconnaissance and then devise invasion tactics. That was the way to do it. The Sergeant surveying a public house near Magdalen Gates was in the first stage of this process, working on the theory that closed curtains and doors did not seal a building. Keyholes were the answer. The aperture was sufficient to see the whole range of wrongdoing. He was in the scouting stage, with his eye squinting to the front door keyhole, when it all went wrong. The door opened quite quickly, it must have been unlocked, and a satisfied customer walked from the premises. That was his intention; he actually swallow dived over the crouching uniformed figure who was well below a line of vision which had not been improved through a prolonged presence inside the establishment. Suitable apologies and discussion over poor lighting, insecure bootlaces and routine enquiries, did nothing to restore any future element of surprise. The landlord knew it was low profile time.

Another Sergeant resorted to the keyhold technique but was considerably embarrassed at the conclusion of his evidence in the Magistrates Court when the defence carried the pub door into the courtroom and there, for all to see, was a Yale lock. This Sergeant with laser vision was later to be known as 'Keyhole Jack'.

Some public houses had a geographical advantage which raised an extra degree of difficulty for the invading forces. The 'Jolly Maltsters' in King Street presented such a problem. Bounded by the river and the Ring Road, with no suitable adjoining premises, it was a challenge. The Sergeant prowling the circumference noted subdued voices, occasional low laughter, glasses chinking, or was it money, or both? He concluded that drinking and gaming was in force and resolved to be amongst them before the evidence was dispelled. He had come fully equipped with the beat Constable, having previously reconnoitred and evolved his plan.

It was long after closing time and standing on the pavement outside the pub was a recipe for discovery. A suitable recess on the opposite side of the road was selected as the jumping off point. It was simple really. Wait until a customer was allowed out through the front door (it would have to be that door unless he had a boat waiting at the rear), time the unlocking process to coincide with take off from the King Street recess, and, before a startled landlord could shut and relock the door, the forces of law and order would be through. The wait began.

The unlocking was obvious, the Tower of London could not have made more noise; the take off was perfect, as was the arrival. The customer was just getting clear of the doorway as two uniforms rushed past and jammed side by side in the opening. A surprised landlord stepped back, leaving the key in the lock, and the inner assembly paused over cards and glasses to fuzzily focus on the commotion at the door. They saw two policemen struggling to extricate themselves from a side by side position in the doorway, legs whirling in an unsuccessful attempt to obtain forward motion, arms pushing against each other for leverage, and elbows digging into the door jamb—vainly trying for further purchase. What seemed liked minutes was only seconds, but those concluding seconds saw a sea of frenzied movement with the Sergeant entering the bar like a cork from a bottle, his assistant reeling backwards to a point whence he had come, the landlord retreating to consult his customers, alias friends, entertained at his expense, and these worthies organising themselves for the impending interview. The landlord's wife added an unwelcome voice to the proceedings which seemed to have lost a certain amount of decorum. Her overriding view did nothing to restore it. Needless to say seizure of evidence was a lost cause. The only seizure that was possible would have been medical and connected with the efforts required to enter a doorway.

The problem with Sergeants, from a Constable's point of view, was that they had been Constables. They knew the ropes. A further problem was that sometimes personalities changed with elevation to the rank. What was once amiable became critical, or worse still, devious. Poachers became gamekeepers. However, they remained in touch with the man on the beat and could be classed as reasonable, worldly wise human beings, with a rapport of some sort with both the Constable and public; unless of course you ran a public house. The real danger lay in further metamorphose to the god like status of Inspector; but that must be another story.

# All Correct Sir

INSPECTORS of the yesteryear were all-powerful beings, each reigning over his own tour of duty, equipped with waspish humour and an awesome vocabulary of condemnation which was used to apprise the Constable on the beat of any shortcomings that came to notice.

The ritual of the meeting between Inspector and Constable was usually instigated by the senior rank—Constables looked for Inspectors but not because they wanted to meet them. Some Inspectors were conversational and known to be relatively harmless, unless provoked, but other members of this exalted rank were damaging to the peace of mind so earnestly desired by the beat Constable.

"All correct Sir", was the standard greeting, fervently hoping that it was, and if it was not, the Inspector did not know any different. A smart salute was a required accompaniment.

A deviation from a statement of "All correct Sir", needed some thought. The Nineteen Beat man who, on scheduled working, found a small fire smouldering amongst rubbish in White Lion Yard in Oak Street used his initiative. He put it out by stamping on it. At four five a.m. he saw the Inspector at Twenty Eight Pillarphone (St. Mary's Plain). Feeling reckless he forsook the safety of "All correct" and announced the extinction of his small fire some four hours earlier. The response was immediate and condemnatory; all fires must be reported to the Fire Brigade. Bitterly regretting his loose tongue the Constable said he would remember it in future, but this fire was small and well and truly out. The Inspector reinforced his point; all fires must be reported: tell the Fire Brigade, now!

The Constable used the pillarphone to advise the Fire Brigade, emphasising that the fire was small and out. Guessing the outcome he walked the short distance to Oak Street, hearing the advancing ding-a-ling-a-ling before he got there. He watched as the fire engine revved noisily outside the 'White Lion' public house and helmeted figures charged up the yard. He noted lights appearing in the public house. Explanations to the leading fireman as to the power of an Inspector were well received, although the bleary eyed crew looked unimpressed. The occupants of the 'White Lion' then joined in the conversation, and they were very unimpressed with the timescale involved. Never tell the Inspector anything he does not need to know, which is everything he cannot find out.

Amongst this ruling junta of Inspectors was the senior Inspector. Senior because he had been there longer, and senior because he had a dominant presence, both visually and verbally.

Heavily built with a powerful barrel chested body, square jawed face, piercing eyes and crew cut hair, he was formidable in appearance and manner. You easily detected his approach, unless of course he was in repose in the back of a police car. Thereby hangs a tale.

'Chesty', as the senior Inspector was called, quite aptly you may think, was treated with extreme caution for a number of reasons, not the least of which was his forceful Sergeant Major approach to any discussion or question. This could be partially circumvented by steering the subject on to football or cricket, but this tactic was of limited value when Chesty was on night duty and given to an extra degree of abruptness.

All Inspectors were, in the name of supervision, dangerous at night, but not all hunted the beat Constable by devious means. With the advantages of pillarphones, fixed points and an allocated car, Inspectors contrived to meet Constables with great ease. No great problem, until Chesty left the station without the car—that was serious.

The Inspectors car was a valuable aid to the detection of the Inspector. It was an ex-traffic ('the mobile') car handed on for the sole use of the Inspectors in their supervisory duties. The Traffic Department had one other car on the streets at night but this was a later model which was instantly recognisable as it swished past with its occupants reclining in an envelope of leather and walnut. A cold dripping Constable on an adjacent pavement would cast covetous eyes and exchange recognition waves.

If the earlier model black Wolseley appeared on the horizon the comaraderie was replaced by increased alertness and caution. This car would contain a man with two pips on each shoulder who would wish to talk about insecures and lights in premises. The hand raised to the dripping helmet would be in the form of a salute.

On the night Chesty left the station without his car he commandeered the traffic car and, not being one for half measures, he also commandeered the crew. Armed with his Trojan Horse he set out to find his beat men.

It was not cricket, some would say it was not British, but it was Chesty and he had the advantage, or did he? Perhaps he only wanted to be driven and was too tired to drive himself to meet his men.

The young beat Constable was pushing his cycle along Magdalen Road when the mobile (or so he thought) came into view and pulled into the kerb at St. Clements Hill without any recognition signals. Two serious looking traffic men stared through the windscreen awaiting instructions from the large figure slumped in the back seat. Only the revolving eyeballs of the driver told the cycle Constable that a state of abnormality existed.

The slow and bemused approach of the young officer was transformed as he perceived the abnormality. The unmistakeable figure of Chesty in the back of the car.

The order of events was a rapid approach, coming to attention, and the best salute one could muster. Speech could be tricky but this depended on Chesty. As it turned out it was impossible because, after the Constable's rapid approach, the proposed sequence faltered. The car window remained closed.

A thoroughly alarmed young Constable found himself peering upon his senior officer without a practical voice to accelerate the proceedings. The traffic men maintained their straight ahead view through the windscreen, and Chesty declined to acknowledge the presence of the anxious figure at the window. A stand off, which seemed to the unhappy man outside the car to be an eternity.

Eventually, Chesty lowered the car window a fraction; sufficient to vent his wrath for a failure to salute and report the correctness, or otherwise, of the beat. Protests that saluting and reporting through metal and glass did not appear appropriate were swept aside and served only to encourage a more in-depth analysis of the young officer's deficiencies. The pocket book was posted through the window, signed and smartly returned. The window returned to the fully closed position, and the Wolseley sped away from the unhappy Constable. He was, however, to receive some consolation from following events.

Kenny (the third to appear with this name), was an older Constable with several years experience, a dour and phlegmatic character inclined to pessimism and common sense. He was at Tuckswood on the Ring Road, a few miles from his younger, and recently discomfited, colleague, when he espied the stationary Wolseley still with its hapless crew and ominous passenger in the back.

It is not recorded whether Kenny saw a trap or pondered the possibility that the Inspector's regular car had broken down. Action was polarised by the view of Chesty's large figure against the rear passenger window.

Kenny headed for Chesty and the traffic crew resumed their study of the windscreen.

Kenny came to a halt at the relevant window which remained closed. He waited on the assumption that the next move belonged to Chesty.

Chesty did not appear to share this view. He remained in the straight ahead position slumped in the seat.

There followed a course of action which to Kenny appeared logical and automatic. Some would call it initiative. If conversation was prevented by a moveable obstruction, then remove the said obstruction.

Kenny opened the door.

The result was electric. Chesty pitched from his leather comfort and headed towards the pavement in a rapid down and sideways movement.

Kenny, jerked from his usual steady and pragmatic view of life, realised in a split second the enormity of what was happening. There was no time for a philosophy of what will be, will be. He tried to retrieve the situation. Of such desperate and spontaneous actions are even bigger disasters born.

The plunging Chesty was frantically grabbed by a horrified Kenny who had completely overlooked the large three cell torch clipped to the top of his uniform in the manner favoured by some beat Constables.

Kenny not only failed to arrest Chesty's progress, he coshed him over the head with his torch.

Chesty sprawled ignominiously upon the pavement and nursed a sore head. Kenny crouched over the fallen figure in frozen horror, and the traffic crew looked through the windscreen in the ultimate test of self control.

What followed is attributable to memories clouded by emotions of embarrassment, mirth and rage, depending upon where you stood, sat or lay amongst the four persons present at this small drama in a deserted city street in the early hours of the morning.

Chesty gathered himself, but not sufficiently to give maximum power to an assessment of Kenny's actions. He hurriedly signed the proffered pocket book and retreated to sanctuary in the rear of the Wolseley, leaving apologies echoing in the night air.

There was a little hesitation in the Wolseley's departure as its crew fought for self control. If Chesty detected that they appeared to be overcoming some kind of fit he did not comment.

*A course of action which appeared logical*

Kenny held the view that the great man had been asleep, lulled into a reclining position supported by the door, a condition induced by the soporific driving of a driver who had no wish to draw attention to himself. Others thought differently.

It is known that the tactic of utilising the traffic car was used on rare occasions by other Inspectors, but they never, never, leant upon the door.

Inspectors, unlike the Mounties, did not always get their man. Chesty probably wished he had not got his on a certain night, but Crackers was not thinking on these lines when he went to Tuckswood Section Box expecting to find the cycle beat man idling inside the station ten minutes or more after the time of scheduled departure.

Finding the station occupied by a lawfully placed Constable Clerk, Crackers sat on the office desk cupboard and commenced an interrogation designed to elicit information concerning the last known whereabouts of the man whom he had confidently expected to catch. The answers he received have gone unrecorded but they were not truthful, because the cycle beat man was crouched in the cupboard upon which Crackers was sitting. Arriving by car traps the defaulter in the station but it also removes the element of surprise.

If "all correct" was one antidote to a belligerent Inspector, another was a smart salute. A little bit of servility made for a quiet life, but in the case of one Inspector it was an absolute necessity. He thrived on salutes and Constables were convinced that he instituted a campaign designed to collect the maximum number during a shift. A young probationer Constable, on night duty in St. Stephen's Street one cold December morning, was sufficiently experienced to know that the salute collecting Inspector was on duty and likely to appear at any moment. However, his concentration was interrupted, not by the Inspector, but by a car pulling alongside sounding its horn.

The Constable tried to remember the law on sounding car horns at night, and had narrowed it down to three different times, before he realised that the driver of the car was an off duty Norfolk County Constable with whom he had been friendly at training school. Forgetting the law on car horns he began a detailed comparison of police adventures with his erstwhile colleague, which in some strange way led to his county friend opening the boot of the car to reveal a record player that he was seeking to sell. Our on duty city Constable picked up the record player for more detailed examination but was then aware of another vehicle driving slowly past. The Inspector. A very interested Inspector who was staring intently at the handicapped Constable.

Should the Constable salute and thereby drop the record player, along with a very good friendship? Should he nod, smile, or pretend he had not noticed the cruising Inspector? Black marks for poor observation and a certain rollicking in the latter case. It had to be the latter, friendships were worth keeping.

The absorbed Inspector nearly collided with a parked car, such was his interest, but he kept going, leaving the Constable debating various stories that might fit the circumstances. He declined his county friend's offer of a citizen handing in found property, and also discarded other fanciful circumstances as unlikely to impress. Returning to the station to report off duty he had still failed to assemble a defence when the Station Sergeant bellowed that the Inspector wished to see him.

Entering the Inspector's office in the manner of a scaffold climbing subject he pondered upon Labour Exchange prospects. The opening lines did nothing to lighten the gloom despite his best salute.

"Ah lad. I want to talk about your activities in St. Stephen's this morning".

The Constable is about to blurt out that a police officer friend was the person involved, hoping that mercy might still be found in the most improbable of places, when the Inspector continues, "I want to say well done".

The shock impresses silence upon the Constable.

"I like to see policemen turning over members of the public, including searching their vehicles. You won't find anything by hiding in shop doorways. Keep up the good work".

A smart salute and quick exit are called for; but the praised Constable is not quite quick enough.

"Shut the door on the way out lad; and I will overlook it this time that you did not salute me earlier on".

It was not always possible to detect Inspectors with ease. The beat Constable who decided to have a haircut whilst on duty was not setting a precedent, but caution was necessary. His preliminary routine could not be faulted. After a careful study of the street, pedestrians and vehicles, he melted into the barber's doorway, pausing for quick secondary glances up and down the street; then briskly entering the shop he hid his helmet and occupied a vacant chair with covering white smock accessory. He settled back, and prepared to debate important issues in politics and sport, but was aware of the intent stare from the occupant of the next chair. He turned towards the white garbed figure and found himself under the steady gaze of the Inspector. They called that one a draw.

Occasionally, a Constable fought back, but revolutionaries often have a price to pay. 'Blondie' was a Constable with a sense of humour (it did not stop him becoming a Sergeant later in his career) and he repositioned the driver's seat in the Inspector's car to a point from which the Inspector was groping and grasping for the controls. This act of sabotage occurred under cover of darkness, and the following night Blondie reported for the comfortable duty of Station Entrance only to find he had been reallocated the gloomy and despairing depths of King Street, Mountergate, Oil Mills Yard, etc.—the dreaded Nine Beat. He was confronted by a satisfied Inspector who proclaimed, "You change the seats. I change the beats".

Inspectors had a nuisance value without leaving the station and their control of the duty sheet was a powerful weapon. Chesty would often flourish a pencil and rubber with a cry of "At the stroke of a pen", indicating that some poor soul would now explore the depths of a beat rating nil minus on the interest scale instead of some originally intended area of passable interest. Certain beats were regarded as uninteresting and hard work. They were carefully allocated by the Inspectors and provided a useful indicator as to the current standing of the officer so allocated.

Entering the Inspector's office on a voluntary basis was not recommended, but necessary when domestic forces were pressuring for a duty change. After an unsympathetic hearing the applicant would escape wondering whether it had been worth it. This wonderment occurred even when the Inspector approved the application.

There was another reason to enter the Inspector's office—pay. Once a week, on the golden day, on or off duty, Constables would present themselves to receive tangible evidence that their labours were for a purpose.

Attending in uniform meant a salute and "All correct Sir", even if it wasn't, for pay parade was not the place to introduce complications. If the Inspector failed to respond there was a follow-up: "Pay sir?".

Recognition of the claimant came in varying forms, as did delivery of the money. A grunt, brief comment on the worth of the claimant (uncomplimentary), or silence, were options that could reasonably be expected; but delivery of the precious envelope, rattling with coinage, had variations of a push, throw or slide across the desk. A sheet of paper requiring a signature would also be heading in the same direction. Chesty had a tendency to off breaks across the table and the intended recipient had to be quite active to field the rewards of service.

Signing and grabbing, or grabbing and signing, whichever came naturally, was followed by a swift departure, thanking the Inspector for his generosity. All to be repeated next week.

Visits to the Inspector's office for duty changes could be hazardous affairs. The man in charge did not like complications, and some recoiled from impromptu decision making.

The Sergeant who went into the Inspector's office, after the late turn shift had been paraded, was seeking to reallocate one of the duty Constables. The traffic car was one short and should be double crewed. A star tour of duty awaited someone who was probably contemplating a much less interesting eight hours.

Chesty was the Duty Inspector but he was not in his office. He was quickly located in the Club Room, following the Test Match on television. It followed that the only person who was 'out' was the interfering Sergeant who kept talking about duties. Chesty summarily dismissed him and refused to allow the problem of single crewed police cars to rise above the respective merits of England and Australia. It was difficult to argue with an irritated Chesty absorbed in a cricket match. The Sergeant retired.

The Sergeant next appeared on the Police Station roof, which was flat and easily accessible, where he very quickly redesigned the television aerial. Within minutes he was back in the Club Room viewing a large backside, the owner of which was bent forward twiddling knobs on a television set that was displaying a severe snowstorm. A vengeful but satisfied Sergeant left, and a now greatly irritated Chesty returned to late turn shift duties. It is not clear when normal service was resumed, both on the roof and below it.

Inspectors could be found in awkward positions elsewhere in the Police Station. Night duty officers were sometimes disconcerted to find the rank in the vicinity of the Station Office, making forgery of the refreshments book a very risky business. Again know your Inspector. If a certain person was in the adjacent corridor it was a stake out. That corridor comprised only bare walls and a height ruler used by Stumpy to assault recruits. The Constable would book in and be half way up the steps to the canteen before a clarion call would bring him back for a detailed discussion upon Greenwich Mean Time, and an embarrassing examination of his wrist watch. The fact that he had made an almost indecipherable and ambiguous entry in the book would not help. Inspectors did not deal in ambiguity.

Upon this scene of subterfuge and insecurity came an instrument of rescue, an aid and boon to the conniving Constable. A one armed bandit or fruit machine, as it was variously known, legislated by the Betting, Gaming and Lotteries Act of which most policemen knew very little, and cared even less. It was placed in the clubroom and immediately attracted its devotees which, to the delight of certain Constables, included a cross section of Sergeants and Inspectors.

The book forgers not only claimed their extra two minutes with a lessening risk factor, some daring and unscrupulous individuals made it three. After all, Civil Defence training had shown that four minutes was a long time.

Assessment of the Duty Inspector no longer rested solely upon personality and track record; the crunch question was whether he played the machine. Whilst he was exercising his right arm in the cause of poverty he was not bothering anyone else. However, you could not please everyone because some addicted Constables could not get near the light flashing metal contrivance which displayed all the generosity of an impoverished Inland Revenue office. Its insatiable appetite for money failed to deter a select number who, clutching a sandwich in one hand and pumping coins into a slot with the other, spent the greater part of 45 minutes staring intently at an assortment of flickering oranges, lemons and other fruit. Occasionally, there would be a triumphant cry of "Three plums", or something similar, indicating that the machine had released part of its enormous gains, presumably as an encouragement to further efforts. Even more rarely, a jackpot would be released with an accompaniment of noise from both machine and persons gathered in the vicinity. This tended to flush the Inspector from his office and, usually, he did not include himself in the cries of congratulation.

The Inspector's office was alongside the clubroom and had a connecting door which no one, other than the great man himself, dared to use. On the night a Constable got the jackpot during his refreshment period, when else, the Inspector arrived on the scene with compelling urgency.

The jackpot arrived with a tremendous whirring, chugging and jingling of coins, accompanied by triumphant cries in which the word "lucky" predominated. The connecting door flew open with such force that anyone behind it would have needed medical treatment. The Inspector's progress towards the dispensing machine and jubilant winner was swift and emphatic, assisted in no small way by the sudden dispersal of the surrounding audience. Congratulatory voices subsided and were replaced by a gruff announcement that he (the Inspector) had spent a long time putting all that money in. The affluent Constable realised with a sinking heart that he was both a winner and a loser.

Checking the Station Office proved to be an excellent supervisory tactic on the night 'Butch' enquired as to the state of events. The Station Office Constable informed him there was "not much doing", but added humorously that he had just thrown a murderer out of the station. Butch was an Inspector with a good popularity and C.I.D. record. He was interested.

Apparently, only a minute or so earlier, a man had called in and reported that he had chopped up some relatives. He had seemed rather vague concerning details and the Constable had bracketed him with others who showed a regular tendency to admit bizarre and horrific crimes: exhibitionists and attention seekers. A failure to elaborate or impress the recipient of the tale had prompted a sharp dismissal from the station.

Butch listened carefully and then disappeared from the station. He found the vague confessor in St. Peters Street and requested a repeat rendering of his awful deed. He got it, and walked back to the station with the man. A telephone call wad made to another Police Force requesting a check of a certain address, with apologies for a possible waste of time. The call back was very prompt, and the caller somewhat excited as he described the scene of carnage that had greeted the enquiring officers. The confessor was formally invited to remain at the station.

Whilst the authority of the Inspector seemed unquestionable the arrival of a World War did redress the balance slightly. 'Snotchie' held the rank, and, whilst there will be no attempt to explain the nickname, it should be noted that he was aware of the importance of his position. He announced it when he wished to reach the Power Station and was stopped by the Home Guard.

"Halt, who goes there?" was a perfect opportunity to state exactly who went there and, furthermore, where he wanted to go—the Power Station.

An unimpressed home Guard followed up with "Halt and give the password".

Snotchie was well and truly halted but he did not know the password. He passed on this lack of information and, in the process, recognised the Home Guard soldier as a well known local villain, known to all rather appropriately as 'Fagin'.

"Blast, you know me Fagin".

"No sir" replied the absent minded Fagin.

"Of course you know me, Fagin" came the exasperated rejoinder.

"No sir, who are you?"

A defeated Police Inspector left to find the password.

The rare occasions when the rank was seen in multiples complicated matters; usually it would happen in the middle of the day and, occasionally, in the evening. There was no collective noun for Inspectors, certainly not a pride, although two members of the rank did once come together with the result that pride went before the fall. Chesty was opening batsman for the police cricket team, he played as well as watched, with 'Shots' as his partner. Shots was a fairly stern Inspector who spoke in short machine gun like bursts, but the nickname related more to his ancestral connections with the village of Shotesham, than the speech. He was of hefty build, although not in Chesty's class.

With two Inspectors at the wicket there was serious attention to the state of the game, with the occasional cry of "Well played sir", usually from someone who looked for a favourable position on the duty sheet. It would have been well played if Chesty and Shots had concentrated on each other, and not sought to take a quick single with anxious eyes upon the chasing fielder. They collided in the centre of the wicket with the lesser built Shots recovering first, leaving Chesty stranded flat on his back and run out. As a furious Chesty trudged from the wicket the toadying "Well played" was changed to "Hard luck sir".

Spectators, and some players, watched keenly as Chesty obtained a folding chair and moved to an isolated position on the edge of the ground to nurse his temper, the state of which was evidenced when he slammed himself down into the chair to watch the match. The chair could not take it and collapsed, leaving Chesty once again spread on the ground and players and spectators engaged in a variety of convulsions. Eventually, the game recommenced and Chesty's temper improved at the after match repast.

Dignity of the rank nearly suffered when a selective canine chose the highest ranking officer on view. The landlord of the 'Ironmongers Arms' pushed his dog out of the main door for fresh air and natural functions. Whether the landlord saw the three policemen standing outside is not known, but the dog did. Whether he saw an Inspector, Sergeant and Constable, or six blue serged legs, is another matter. He chose the Inspector, who was Stanley, one of the more likeable representatives of the rank and destined for even greater things in his career. This popularity meant that Stanley received only a spattering instead of a soaking for the Constable warned him that the disrespectful dog was standing alongside operating on three legs. Cyril was the Constable and he later observed that certain other Inspectors would have received the full quota before he had been moved to speech. Cyril had, it will be recalled, survived being led astray on Seven Beat by Sid and the landlord of the 'Walnut Tree Shades', but it was entirely coincidental that he should again be lurking outside a public house.

Smartness of appearance was a trademark of one Inspector, not that the others were scruffy, and he enhanced his appearance on early turn by shaving in the Police Station. He then went one better by visiting a dry cleaners where he waited trouserless in a back room whilst his creases were professionally applied.

Although Inspectors were omnipotent they were not completely invincible. If lesser ranks were presented with an opportunity they would not turn it aside. The prime example was the meat delivery—the meat may have been prime as well, but that depended on who was receiving it. It all related to the proximity of the market which was a handy shopping area for all ranks, although the Constables had to be secretive in their dealings.

An Inspector patronised the meat stall in the morning, but needed to arrange delivery to his home. Simple, use the mobile. This arrangement worked well from everyone's point of view. Everyones?

The Inspector purchased a nice joint for himself and his wife, plus a large piece of what was probably whale meat for the dog. The latter purchase was wrapped in newspaper to distinguish it from the family joint in brown paper. The traffic car was then consigned to the task of delivery, which was duly carried out; but not before the wrappings had been exchanged, and the newly designated family joint had been tenderised by being hurled against a wall in the Police Station.

There were no recriminations. The Inspector and his wife remained pictures of health, not to mention vitality, whilst a certain dog thought our policemen, the mobile crew in particular, were truly wonderful.

It was probably the same crew that regularly delivered a newspaper to a very senior rank, you did not have to buy such items when very high rank was achieved, and just as regularly managed to infuriate the alsatian dog inside the house by waggling the newspaper in the letter box. That very senior rank often received his news through chewed newsprint. It seemed that Inspectors with dogs were vulnerable.

There was nothing wrong with Inspectors, provided you knew where they were and everything was all correct—"Sir"!

# Leave it to You

VERY SENIOR ranks, Superintendent upwards, could be found in different places, but mostly in the Police Station. They comprised a mixture of personalities and power likely to cause embarrassment or discomfort to the backbone of the force. They were similar to guided missiles in that they operated to deadly effect from a distance; that is not to say they were not effective from close range—in such cases they could be devastating.

The higher echelon was for many years, the Chief Constable, Deputy Chief Constable (holding Superintendent rank) and Superintendent. They issued written orders, made public declarations, and, on their rare excursions from the station, received salutes from the beat men who had not seen them coming soon enough. There was, however, some qualification to the stated rarity of these appearances. The Chief and the Deputy were special occasion or fine day performers, but the Superintendent, that was another matter. He was prone to occasional forays into the streets to demonstrate his supervisory powers and was consequently more dangerous; also, both he and the Deputy made for a delicate existence in Bethel Street Police Station by having resident accommodation on the top floor.

The inconvenience of having the hierarchy living above was more likely to be demonstrated at night, as the man who pressed the wrong button on the telephone switchboard had found out. Excessive noise at night could prompt an enquiry from above, and the last thing a harassed Station Sergeant wanted was an irritable Superintendent querying the inability to quieten someone who was reaching for the high notes with a powerful but slurred voice. The "do not disturb the Superintendent" campaign reached an incredible peak with instructions, believed to have emanated from Inspector level (following acid comment from above), that vehicles leaving the station in the early hours of the morning were not to start engines, or shut doors, until they were clear of the station area. This meant that vehicles initially headed for St. Peters Street, because it was downhill, with flapping doors and pushing, perspiring, cursing drivers. The swearing should have awakened the Superintendent.

The Superintendent was the one to watch for on the streets but for

104

very many years the holder of this post was not difficult to detect, principally because he had a habit of walking in the middle of the road. Affectionately known as 'Milky', he was trim in appearance, formal in manner, and keenly considerate in conversation. His supervisory visits to B Division were famous and can only be likened to a victorious troop commander entering a liberated city. He would proceed to Magdalen Gates Police Station via the centre of Magdalen Street, with traffic respectfully giving way to his imperious progress. However, increasing traffic and shortening tempers and, therefore, increasing risk, made this a less frequent exercise as time went by.

Beat officers appreciated Milky's centre of the road route. It gave them ample warning and those unofficially in Magdalen Gates Police Station could escape long before a querulous voice demanded to know the reason for their presence. The centre of the road did, however, give a commanding forward view of both pavements, and brave, or foolish, was the Constable who faded into an alley thinking he had not been observed. As likely as not, a gimlet eyed Milky had marked his disappearance for a pointed interview at a later time.

The centre of the road was not a guaranteed approach. One officer failed to detect Milky simply because he did not look at the top deck of a passing bus. He later received some advice on appearance and working a beat which brought about a renewed interest and future study of double deckers.

The Chief and Deputy Chief Constables were Olympian figures, glimpsed on occasions, rarely outside the station, who came into prominence when an all supreme being descended on the Force once a year. The HMI. The man who came to inspect the Force to reassure the Home Office that all was in order and the Chief Constable was not running a mickey mouse outfit.

As ranks progressed upwards to HMI (Her, or His, Majesty's Inspector of Constabulary) power increased and contact with the Constable decreased. You had to be lined up with three quarters of the Force to speak to the HMI, although if you were suicidal you could request a private audience.

The main parade was in the Fire Station yard, and the great man would pass along the ranks accompanied by the very senior officers of the Force who would be displaying a mixture of anxious and threatening looks depending upon whom they were gazing at the time.

If the HMI deigned to speak to one of the rigid figures his standard opening remark was "Had a good year?" Woe betide the man who had not had a good year. He would answer to the Superintendent later and the substance of the next year was guaranteed.

The HMI was an ex-Navy man and looked for campaign ribbons that might lead to a naval conversation. When he found one he would depart from the good year routine and relive the glory days of the Empire. Spotting an indicator during one of these nerve racking routines he stopped in front of the beribboned Sergeant.

"Navy man?"

"Yes sir".

A direct hit. The HMI followed up with a query concerning the Sergeant's role in that service.

"Stoker sir". Then before the HMI could warm to the theme he added "Merchant Navy sir".

The interview was over. The HMI passed on.

Moving along another line in the parade the HMI tried a random strike and asked a Constable to identify his job during the war.

"Stoker sir".

The HMI brightened. "Royal Navy" he asked, not wishing to be caught again.

"LNER sir" came the reply.

The HMI gave up.

The Traffic Department—'the mobile', were also lined up in the Fire Station yard with highly polished Wolseleys and Nortons on display. Normally, the HMI took only a passing interest in these fine examples of mobile power (the vehicles that is) passing a peremptory glance over the mechanised pride of the department; he may have been more interested if they had floated. However, during one particular visit the department had put itself at risk, probably with the comforting knowledge that the HMI did not delve deeply into the non-sea going transport. One of the Wolseleys had its engine removed for servicing, which was extremely bad timing with the inspection looming up. On the day itself the means of propulsion had not been replaced and the vehicle looked distinctly out of sorts with the front end appreciably higher than the rear. Highly polished, gleaming and impressive it might be, but, it obviously did not have an engine, which meant explanations to the HMI as to why it was off the road, and for how long. Policemen did not like giving the HMI explanations. They led to questions, awkward ones.

Initiative triumphed. Sandbags were acquired and the engine compartment was suitably stacked with the appropriate weight. The car was placed in line with its stablemates, and the inspection proceeded with a certain smugness amongst members of the Traffic Department. This was quickly replaced by consternation as the HMI studied the gleaming vehicles and crews standing alongside. Had he received information? Was the balance of the car wrong? He seemed very interested in the sandbagged Wolseley.

The HMI spoke to the crew (a bit of a misnomer) of the incapacitated Wolseley and then—horror of horrors—he asked for the bonnet to be lifted. You do not question an HMI, especially with a frowning Chief Constable standing alongside; the bonnet was opened by a traffic man who earnestly wished the ground would do likewise.

The HMI silently studied the sandbagged engine compartment whilst the Chief Constable fought against an on the spot coronary. The crew studied cloud formations, and the remainder of the parade tensed in anticipation. The game was up.

"Haw, haw. Running your vehicles on sand now Chief Constable" guffaws the HMI. He walks on, still guffawing and feeling rather pleased with himself. The Chief Constable follows, smiling weakly. He will make his comment later, when the HMI has gone.

Later, the parade moves to the parade room, minus vehicles of course, where probationers are ordered to identify themselves and produce pocket books to indicate the measure of their public service on a certain date selected by the HMI. Reports referring to that date, and relevant incidents, are then hastily produced to demonstrate the efficiency of the whole tour of duty. A call by the HMI for a probationer to describe a worthy deed is quickly answered, as the HMI knew it would be, by a Constable who has been planted (even if it was his day off) and suitably briefed. He stands up and recites parrot fashion how he responded to an alarming situation in the best traditions of the police service, giving graphic detail of the final victory over those who would dispute the peace, good order and laws of the land. He is encouraged by regular nods from the HMI and a broadening smile from the Chief Constable. The smile strengthens as the HMI makes his morale and motivation speech. All is well. The HMI assures the audience that they really are the finest and moves off to sort out the C.I.D., who are trying to find all sorts of reasons to absent themselves from the Police Station. Everything else returns to normal with the Traffic Department de-sandbagging a Wolseley.

If anyone thought the lessons of sandbagged Wolseleys were learnt in the C.I.D. they were wrong. The HMI caused as much panic and confusion there as anywhere, especially in the Scenes of Crime room—his favourite hunting ground. He liked to ferret amongst stored exhibits for labels and explanations. Frequently he was short on both.

A wary Detective Inspector instructed that everything should be properly labelled prior to the HMI's visit. He was, therefore, not too worried when the great man selected a jemmy and, holding it aloft, called for the crime report that related to this exhibit. The jemmy was labelled, and the Detective Inspector nodded to the anxious detectives standing in the background to comply. Whether he noticed they were trying to stand behind each other is not known. If he did he might have had a twinge of alarm, but if he had known why they were abandoning the front row he would have had a breakdown. The jemmy had been labelled shortly before the HMI's arrival, specifically because he was coming, and no one knew where it came from, or what it related to.

Two detectives, victims of the Detective Inspector's nod, slunk away from the HMI's circle with visions of resignation from the department, sudden illness, or a total denial as conspirators in a planned deception of the highest rank in the police service. Finding little comfort in any of these alternatives they galvanised the brain cells into action and grabbed a typewriter before disappearing into another room. Ten minutes later, with the HMI holding court on another subject, they appeared with a crime report and a prayer. The report received a glance and a nod before it was returned, and the HMI returned to the theme upon which he had been

107

pontificating. The prayer had worked.

The following year the problem of exhibit hunting by the HMI was solved by all potentially embarrassing articles being loaded into the crime car and the vehicle being consigned to innumerable laps of the Ring Road until the coast was clear. Pessimists said he would probably ask to see the crime car and they would have to invent a crime that it was attending.

The HMI was a policeman, but not a member of the Norwich City Police. Other policemen fell into this category and, although they were less auspicious, they sometimes presented problems; or a different way of thinking which amounted to the same thing. They had jurisdiction but were not desirous of contact with the public in the city, usually on the grounds they were just travelling through. They were officers of the Norfolk County Police, a separate force that knew all about such mysterious things as diseases of animals (Form D and the bucket of disinfectant), pig licences (not for the pigs—but for the owner to move them) and poaching.

County officers wore a slightly different uniform, less silver on show, carried helmet chin straps in the down position (they were no fools—less chasing and loss of dignity) and drove dark green Riley Pathfinders instead of black Wolseleys. Their wives ran a twenty four hour police service from the home address, and, when reports were submitted, the crawling vernacular used by police officers, respectfully, favourable consideration etc., went a stage further—they commenced "Sir I beg to report". Visions of the beat man on his knees proffering his written offering to the Inspector.

County officers working in the dormitory area around Norwich found themselves in a Berlin situation because the Divisional Headquarters was in Thorpe Road—Sixteen Beat on a cycle in the city. Pay day, therefore, produced the interesting situation in which they had to navigate the city streets from Hellesdon, Costessey, Sprowston, Thorpe and other outposts, to claim their money. As they passed the city beat man a standard form of greeting evolved.

"Morning, city".

"Morning, county".

Greetings were exchanged with great solemnity.

There were occasions when the boundary played a part in the police action that was to follow. Bodies found in the River Yare were the responsibility of whichever side the corpse was discovered. This resulted in some judicious prodding from bank to bank, followed by a telephone call to the Force on which side the corpse had been successfully propelled. Finding bodies in the river was not a problem. It was getting them out, and transporting and storing them, that became a distasteful task, especially if discovery had been considerably delayed.

The same principle applied to traffic accidents, except that the end result could not be shifted over the appropriate demarcation line. This in itself did not prevent disputes or, put in a more diplomatic way, discussions.

Officers who did not receive information directly from the all seeing public, or summoning pillarphone, could find themselves dealing with an incident in other ways: either coming upon the scene or having the fait accompli of it happening in front of them. The latter happened to a county officer and the former was the lot of his city counterpart. The demarcation line was suddenly important, and in this case, debatable.

The Norwich Ring Road created both the boundary and some geographical difficulty. The Aylsham Round roundabout was completely within the county, as was several yards of this road on the city side. For reasons of historical complexity, the dividing line ran from a point well into Aylsham Road, through shops, houses and gardens, to a point in Mile Cross Lane (on the Ring road), some half mile distant. Because of this aberration of city/county planning a metal post was inconspicuously placed in Aylsham Road, purporting to show the boundary line. Such a post should clearly show where responsibilities began and finished. Not so. Policemen can complicate the simplest of issues.

The traffic accident that was to cause a diplomatic incident occurred in the early 1960's and fell into the initial care of the county officer who witnessed a van attempting to negotiate the roundabout at a speed that defied all four wheels to remain on the ground. The offside wheels received an airing at an early stage, but progress towards the Aylsham Road was maintained successfully on the nearside wheels whilst an elevated and horrified driver attempted some form of remedial wheel twirling. It does not require a degree in mathematics to know that the outcome could only be a return to four wheels or a loss of adhesion from the two wheels that were performing so well as the vehicle continued into Aylsham Road.

The result was an emphatic loss of the two running wheels, a brief sideways contact with the road surface, followed by completion of the revolution with the van continuing its erratic journey along Aylsham Road on its roof and other side. Slowly it skated to a halt. The driver emerged from his upside down world and gloomily surveyed the trail of metal and glass leading back to the roundabout. His gloom deepened with the instant appearance of a cycle pushing policeman (county variety, but he wouldn't know that), followed within what seemed only seconds by a motor cycle officer.

The Constable on the Velocette was the Mile Cross Twenty and Twenty One Beats, engaged on property checks, and he came upon the accident without warning. The van's wheels had only just stopped spinning and glass was beginning to be crunched under the wheels of other vehicles, driven by neck craning drivers who determinedly drove through the wreckage and nearly into each other. Observing the county officer talking to a young man who had the air of someone who had recently owned a perfectly serviceable van but was now viewing the rusting, oil stained underside of a memory, he stopped to seek more information and make the token offer of help. Curiosity was always at a high point when someone else was doing the work.

"What happened?" followed by "Need any help?" was the usual two pronged opening gambit.

In this case the answer to the first made the second superfluous.

"No injuries. You've got plenty of witnesses. Leave it to you".

The words "Leave it to you" appear many times in a police career. They are a portent to work without assistance. This one, however, was out of order and the city representative of law and order informs the county representative accordingly. There follows a discussion upon the location of the city/county boundary in which reference is made to the aforementioned metal post, triumphantly pointed out by the city man with the indicating arm completing a sweep to the wreckage leading from the roundabout. At that juncture the city argument was winning hands down with no apparent comeback from the opposing side.

"Absolutely right" says the county man studying the metal post. "That's the boundary all right. And the van is on the city side".

A quick reply from the city advocate emphasises the trail of wreckage from the roundabout and the rolling antics of the van within the county, before it inconveniently slid into the city. This eloquent, and believed convincing, final speech fails to impress the stolid veteran of much county service who looks upon his much younger brother officer in the manner of a schoolteacher dealing with an awkward child.

"County". He waves expansively to the far side of the Ring Road.

"City. And there is the vehicle". He gives a short arm jab towards the van.

With these concluding statements the county officer mounts his cycle, and with a final comforting cry of "See you", heads back into county territory.

The driver of the van has been cheered up by following the legal and geographical discussions between those whom he had expected to concentrate on his recent driving exploits, although he is unsure whether his stiff neck is a result of following the debate or the accident itself. At least he now knows he is a city statistic.

Traffic accidents could provide a study in human relations that would do little to engender much faith in the human race a a whole, but would allow a certain wryness in assessing reoccurring patterns of behaviour.

"Any witnesses" is the cry to the rubber necking circle seeking the best view of someone else's misfortune. A visible shrinking of the circle might sometimes be interrupted by a self important voice making an announcement which amounts to seeing nothing, but wishes, nevertheless, to provide some opinion upon the event under examination. Little time is wasted on this voice of the people, especially if some genuine witness offers his, or her, services. Grab him, or her, before an occlusion of memory is prompted by the realisation of the tortuous and inconvenient path that will follow this public spirited action. It also helps if any all seeing witness is exiled before the opposing drivers home-in to assess, or influence, this potential threat, or aid, to their own assessment of the accident.

Direct the traffic? Not to bother, some bystander, whose life has just

*A geographical discussion*

taken on a new meaning, will adopt the important role of signalling to drivers who do not wish to hurry past until they have savoured every last detail for elaboration as soon as they arrive at their destination.

Another bystander often appears with a broom to take on a road sweeping role. He can be left to share the limelight with the traffic signaller whilst the policeman sorts out drivers and witnesses, and chalks around the vehicles; or if it is raining, asks another enterprising bystander to hold the end of the tape whilst he takes the measurements that will obviously be unobtainable when the vehicles are moved. Add chalk and tape to the unofficial appointments of the all round beat officer.

Statements have to be taken from all concerned, except of course tape holding, road sweeping, traffic signalling bystanders. Praise be to the inventor of the biro. A rain sodden book containing a statement remains slightly legible, although subject of much eyebrow twitching when produced in Court to support the typed copy. It is at this point that the finer points of the accident will be discussed without appreciation of the sweeping rain, gloomy street lighting, frozen fingers, arguing drivers assessing their damage, complaining witnesses who want to be on their way and have just realised they didn't see anything after all, curious bystanders obstructing views and movement, and, finally, but most importantly—the detailed examination at the scene of every document relevant to that person being on the road with that vehicle; if they are not available it's another form to fill out.

The policeman who negotiates the pitfalls of dealing with stressful people in an accident situation will later compare the statements to

111

ascertain the truth of the collision; an ideological view that is often a road to disappointment; he should not be surprised to find that, if the versions given are correct, either no one is to blame or everyone is at fault, with the exception of the statement maker. Sometimes the statements reveal that the vehicles did not collide after all.

The paperwork is later given to the Sergeant for his signature and comment. The former is not so easily obtained as the latter. However, after a frowning concentrated study, he compares the handwriting unfavourably with a Chinese physician and, with a final grumble that the whole thing looks as if it has been written underwater, it has, he signs the offering. Sergeants did not like Traffic Accident Reports. They contained too many complications and pitfalls.

Traffic accidents were not all gloom and distress and the fish lorry that scraped alongside a traffic signal box at Mousehold crossroads presented opportunity to those with an eye to the advantages of the profession. (Quickly evident at the St. Stephen's Co-op). It also permeated the night air with a distinctive aroma as boxes of plaice fillets cascaded over the grass verge. Broken boxes were condemned on the spot by a disconsolate transport manager attending the scene, but his fears concerning the clear up problem were dissipated as the Norwich City Police gave the matter its best attentions and spirited away a large quantity of unwanted fish. Wreckage was cleared and normality restored in a quarter of the estimated time, and a certain police car still contained a detectable odour when it was, a long time later, sold at auction.

If the fish lorry accident attracted policemen the cyclist who fell from

*The routine of weather—looks as if it has been written underwater*

112

his machine, shortly after six a.m. one cold and frosty morning, had exactly the opposite effect. He started with more than enough; four to be precise; cycling home from night duty as a gossiping pack, wending their way from Bethel Street Police Station and the rigours of night duty. They were moving steadily towards St. Giles Gates, a five road junction which was to be of some significance to the cyclist.

It was not unusual at shift changeover times to see groups of cycling policemen radiating out from Bethel Street, gradually diminishing as individuals pursued their own specific homeward paths; but it was a vulnerable time. The public understood what it could see, namely, a uniformed policeman. On or off duty did not come into the reckoning, a policeman was a policeman and if you found one, provided of course you actually wanted one, there could be no discussion or reference to unavailability. What you saw is what you got.Unless you were a bemused cyclist sitting in the middle of St. Giles Gates.

It was not a serious accident; one of those minor skirmishes that take up a lot of time to no effectual result; but it was a traffic accident requiring the full attention and comforting ministrations of the police, provided they knew about it. The cyclist thought they knew about it because they were there at the time. He had only touched, or possibly just missed, but definitely been thrown off course by a passing car (probably did not expect to see a vehicle at that time in the morning), and, after losing control of his machine, he had slid into the centre of the confluence of five roads where he sat taking stock of the sudden turn of events. His unnerved gaze perceived that he was not alone; a group of cycling policemen were bearing down upon him with all the solemnity and orderly cranking of pedals that goes with the importance of their job. Never has one accident had no such assistance so readily available.

The ex-cyclist sitting in the road regrouped his senses and stared expectantly at the ready-made 'flying squad' who had stopped gossiping and appeared, in his opinion, to have concentrated a collective attention upon him. Without faltering in their pace, and now seemingly intent on other things more distant, the cycling group moved to both left and right, passing the solitary recumbent figure without speech or incident. Without a backward glance they cycled on into Earlham Road, disappearing into the distance and leaving another early morning traveller scrambling to his feet, locating a cycle, and reappraising the local Police Force.

The sequel to this interesting event appeared the following night when one of the cycling policemen was posted to Eight Beat and went into the Bus Station for a cup of tea with the night duty mechanics. He was quietly imbibing the warming liquid, and listening to all manner of tales from garrulous workers, when an aggrieved individual insisted on castigating the police on the grounds that a number of them had cycled past him as he lay in the middle of the road following an accident. The Constable choked on his tea, sympathised with the disgruntled victim, muttered something about the Force not being what it was, and remembered he had some property to check. A case of leave it to you.

# Special Duties—or Just Different

CHECKING PROPERTY and directing traffic was the staple routine of the city policeman; opportunities for more specialist work being limited and dependent upon the views of senior ranks.

To escape the dictates of the daily duty sheet it had to be a department, preferably one of the big two—'the mobile' or C.I.D., otherwise it was a case of hoping that the Inspectors pencil slipped in the right direction to favour some of the generally unfavoured.

So what were the desirable, the much sought after, interesting, job satisfying duties that avoided the arm being pointed at a vehicle or door handle? On the duty sheet eager eyes would seek out 'plain clothes', 'crime car' and 'river patrol', before reluctantly searching the beats to find the area where the public would utilise the subject's talents over the next two weeks.

'Plain clothes' was a six p.m. to two a.m. duty, allocated to two men who were detached from normal night beat duties and allowed to walk freely around the city. This patrol distinguished itself in 1958 when it captured two burglars in a Magdalen Street cafe after a terrific fight on the premises, but criminals were not always available and, with no door handles demanding attention, other means had to be found to occupy the time.

The Fifteen Beat man, working the somnolent depths of Calvert Street in the middle of the night, was in the near comatose state that formed an integral part of the Fifteen Beat syndrome, but he was on time as he progressed along the door handles of the street that time forgot. It was dark, very dark on Fifteen Beat, and very cold. It was also quiet, very quiet. With his concentration dulled by the repetitive doors, dismal alleys and gloomy street, he was suddenly aroused by a loud bang and the sound of running feet. Regrouping his senses he flashed a speculative light in the general direction, saw nothing but heard another bang with receding footsteps. He set off in pursuit of the unknown, matching his running feet to those in front. The traditional cry of "Oi, stop!" was uttered more as a matter of form than in the hope that someone was actually going to comply.

The chase was concluded in Muspole Street when the running feet

114

went down a yard near the Pitt Street junction. Just as well they did, for the greatcoat was proving too much for the pursuer and he was contemplating an honourable defeat and return to orderly scheduled working. On reflection, it was slightly strange how the fleeing phantom managed to make so much noise whilst maintaining an exact unseeing distance ahead; he, them, or whatever, was always just around the next corner or just out of viewing distance, which admittedly was not very great in this poorly lighted disreputable part of the city; but now the noisemaker was trapped for it was a one way in, same way out yard.

It was noisemakers, two at least; the out of breath policeman framed in the entrance to the yard could hear low conversation which initially sounded like giggling. Approaching slowly he probed the yard with his torch and in what he hoped was a strong commanding voice, but actually came out as a nervous croak, he said, "Come out. I know you are there". More banging, shuffling—then laughter. They came out—two plain clothes men with nothing better to do. An interesting conversation followed, with the Fifteen Beat man hoping that his number would one day land alongside the magic words on the duty sheet—'plain clothes'.

Crime car driver was another night duty prize, and a splendid escape from the uniform operational routine. It was a passport to working with the C.I.D., even if it was only as a chauffeur. The idea was that the insufficiency of detectives at night would be made up by a driver. The night confusion really arose was when no one could find the crime car and that included the driver. He claimed to have parked it in Guildhall Hill and it was eventually decided that it had been stolen, although when the Duty Inspector was so informed he immediately cast aspersions upon the character of a certain detective. Many harsh words were spoken before the vehicle was found two miles away in Grove Road. No one ever deduced how it got there.

River Patrol was a grand sounding title for a pleasant day duty performed in the summer months. It was allocated, via the duty sheet, to a lucky Constable who would act as an assistant to the regular on the launch: this was one of the mobile drivers, working on the theory that it was a driving job.

The original police boat was an old forbidding looking black rowing boat of impressive size which was kept behind the laundry near Mile Cross Bridge. In the 1930's a certain Constable was given the responsibility of rowing this ominous looking craft along the river for the specific purposes of body recovery or impressing the locals on the banks. These were the early days of a police presence on water, although it is disputed by some who claimed that Inspectors always walked on water.

The later police launch was demonstrative rather than effective and although it was a nice sideline, weather permitting, it could not be viewed as a career prospect. Occasionally, exuberant speed boat drivers had to be rebuked, and, there were times when the distasteful duty of recovering bodies was experienced, but these were minority events. Differences between Norwich City and Norfolk County officers as to which side of the river the body was located did not matter when the River Patrol was available.

The boathouse was located at the Ketts Hill mortuary, and jurisdiction extended along the navigable waters of the Wensum and Yare as far as Hardley Cross. No A or B Divisions, no predatory senior ranks; just a pleasant day out saluting holidaymakers and eating sandwiches in the reed beds away from it all. Not always so. It could go wrong on water just as well as on land.

On a fine summer's day two Constables set out in the launch from Ketts Hill with specific instructions to assist at the Whitlingham Regatta; an event of some importance to the boating types who would flock to this stretch of the river in considerable numbers. Our ambassadors of the river had plenty of time and it was natural they should seek to foster police and public relations at a select watering hole, otherwise known as riverside public house. It was a popular public house and the room in which the crew sought to refresh themselves became the centre of attention for a number of Northern holidaymakers claiming to have some ability at the game of darts.

A noisy, cheerful relationship was forged over bear and darts, with the holidaymakers notably impressed by the prowess of the Norwich policemen in both departments. Eventually, it was time to leave and, to a chorus of hearty farewells, the River Patrol cast off in the direction of Whitlingham Regatta. The occupants of the launch felt very happy, until they found they were late for the regatta which had already started. To add to their misfortune a freighter had blocked part of the river forcing the finish line away from the spectators. Things were suddenly going badly; but no matter, the regatta organising committee did not appear to be laying blame. They ignored the belated arrival of the River Patrol and invited its crew to the club house for drinks. The crew accepted.

At the club house the police made another impression. The allocated Constable was overcome with the generosity of the committee and decided to remove his cape to allow more arm movement. The generous twirling movement that effected the removal of the garment also cleared the table of drinks, which meant future generosity was going to be limited. There was a distinct possibility that relationships might fall into the same category and it was time to inaugurate some more farewells. Everyone parted on the best of terms. There was a lot to be said for River Patrol.

Underwater, as opposed to over, was normally not too much of a problem, for neither criminal or policeman had much desire to explore beneath the surface. However, the need arose when bodies refused to come up and thieves hurled their ill gotten gains down. The forerunner of a modern diving squad was a volunteer frogman working on the principle that it is in there somewhere, go and find it.

The frogman, singular, brings us back to the Traffic Department, for Donny was the pioneer in this field—or perhaps lake or river is a better expression. He was a keen, strong swimmer, who, with borrowed equipment, had frequently been called to watery situations to retrieve articles and persons. After some publicity the Watch Committee

116

authorised the purchase of a proper diving suit, thus recognising the post. Those early days did, however, lack some sophistication, especially noted when those on the bank wished to communicate with Donny who was in the murky depths. Whether a proper lifeline had been included in the budget, or was even available, is not known, but the hurling of stones became the most efficient communication of the time. Small stones and near misses to attract attention was required. Anyone outside these terms of reference was likely to incur Donny's wrath.

Riot Squad had received some earlier mention and it featured notably under that title in the 1940's to 1960's period. That such a concept is also a feature of modern policing could be said to show that some things do not change. What does not change is contingency planning and that is what the Riot Squad was, and still is. If trouble is anticipated then prepare for it. Weekends or bank holidays, festive occasions or the like, pubs and certain areas were likely to demonstrate the tendency to alcohol induced disorder, therefore, find a vehicle and put some policemen inside, usually with a Sergeant in charge, and tour the trouble spots. With radio communication a trouble shooting flying squad was in being. Quite often it was used for convenience work and the night the Nineteen Beat man was delayed by a drunk in Westwick Street was no exception.

On a cold Saturday night, with the rooftops already white with frost, the Riot Squad was not over employed. There were few drunks moving around or laying about in the open, and, in view of the identity of the Station Sergeant, it was also unlikely that any were in the Police Station.

The Riot Squad of that night was very conscious of the Station Sergeant's wishes in respect of drunks—he didn't want to see any. It was, therefore, with mixed feelings that they obeyed the instruction to go to Westwick Street and assist the Nineteen Beat man who had a drunk.

There was some initial difficulty in finding the Nineteen Beat man but, eventually, he was located behind the tyre company premises busily engaged in drowning his drunk. That was how it appeared to the Riot Squad and in practice their arrival probably prevented the beat man's enthusiasm going too far. The drunk was inverted in a water tank used for the identification of punctures and although he was hauled upwards at intervals to obtain a minimal supply of oxygen he was quickly ducked beneath the surface again. The Nineteen Beat man also knew the identity of the Station Sergeant and had no intention of making an arrest.

The squad saved the drunk from a watery end and debated the next move, until a Constable recognised the sodden figure oozing water at the feet of the uniformed assembly. He knew his address in Devonshire Street and that was not very far from Westwick Street. It was decided. Everyone's interest would be served by running him home, promptly, before he became an icicle.

The Nineteen Beat man returned to his scheduled property checks, calculating the time lost, and the Riot Squad loaded a saturated drunk into the back of the van. Delivery to Devonshire Street was quick and without incident. A street of terraced houses, pocket handkerchief front

*The intruder was both wet and unconscious*

gardens and complete silence. At the indicated number there was no reply
to the knocking, which was unusual for normally when a policeman
knocked the street was liable to turn out; must have been the clandestine
nature of the operation that subdued the police approach to the house.

The negative response at the house was not a complete bar to further
proceedings for the front door was found to be unlocked. It was
tentatively opened to reveal a small living room and convenient settee.
The solution was obvious; place him inside in the warm to sober up; he
wouldn't remember anything about it tomorrow.

A drunk was quietly loaded onto a settee followed by a stealthy exit.
The Riot Squad went  off to ingratiate themselves with the Station
Sergeant and that should have been the end of the matter. Not quite. The
Station Sergeant had another job for them. Go to Devonshire Street
where a householder had discovered a man in his front room. The intruder was both wet and unconscious. The squad hurried back to a certain
address where a perplexed householder was most impressed at the speed
and efficiency with which they removed the intruder. He was not enlightened.

Vice, in the form of prostitution, was regularly dealt with by the
policewomen on the grounds that it was all to do with women, although
someone did point out that men had a part to play. Sometimes, the Nineteen Beat man shouted at the lurking figures in Rose Lane and, provided
they gave up lurking, honour was satisfied; and, sometimes, the Sergeant
appeared to dispense cautions to those who failed to see him approaching.

Johnnie was a Sergeant prominent in figure and voice. Normally, those who did not see him coming were afflicted or otherwise engaged—the latter example having been provided by nocturnal fishing and knife grinding on the beat. Largely built, ex-RAF aircrew, with the moustache to prove it, he had a formidable, and when necessary, noisy presence. It was often necessary, although the night he approached a prostitute in Cattle Market Street in the company of the Nine Beat man he was more visually obvious. Amazingly, she failed to appreciate his presence. He resolved to give her a caution, which would have been quite unforgettable, but she stood her ground, compounding a defiant attitude by refusing to give her name and address. She was 'invited' to accompany Johnnie to the Police Station.

On the way to Bethel Street the lady of the night urgently sought to use the Cattle Market public toilet. This created the spectacle of Johnnie standing outside holding a handbag as if this was nothing unusual in the line of police duty. No passer-by dared to comment.

Eventually, they arrived at the Police Station where the policewoman on duty was Beryl, worldly wise and experienced, but due for a shock in this case. Beryl removed the prisoner for searching and Johnnie rummaged through the contents of the handbag in an effort to trace her identity. A bus ticket to a nearby village was found and a telephone call was then made to the worthy member of the County Police who operated a twenty four hour service in this area. He responded promptly, listened and replied, "That's not a her, it's a him. You've got Reggie".

Beryl was about to make the same discovery but a shout from the Station Office stopped her.

Reggie was committed to a local hospital and Johnnie stared suspiciously at prowling prostitutes for some time afterwards.

Policewomen often went on expeditions to snaffle some of the regular prostitutes, keeping observation from their own private car. The policewoman who captured a well known prostitute, of more than ample proportions, was committed to taking her to the Police Station, but had only her own rather small vehicle which had been used for observation purposes. She loaded this immoral heavyweight into her mechanical pride and joy only to see her crash through the floor. The Police Force paid the sum of £6 to compensate for a restructured vehicle.

John was a night duty Detective Constable, who, accompanied by another officer, was driving the C.I.D. car through Cattle Market Street when he was compelled to stop by the sight of a body slumped outside the 'Buff Coat' public house. Not a murder but a totally drunk prostitute known to, and unwelcomed by, Station Sergeants. She could not be roused and John went off to the nearest pillarphone to advise the Station Sergeant that it was necessary to remove her to the station for her own safety. He received some advice in return which concluded with the phone being slammed down at the station end.

Returning to the 'Buff Coat' John initiated his own solution. On the other side of the road was the Cattle Market (after all it was Cattle Market

Street) and immediately opposite, pig pens; liberally covered with straw. The unconscious prostitute was carried over the road and propped in a sitting position inside a pen. She was covered with the cleanest straw that could be found, how clean is a matter of detail and degree not relevant to this account, and with her head uncovered was left to pass the night away. She survived none the worse for her experience, although there was a possible shortage of customers for some time afterwards.

Prostitutes who gave up street work did not automatically cancel police interest. The house they operated from would quickly draw attention to itself through the heavy visiting traffic. These houses of ill repute required police observation, an ideal job for the plain clothes patrol; but what the plain clothes patrol knew of surveillance techniques was probably gained from American films; it certainly did not come from police training because there wasn't any.

Two plain clothes officers, hiding behind the hedge in St. Matthews Churchyard, were taken aback when the house they were watching in Rosary Road suddenly disgorged a number of American servicemen, who, with threatening gestures, surrounded the watchers. They were more than taken aback because they were taken to Ketts Hill Section Box by three oversized specimens of our noble allies. Apparently, they did not believe the English police would act as 'peeping toms'. The Duty Inspector arrived and restored the special relationship, as well he might because he had given them the observation duty in the first place. Two discomfited plain clothes men were even more concerned to find a knife of Davy Crockett proportions lying on the wall surrounding the Section Box, just as if it had been placed there by someone entering the station.

The darkness of a yard at the rear of a Duke Street house seemed a good observation position to another plain clothes patrol seeking evidence of a bawdy house, but they were forced to re-think their strategy when an upstairs window opened and a large quantity of water fell upon one of them. He thinks it was water.

Other special duties manifested through unforeseen occasions. In 1963 the conspiracy to collect insurance from the destruction of a cafe in Exchange Street gave rise to a long running observation duty upon one of the conspirators in a city hospital. He had got it all wrong, and, although in no apparent state to walk from hospital care, he had to be watched and any pronouncement noted. He actually made several but they were mostly irrelevant, if not obscene and physically impossible. It was a long time before his blackened figure was able to engage in some form of reasonable interview, and, such was his normal disposition, he was not inclined to favour the uniformed bedside watcher with anything other than his own strong anti-police feeling. It was this jaundiced view of authority, evidenced by previous misdeeds, that had made him so suitable for recruitment by a cafe owner who had bought a going concern that, after a period of his proprietorship, was no longer going. The plan was that it was to be going—up in flames.

Three local men, with a limited degree of success in criminal matters, had responded to another's wishes by visiting the cafe in the early hours and pouring petrol through the letter box. Two walked away leaving the hospital destined conspirator to apply the necessary ignition. This he did, but the resulting explosion made sure that he did not walk away, indeed, he became the only known person to cross Exchange Street without touching the road surface—unforeseen progress which was halted by the Corn Hall opposite. The whole affair caused great activity in the C.I.D. and set up the long running hospital duty. It also closed Exchange Street and removed a cafe much frequented by certain C.I.D. officers.

Football duty was special but foreseen. It was special, desirable, and available to the night duty men. That requires further explanation because, although Norwich City sometimes played as if it was dark, it really meant that the selected night duty men reported back on duty for an extra tour on a Saturday afternoon. Genuine overtime money paid by the football club.

Take a chair, sit in the corner and watch the match; try not to get too excited (usually not difficult); stand up at half time and full time—even walk around—wait until the crowd has gone and report off duty. All with a crowd of 30,000 and a team bottom of the Third Division (South).

In 1959 everyone got excited. An FA Cup run with famous names falling to the footballing skills of the yellow and green from Carrow Road. Manchester United, Cardiff City, Spurs, Sheffield United—all vanquished in the pursuit of a Wembley dream. The local population rose up, took notice and demanded tickets. Contingents of police paraded on duty at Carrow Road to control ticket queues; extra numbers were drafted in for the matches and the city developed a single talking point. As the fever increased, rent collectors failed to collect, oversized canaries appeared in shop windows, the brewery horses were draped in yellow and green, footballers achieved god like status (similar to Inspectors) and police dignity evaporated. A Constable standing on a biscuit tin (he was below Stumpy's height requirements) waving his helmet as the winning goal was scored against Sheffield United was observed to lose his balance and disappear amongst a similarly delirious section of supporters.

The demand for tickets did bring out the worst in some supporters, principally when ticket queues learned that tickets were running out. Those at the back would attempt to make the front, and those at the front would resist the attempt. This was unfortunate because the queue wound around the club car park which had a common entry and exit of road width only. It made the queue look reasonable, until it was realised that several hundred people were in the car park, and what you could see, was going to be unattainable for a very long time. It had to happen; the back section bisected the car park entrance and joined the front section, leaving a distinctly unhappy middle section. Chaos ensued, with helmets bobbing around in all sections, until there were no more tickets to fight over.

On another occasion an ill judged announcement that tickets were running out resulted in a concerted rush which lost the club a very good fence.

The black market in tickets brought strange people into the city. They talked out of the corner of the mouth with a funny accent, and kept giving sidelong glances as if expecting an ambush from unknown quarters. They called the locals "Guv", and flashed wads of tickets before their startled eyes. Some were quickly disptached by broad shouldered countrymen whose interests ranged between tractors and Norwich City Football Club. The manner of the dispatch varied from a polite "No thanks" to a passing arm movement which left the furtive vendor sitting on the pavement surrounded by fluttering tickets. These vendors did not complain to the police but one of their intended customers did. He was upset by the effrontery of a ticket spiv and complained to the nearest policeman, who just happened to be other than a crowd supervising Constable. It was Milky, always liable to be on view at major public events, and on this occasion he would not have been criticised if he had summoned a Constable to deal with the complaint; more or less expected of very senior officers. He did no such thing, but marched up to the indicated street entrepreneur and demanded to see the tickets in his possession. The spiv, taken aback by Milky's sudden and forceful appearance, handed over a bundle of tickets for inspection. There was no hesitation in the sequence that followed. Milky walked away, tore the tickets to pieces and scattered them from the ramparts of Carrow Bridge. The spiv was advised, in true Western parlance, that the place was not big enough for both of them. Problem solved.

For non-students of football history Norwich did not grace Wembley and life returned to normal. Rent collectors even managed to recover some back money.

Another specialism was police dog handler. Not everyone was used to having these animals on their own side but 1959 saw an enlightened attitude with two allocated alsatians and handlers. Much was made of an early failure when a local criminal, who had been pursued into undergrowth, was not discovered by the searching dog. It was not so much the failure to find him, it was his later complaint that the dog had cocked his leg over the bush in which he had been hiding.

Even greater discussion followed the dog's handler attendance at a fight in Davey Place in which the mobile and beat officers were desperately trying to subdue a particularly fractious group of young men. As more officers joined the fracas, and victory became certain, time was taken to look for the dog. It was spotted lying under a parked police van watching proceedings with a look of intense interest.

Searching for intruders on premises was, of course, a strong point for police dogs, and it was much welcomed by officers who did not fancy being ambushed. The dog summoned to the scene often distinguished itself but occasionally got its priorities mixed up. The alsatian pushed into a supermarket was unused to the new help yourself display racks but quickly adapted and returned promptly to the handler. Whether it was choice cutlets or dog meat in its jaws cannot be recalled but it was definitely  something that was for sale and far removed from a burglar. Never let it be said that police dogs were not intelligent. Another example of their brain power was their biting record: although they sometimes bit policemen, there is no recorded case of the victim being other than a Constable.

The dogs did have many triumphs and successes and when they failed it was not always their fault. Stanley was the pioneer and first well known dog handler, and both he and a succession of dogs had a creditable record. It was, therefore, fortunate that he was immediately available and in the company of the C.I.D. when the call went out that intruders were believed to be on the premises in Botolph Street. To be exact it was two a.m. and Stanley was in the Bethel Street canteen with John, the night duty Detective Constable (who lodged prostitutes in pig pens).

John left to collect the C.I.D. van with a "I'll see you there Stanley". Stanley followed to collect the dog van.

At that time of the morning it was very quick progress to Botolph Street and detective and dog handler arrived close together. Sure enough the rear of the premises had been forced. The next move was obvious.

"Put the dog in Stanley".

Stanley moves to acquiesce but two minutes later he returns from the van to report that he cannot find his dog. There follows a detailed conversation with the question from Stanley, "Is it you C.I.D. buggers playing tricks again?" John protests his innocence and they search the building without the dog.

A quick return to the Police Station allays the fears of a worried Stanley. The dog is asleep under a canteen table.

Horses could be categorised with dogs: they turned up when they were not wanted, had a knack of making life awkward, and they joined the Force. The joining was irregular and part time, dedicated police horses fading away after the First World War.

The cavalry supplied horses for special events the most notable of which was the 1937 Coronation Parade through the city when the Deputy Chief Constable rode a white charger and gave a fine display of horsemanship, mainly due to his position immediately in front of the band.

Later suppliers were a Tuckswood riding stables, and a local brewery who provided a team to pull the city coach on ceremonial occasions; usually the opening of the Assizes when the Lord Mayor and Judge of the High Court rode in splendour and discomfort between the Guildhall, Cathedral and Shirehall. The coach would be expertly steered by ornately dressed flunkeys, alias brewery drivers, who did their best to prevent the procession from hesitating outside public houses with the relevant brewery allegiance. This required extreme concentration because the horses could not tell the difference between the Lord Mayor and a barrel of beer. The hesitation was pronounced the day someone forgot to sand Gaol Hill, and the illustrious passengers found themselves with the same view for some time.

Heading many important processions was a lone horse acquired from the Tuckswood stables and ridden by a policeman with the necessary equestrian expertise. Three officers undertook this prestigious duty from the end of the Second World War to the eventual passing of the Norwich City Police. Sid (of 'Walnut Tree Shades' fame), who spurned the stables offering and supplied his own popular and well known horse—'Starlight'; Alfie, a War Reserve officer, and Paddy, one of the regular beat officers. They received admiration but little envy from the many officers who viewed horses with suspicion, especially those who found them when they didn't want to.

Using a hired hack was all right in most circumstances, but when you put it up against the finest police horses in the world you might reasonably expect a modicum of difficulty. Few would dispute the qualities of the Royal Canadian Mounted Police, and their visit to Norwich was justifiably seen as an important event requiring an appearance by a Norwich City Police mounted officer in the vanguard of their procession. Alfie was the nominated outrider and he duly collected his steed from the Tuckswood riding stables, then briskly clip clopping his way down to Thorpe Station he met the de-training company of upright impressive looking men, resplendent in scarlet tunics, astride powerful snorting beasts that were anxious to stretch fetlocks, or whatever horses stretched after a confining train journey. Alfie's horse was not so anxious after the long journey from the stables and it had drawn the short straw anyway, for Alfie was unquestionably the heaviest of the police riders.

From Thorpe Station the colourful troop was to ride to the Royal Norfolk Showground and the horses set off at a brisk trot, or should it be a canter, with tossing manes, rolling eyes and the odd frisky pirouette; whilst the riders sat in a stiff erect position, gloved hands holding pennanted lances to one side and occasionally tweaking reins as bottoms rose and fell in unison. A stirring sight much appreciated by the cheering, waving crowds. Alfie trotted along in front enjoying the reflected adulation, and, who knows, he may have momentarily transported himself in his mind to the Rockies.

A great part of the route was uphill and Alfie's horse knew little of the Rockies. It was a flatlands Norfolk horse and by the time the Dereham Road was reached it was fed up and tired. The Mounties continued to bounce up and down and there was no sign of the pace slackening; if anything the long straight Dereham Road and lessening number of spectators encouraged a quickening speed making the end inevitable for Alfie. His horse expired, not totally, but physically and temporarily, appropriately within sight of the county boundary. Alfie knew he was not going to make the showground. He pulled over to the side of the road to avoid the ignominy of vanishing into the eagerly cantering red stream immediately behind. His mount gasped great lungfuls of air and, with heaving sides and trembling legs, fought against total collapse. The Mounties swept past as Alfie lurched to the ground in the interests of kindness to animals. This was a case where the Mounties got their man, but then lost him.

Special duties were all very well but sometimes they were just a bit too special.

# Man Versus Machine

THE MOST magnificent, contrary and formidable representation of the Norwich City Police was mechanical. GLT 1 was not just a number, it was a means of transport; it was an institution. Ironically, today, its number is worth more than the vehicle ever was, but that is a mercenary view that does not do justice to the sterling work performed by the vehicle.

To the uninitiated it was simply a two ton Bedford truck in dark blue with a closed back. Unmistakeably a 'Black Maria'; but originally an ambulance and a National Fire Service vehicle, now passed on to the police as surplus to the requirements of a developing Fire Service.

GLT, as she, or he, or it,was known, provided a comprehensive service, which included hauling cycles, car engines, drunks, corpses, prisoners and policemen. It was the Pickfords of the Norwich City Police. The rear compartment was a history of events, incidents and a miscellany of property. The front compartment was where the buck stopped and the stress began.

Driving GLT required confidence and an iron resolve but, it had a select band of mentors who nurtured it in a way that disguised the cantankerous nature known to others. It could often be seen progressing through the city streets pretending to be a normal vehicle without any hint of latent aggression.

The select band in question was a cross section of the Traffic Department, including some of the mobile drivers who managed the quantum leap from Wolseley smoothness to Bedford abrasiveness with praiseworthy composure. They were, however, with assorted other officers, the irregulars, for GLT spent much of its running time in the hands of stalwarts such as 'Bodge' and Herbert, two veteran officers who performed Traffic Department duties outside the mainstream of motor cycle and patrol car driving. Herbert and GLT became synonymous for many years and he pursued the extremes by also becoming the Chief Constable's driver—not of course in GLT.

A tall and craggy individual, Herbert had the stature of the envisaged old time policeman and in this sense he shared an historical affinity with

125

GLT. They worked well together and could regularly be found visiting the Section Boxes, collecting cycles which some enterprising member of the public had found; or perhaps the massive police uprights which required some form of attention in the workshops. Herbert wore a grey smock over his uniform and, although GLT was not labelled, it was obvious to all whom he and the vehicle represented.

Because of the awesome reputation of the vehicle a test of potential GLT drivers was deemed necessary. The best of two falls or a submission with a Chieftain tank might have been a useful baptism but it was decreed that the victim should go straight in at the deep end. "There it is. Get in and drive it."

It was possible to actually request this induction and it was usually granted as a disguised examination of nerve and sanity. Normally, requesting anything outside regular beat work was viewed with suspicion and refused on the grounds that those above made the decisions and knew what was best for those below.

The test could be harrowing or merely stressful, depending upon the start, or to be more precise—the temperature of the beast itself. If it was in the Fire Station yard, and unused over a significant period, quite short in winter, then the engine and everything connected with it was cold. If driving GLT was a fight, driving a cold GLT was war at its very worst. It responded to low temperatures with all the stubborness of setting concrete. The engine ticked over like falling granite and the gear lever discounted every notch in the metal case that served as a gearbox.

Warm or cold, moving the steering wheel was a full scale keep fit exercise, although there was ample time if you took into consideration the creeping acceleration. Not that the steering wheel mattered very much when the engine was cold because the first quarter mile needed two hands to shuttle between reverse, first and second gears. As straight a route as possible was a distinct advantage in the early stages of the journey.

So to the induction or test. The examinee ponders upon what he has heard. Can it be true? Policemen were known for both humour and exaggeration. With conflicting emotions of apprehension and resignation he seeks out Donny, the Traffic Sergeant who was regularly designated to test aspiring GLT drivers in the 1950's and 60's.

They walk from Bethel Street Police Station to locate GLT parked in the side road by the Fire Station, fresh from cycle carrying adventures with Herbert. Good old Herbert. Many an officer made this statement upon finding a warm GLT.

Climbing aboard, it is necessary to carry out the cabin drill of lining up the mirrors, checking the controls, and praying. The silver coloured card hanging from the windscreen bracket does little to boost the driver's confidence. It is entitled 'In Loving Memory'.

Starting the engine is no problem. Use the self starter, ignoring the clothes peg which dangles on a piece of string and is intended to keep the choke out. First gear is selected by moving the gear lever in a hopeful forward direction thereby bringing into play arm muscles that have long been neglected and will shortly rival aching leg muscles, one half of which are currently holding down a clutch pedal that is fighting to rise from the floor.

Handbrake off, not the most delicate of instruments, and the clutch comes in with all the subtlety of an exploding cannon. GLT is rolling and the driver is sweating.

The early stages of the trip can be deceptive. Heaving the wheel round, pushing the accelerator and footbrake, and studying the minute view of life to the rear; it is all fairly steady and uneventful until a rising speed calls for a gear change. Now for the crunch—a carefully chosen and most descriptive word. GLT had what was called, most aptly, a crash box. In simple terms gear changes required double declutching, something which held no fears to seasoned drivers who had not been reared on syncromesh gearboxes. Others found it an exercise in physical and mental stress.

Engine note rising, floor the clutch, gear lever to neutral, release the clutch and then slam it down again, gear lever to new position, release the clutch. Fine, except for two things. Firstly, the head turning grinding noises that indicated the sequence was not to GLT's liking, and secondly, the protracted timescale in obtaining the higher gear meant that it was no longer required because the engine speed had fallen. Further attempts at the sequence, intending to return the lever whence it came, result in a no man's land position. All this time GLT rolls along at a decreasing speed and Donny views the proceedings with increasing disquiet.

So our new driver chases up and down the gearbox and hauls GLT round the test circuit of suburban roads under the patient but despairing gaze of Donny, not to mention other drivers and pedestrians who view the stuttering progress with some incredulity. The return journey shows improvement in sequence of movement by both vehicle and driver, but the gearbox continues to evade all attempts at a rapid, or even correct, selection of ratios.

A sweating nervous wreck of a policeman finally drives GLT into the Fire Station yard and manages to park alongside the pride of the Fire Service without souring relations with the sister service. The whole experience is recorded as a points victory for the new driver on the grounds that GLT failed to deliver a knockout. Donny's assessment of the gear changing shows that GLT won quite a few rounds but the important thing is that the driver has passed out on the vehicle, almost literally.

There was a post war period when another notable character obtained his master's degree on GLT. Bert had already displayed resolve and initiative in chasing drunken drivers and frightening Sergeants. Now he was briefed to instruct officers on police vehicles, and this naturally included the big one—GLT. Soften them up on normal vehicles first, before moving on to the supreme test. He was allocated three pupil drivers at a time, learning over a two week period, with the freedom of Norfolk and Suffolk. The Traffic Inspector who allowed this licence of movement probably reasoned that accident statistics could be shared with neighbouring forces. The concession to the wearing of plain clothes by the foursome might also have been in anticipation of embarrassing situations.

After the pupils had been endowed with senses of confidence and ability through driving the lesser vehicles Bert would head out onto long country roads with GLT. Far from the city streets learner drivers would find less gear changing and higher speeds, a thundering 45 mph with just the need to hang on to the steering wheel and steer the monster in a relatively straight line. Unfortunately, Norfolk roads did not stay straight for very long and a hint of relaxation by the driver could mean a sudden burst of human activity in the cabin as a road situation developed beyond the capabilities of the speeding Bedford and grim faced driver. One such example occurred as GLT charged towards a steep decline with the novice driver finding himself in no man's land in the gearbox. Bert advised, then instructed, and then implored the driver to find third gear. To be fair, the now very alert pupil tried, going through the motions with much enthusiasm and noise. His efforts were concentrated by the sight of a sugar beet lorry loading at the bottom of the hill, something which made a distinct impression on his passengers and prompted Bert to begin hauling on the handbrake, at the same time demanding that the driver's foot come off the accelerator, which was in any case irrelevant without a gear to go with it. The rear passengers blanched at the looming lorry, considered baling out options, but clung to fresh hope as a cog ripping third gear was discovered and speed decreased.

A police Bedford steered around a sugar beet lorry with four white faced and very active policemen on board, two driving and two praying. The enormity of any collision would only have been rivalled by the paperwork that would have been involved. What the sugar beet workers thought of the express juggernaut is unknown—it kept going.

Even at a lesser speed confusion could be induced by a gearbox that refused to accept the tentative probings of a new driver. You could not go much slower than the speed required for a reversing turn into a side road. Bert had ordered this particular driver to stop on the offside of a country road, just beyond a side road, and, by means of wing mirror and looking back through the door window, to reverse into the side road.

The reversing manoeuvre necessitated some body contortion and clutch control, but first it needed reverse gear. Straightforward in a stationary vehicle but not when previous driving has destroyed the driver's co-ordination. Our potential reverser removed his trilby hat to allow better rearward vision, hanging it on a convenient knob in a rather absent minded way, before looking to find reverse gear. To the amazement of his colleagues he failed to reverse the vehicle not because he could not find the appropriate gear but because he could not find the gear lever. An extremely flustered driver was shown the lever nestling under his trilby hat. GLT did have that effect on newcomers.

The county expeditions with trainee drivers on board were not all driving traumas. As Christmas approached there appeared an opportunity to enhance the festive decorations with berried holly from the woods at the side of the Watton Road. GLT was duly parked on the grass verge whilst one of the team climbed a well berried tree. He was enthusiastically cutting off branches and throwing them to the others, who were quickly loading them into the vehicle, when a shouting, waving figure appeared and was quickly identified as an irate farmer. Discussion seemed inappropriate in the circumstances and a rapid tree descent was followed by the quickest standing start in the history of a certain police vehicle.

The versatility of GLT was both appreciated and regretted. Appreciated by those who resorted to its goods vehicle role—it was said that there was not a demolition site in the city unvisited by this capacious vehicle, just brush the bench seats afterwards; but regretted by those who were involved in the troop carrying role, namely, the troops.

Short distances in the back could be endured, in fact they had to be. Prisoners received little sympathy, but a collection of policemen huddled in the rear compartment deserved some consideration after a journey which ably demonstrated that the extra weight did nothing to smooth out an iron suspension. Riot Squad duties usually went to a police van, a more humble but accessible and maneouvrable vehicle, although for a very long period the vehicle employed in this role had only a six volt battery, which occasionally provided the spectacle of uniformed officers pushing with driver and prisoner peering out. There was at least one occasion when the prisoner was made to push as well.

GLT was used in the Riot Squad role when youthful members of the West Earlham Estate were making their presence felt in the neighbourhood. Various suburban areas of the city went through phases in which unruly adolescents disturbed the peace or found more specific ways to bring themselves to the attention of less exuberant citizens. West Earlham suffered its share of juvenile nuisance without an undue amount of extra policing, until some youths obtained a chemical substance which reacted powerfully with water. The effect was sufficiently attractive to prompt a gang tour of roadside drains, and for GLT to appear on the estate carrying officers who had been briefed to persuade those concerned that flying drain covers was not really a good idea.

The sight of GLT parked at the West Centre, with rear doors open and two rows of policemen sullenly staring out upon curious youths looking in, is given credit for the sudden outbreak of peace in the area. The more likely explanation is that the stock of the chemical substance ran out.

From Bethel Street to Earlham is survivable, from a temperament point of view, but those officers who were delegated to travel to Great Yarmouth to assist the borough officers quelling 'mods' and 'rockers' on the sea front were less than happy after 22 miles in the rear of GLT. Many a disorderly youth failed to understand the reason for the bad temper of the Constable who leapt upon him.

The public obtained a ride in GLT when they achieved prisoner status, usually for a violent, disorderly or drunken offence. This did not normally include betting and gaming legislation, although throughout history its complications have infuriated both police and gamblers to a point where violence and strong drink might be considered.

Whatever the intricacies of the law on the subject there was no doubt that a betting shop in Oak Street was operating illegally. Someone of high rank had no doubts because they decreed that it should be raided and the law, whatever it was, should be enforced. Special tactics were required, namely, a swift entry, quick round up of inhabitants and rapid departure. Sort it out at the Police Station rather than interview and counter interview on a tricky legal subject on hostile premises.

The need for a capacious and impressive vehicle to transport the betting fraternity found on the premises was readily met by employing GLT. It showed they meant business. GLT always looked formidable.

It happened as planned. GLT pulled up outside the premises as a group of policemen rushed through the door. With its engine ticking (or grinding) over it waited as interested bystanders collected and unhappy punters filed from the shop: some with the housekeeping still intact— thanks to the timing of the police entry, others pondering upon the double misfortune of the selection of a debilitated horse and seizure by the police for unlawfully making the choice.

The short trip from shop door to Bedford truck left little time for argument or protest. Doors were slammed, an engine revved, and suddenly: it was all quiet in Oak Street. Inside GLT, and during the unloading at Bethel Street, there was the usual query and display of indignation, with threats of legal action for false arrest, and plaintive cries of innocence from amongst an unhappy group of passengers. Nothing out of the ordinary, except for one man who appeared very sprightly for his apparent 70 plus years. He was quite voluble in his declarations of innocence and at the Police Station he made such a fuss the Station Sergeant, who was not pleased to see a truck full of prisoners, placed him in a cell whilst more equable punters were interviewed and sent home with threats of a possible future court appearance.

The old gentleman seemed rather upset at his incarceration and was not mollified by the passage of time. An interview was postponed and he was left to reflect upon his impossible attitude.

The Station Office became quite busy and the Station Sergeant found himself assisting a sweet old lady who wished to report her husband missing. Something out of the ordinary had obviously befallen him because he was a very orderly man with precise habits. He should have been on his way home several hours earlier and it really was a matter of concern. The Sergeant became quite involved and noted details of the route he would have walked, his description, and so forth. Route? Walked? Staring him in the face was—Oak Street. The time was right. Description? Spot on. A quick visit to a cell and one missing person was found as a steaming, outraged citizen who had been walking along the pavement when a crowd of mixed police and public had emerged from a shop door and swept him into the back of an uncomfortable lorry, following which no one had wanted to listen to him. They listened now all right. Feted and cosseted in the canteen, he was eventually driven home in the Inspector's car with profuse apologies which would hopefully divert any official complaint of kidnapping by the police. Betting and gaming was definitely complicated, and a ride in GLT did not help.

The life of this notable vehicle was not incident free and it did not emerge unscathed from some of them. 'Popeye' was a well liked burly Sergeant with an infectious sense of humour (the nickname reflected the joviality), but an element of seriousness was necessary when he assaulted and dented GLT. To be more exact it was the prisoner who carried out the assault but he would plead circumstances beyond his control.

Popeye and others attended a ruckus at the Samson and Hercules Ballroom in Tombland, and GLT was dispatched to collect prisoners and walking wounded. No real problems. Antagonists, protagonists and cheerleaders were swiftly sorted, and Popeye headed from the ballroom towards GLT with a principal offender under his arm. The speed of his approach was hastened by him tripping at the top of the Samson steps and further impetus was provided by the prisoner whose legs had to follow the rest of his body which was being steered by Popeye's armlock. If Popeye wished to remain upright, and he did, his legs had to catch up with the rest of the body that had gone on ahead as a result of the trip. Speed overtook steerage and the headlong rush to GLT failed to find the interior of the vehicle. The prisoner, in his head down position, had no chance, and he butted the side of GLT with sufficient force to dent the bodywork and leave Popeye wondering how to phrase the appropriate report. The prisoner's headache was in real terms whereas Popeyes' was in a literary sense. (No lasting damage, Popeye later became an Inspector).

Other prisoners have, at various times, failed to find the centre door opening at the rear, rebounding from the adjoining bodywork as they disputed the right of the propelling officer to place them in the vehicle. In such a case, two Constables struggling to persuade a prisoner to enter GLT outside Bethel Street Police Station were constantly thwarted by the unco-operative splaying of arms and legs at the door opening. A Sergeant patiently watched this obstructive routine before offering to help. He took hold of the resisting prisoner and aimed him at the opening, but with a degree of inaccuracy which evidenced with the man slamming into the rear of GLT. Apologising profusely he began another attempt only to be cut short by the object of the exercise declaring that he would place himself inside—"thank you very much", further assistance of the kind just experienced not being required.

Others can produce evidence of GLT being the aggressor. Ronnie was the Station Entrance Constable on night duty who, in the early hours of the morning, was deputed to drive GLT to its regular parking place behind the buildings opposite Bethel Street Police Station: crumbling and awaiting condemnation they, nevertheless, served very well as a store for various items of property that fell into police hands, mainly' cycles. It was also a handy off the road spot for GLT.

131

Backing up to a decrepit building Ronnie went just a shade too far and the flat rectangular end of GLT lightly touched against a flint wall that had seen much history but little motorised transport. Unfortunately, GLT had been totally repainted only a few days previously and Ronnie left the cabin with visions of long reports and minimal sympathy.

A careful examination of vehicle and wall showed that all was status quo. No apparent damage to either. A career was restored and it was suddenly a nice night again.

Only another policeman can understand the relief that attended that examination. Ronnie climbed back into GLT and thankfully moved forward. There followed a colossal roar as the wall fell down. A column of dust rose high in the air and the Station Sergeant, and most of the night duty firemen from the adjacent Fire Station, rapidly emerged into the street wondering how they had missed the declaration of war.

The enquiry that followed the demise of the wall took due note of the aged brickwork and the vibration of nearby heavy vehicles, and completely overlooked the effect upon GLT's new paintwork.

The C.I.D. also wounded the beast when a Detective Constable, who should have known better, borrowed it via a Station Sergeant, who should also have known better, and loaded it with five stolen car engines, three of which dropped through the floor of the vehicle as he was tentatively proceeding along the Dereham Road. Further C.I.D. use was frowned upon.

*A shade too far*

132

GLT was also an unofficial transport for policemen requiring delivery of recently acquired goods, and in this guise it was extremely useful to the keen gardeners and D.I.Y. members of the force. It is true that other police vehicles were sometimes so employed but they did not have the capacity of GLT, neither did they look the part. Half a dozen lengths of four by two in a Wolseley would have been sacrilege. This ignores the occasion when an officer's television aerial was strapped underneath a patrol car, and another time when a large harmonium was transported on the Wolseley rear seat in a transaction organised by Bert and Popeye, only for a passing lady to take fright as she mistook it for a coffin.

Unauthorised trips sometimes fell to other vehicles, but GLT could still have a role to play. Bodge took the motor cycle combination when a stationbound Sergeant urgently needed delivery of a number of plant pots to his home in a small, little used, suburban road. When acquiring motor cycles for the force someone had the brainwave of attaching a sidecar to a B.S.A. machine, creating a handy all purpose vehicle for general duties and the Traffic Department. There was no intention to frighten the public by patrolling the city streets with it. It was simply a dogsbody vehicle with limited uses. Moving plant plots was one of those uses.

Bodge delivered the pots without incident but, after placing them in the appropriate greenhouse, he did not dally, mainly because it was a narrow road and even a motor cycle combination could cause an obstruction. The fact that he was on an unauthorised mission also counted.

Quickly returning to his machine Bodge started the engine, let in the clutch, opened the throttle, and roared across the road into a fence post which promptly crumpled under the frontal assault.

The whys and wherefores of the loss of control are immaterial. Neither was it any solace that the evidence, namely the pots, were no longer on board. An accident in a police vehicle was big trouble. It was the forerunner to enquiries that made the Spanish Inquisition look like a weather comment.

Bodge also had to take into consideration that the trip was unofficial, and a certain Police Sergeant was likely to find that a neighbour with a dislocated fence post was not disposed to a cooperative neighbourly understanding of the situation. Even if he was, the enquiring Inspector would firstly ask what the vehicle was doing in this particular backwater and, secondly, he would comment upon the nearness of a certain police resident, who just happened to be on duty at the time. The conspiracy had no chance.

A good point was a damage assessment of the motor cycle which showed it was no worse than before and, by itself, would not reveal the altercation with the post. The post, however, was definitely unwell and only a replacement would suffice.

Bodge was of the same mould as Herbert, made of strong stuff these GLT drivers, and he set about plotting his escape from the situation. It was clear what he had to do. He was not in this predicament alone and

Thirteen Box (what an appropriate number) was nearby, at the junction of Elm Grove Lane and Angel Road. Policemen could be very adroit, some would say cunning, in the face of adversity.

The instigator of the trip was consulted with his own liability being fully outlined. He was, after all, the owner of the pots, and, he was in a position to take GLT out without questions being asked.

The pot owner was not happy over Bodge's indifferent motor cycling, and even more unhappy over the prospect of an irate neighbour and investigating Inspector. It is, therefore, a fact, for which there is no preliminary detail, that he arrived at the scene with GLT and a new fence post. The original scene was quickly restored, although it is a matter of some vagueness as to the attention that was drawn to a police Black Maria in a small side road with two policemen mending a fence. Neither is there any accurate record of knowledge by neighbour or Inspector. Both should have been happy, even if they knew about it. The neighbour had a new post and the Inspector would not be looking for unnecessary work.

It must have been some consolation that it was not GLT that collided with the fence. The repair work would have been beyond the two policemen.

GLT eventually went the way of the dinosaurs, and the Norwich City Police: into oblivion, but it is not easily forgotten, for many and varied reasons.

# Trenchcoats and Trilbys

SOME WERE chosen to move into other spheres of police work, which included the heady heights of the C.I.D. This meant farewell to the uniform, traffic, insecures, flashing pillarphones, and all the routine of being the friendly bobby on the beat; but a salutary thought for our chosen one, perhaps it is only a temporary escape into the independence, glory and mystique of the world of the detective, the powered reasoned thinking against the contorted machinations of the criminal mind: very likely if the chosen one believed in Sherlock Holmes, Hercule Poirot and other manifestations of the art of detective work. A move to the C.I.D. would show him the real world in very quick time. No matter, it was recognition at last, but pause for thought—how and why had this sensational turn of events taken place? Where had the mistake been made? There follows a spell of furious thinking, with comparisons of similar names in the force, which is in turn followed by the realisation that it was intended; no mistake; the C.I.D. beckoned, or put more accurately, he was heading in that direction.

The imparting of such momentous news as a transfer to a specialised department usually meant a speech by a very senior rank and in the projected example it is the Chief Constable. He leans back in his chair staring fixedly at the rigid Constable before him. The summons to the inner sanctum was not prefaced with clues, and a catalogue of previous misdeeds have been fighting for supremacy in the mind of the Constable as he marched through the door following a dutiful knock and responsive green light from the adjacent traffic light system. The best imperial salute and the traditional opener.

"You wanted to see me Sir".

The fixed stare is not a good sign but the opening remark is more encouraging.

"You can stand at ease".

Constable relaxes.

"I'm putting you in the C.I.D."

Constable nearly collapses.

The Chief Constable ignores a spluttered "Thank you Sir" and goes

135

on to make some praiseworthy comments upon the career of the thunderstruck Constable advising him that he will be given six months as an aide in the department, following which he will be assessed as retained or rejected. He points out rather firmly that he expects certain abilities that he had detected (but the Constable is quietly unsure about) to be confirmed in the C.I.D. The Constable takes the point; Chief Constables do not like to be proved wrong.

The embryo detective realises that the interview is over and, after putting up another quality salute, he marches into the corridor to collect his thoughts, the most predominant of which is that he has become a chosen one. Officers in the Norwich City Police did not apply for postings or indicate any ambitions, self assessed talents, attributes or qualifications, or anything that may have been considered useful in furthering the efficiency of the Force. To do so would earn a label of "Who does he think he is?" and firm opposition to the desired movement. You were picked or not picked.

Most beat Constables hoped with all the optimism of a football pools regular that one day they would become a mobile officer. Some thought of the C.I.D., but this department was rather like the planets—somewhat distant in vision with its stars seen only at intervals. Some of these were also distant, being seen as mysterious figures who entered and left the station at irregular intervals garbed in trenchcoats and trilbys. They lived on a higher plane in the station, above the canteen and operational floor of the uniform branch, but could often be spotted carrying a tray of tea back to their eyrie.

Members of the public who called into the station to report a crime were informed in solemn tones that it was a C.I.D. matter and dispatched to the upper floor to talk to a real detective, who would turn out to be an aide given six months to prove himself.

The new aide, fresh from the Chief Constable's interview, makes an exploratory visit to this upper floor where he views a member of the public shuffling his feet in the doorway of the main office, attempting to attract the attention of numerous inhabitants who have developed an intense interest in a typewriter, or file of papers, and are apparently oblivious to the coughing and twitching in the doorway. A few antiquated typewriters are on view and figures crouch over them going through a one finger, woodpecker like routine which projects a picture of intense concentration, combined with the suspense of waiting for the next key to be slammed down by a hovering finger. The telephone rings and there is a pause in general conversation and typewriting. Sidelong glances measure the distance between the telephone and various candidates to take the call and, eventually, a reluctant figure rises from a typewriter and answers the demanding instrument. Another resigned denizen of the room asks the convulsing figure in the doorway if he can help him. The prospective aide will learn that answering the telephone, and speaking to the public who visit the department, is risky and a recipe for extra work that he will not find extra time for. It was a simple process: receive details of a crime, by

136

telephone or personal call, record the same on a crime complaint form and sign it; the Detective Inspector notes the name of the officer on the form and marks it back to him for investigation. You could get a lot of work sitting near the telephone or the door.

The exploratory visit is also useful because the new aide manages to overhear the Detective Inspector bemoaning this particular aide's impending arrival. Apparently he does not share the views of the Chief Constable and is wondering whether some kind of temporary insanity has afflicted him in making his current choice.

The day arrives when a certain number is missing from the duty sheet and its owner introduces himself to the C.I.D. He is allocated a drawer near the telephone and the door before he is invited to step into the Detective Inspector's office where he listens to a short address on the need to work hard and justify the Detective Inspector's selection. He is informed, in very serious tones, that he is being given his chance because the Detective Inspector has been keeping an eye on him for some time and had specially asked for him. The Constable thanks him and keeps his knowledge to himself.

Returning to the main office, the new aide finds that the freshly allocated drawer has already attracted several pieces of paper; all of which contain a direction for him to make enquiries into a significant crime, which include helmets missing from parked scooters and an epidemic of milk missing form doorsteps. Well, a budding detective has to start somewhere. When Bags was elevated to the C.I.D. on trial his keenness, of which some mention has been made, was the subject of enquiry from another officer who asked how he had got on with the first crimes allocated to his all too evident enthusiasm. Bags replied, rather mournfully, that there was not too much scope in a rabbit missing from a hutch at Lakenham and the disappearance of the St. Stephens point duty officer's mackintosh. How did the point duty man lose his mackintosh from the centre of the road, under his very eyes and in view of four lanes of traffic? Bags never found out and didn't think it was a fair test of detective ability.

The pattern was quickly established. The new aide would open his drawer to discover a pile of minor larcenies demanding his enquiries; helmets and milk would continue in the company of cash from household electricity and gas meters, apples from orchards, Road Fund Licences from cars, wallets from unattended clothing, lights and pumps off cycles, various bits from parked cars, and so forth and so on—all requiring comprehensive enquiries and a full page report detailing exactly what those enquiries were. The art of verbosity on paper is quickly learnt. The report finishes with the lying platitude "enquiries will continue".

Aides soon found that the serious crimes of burglary, fraud, and larcenies when something expensive was stolen or the loser was someone important, were allocated to the seniors—the department elders who had been around a bit and had the ability to solve a crime by reading the report and offering a shortlist of names of candidates, amongst which would be the perpetrator. Sometimes, they proved they were right by appearing in the office with one of the names, who would, sometimes, be making confirming admissions.

A few of the elders were willing to demonstrate ability in the interview room to lesser mortals who were finding the technique of conversation with the suspect an elusive art. Assistance varied between the kindly father figure of Tom, who had the ability to charm the interviewee to the point of dedicated friendliness, and even bring tears to the eyes of the listener, to the brusque entrance of another established detective who interrupted an interview armed with a piece of cardboard upon which was the imprint of a shoe. Quickly examining the prisoner's shoes he announced to the frustrated interviewer, "Yes, they are the shoes, No doubt", before a door slamming exit. The suspect was then left with much food for thought; but the involuntary exclamation that followed this visit was not what was expected. "He's got it wrong" blurted the object of the exercise, who had spent the past two hours denying everything except his name. "I wasn't wearing these shoes when I did the job".

The new aide believes that he has arrived unnoticed by senior members of the department. His first Sunday on duty proves him wrong. He starts at a low point by churning out dealer's circulars on a machine in the corner of the main office, apparently ignored by duty detectives who sprawl around the office solving crime by assessment and speculation. At ten a.m. there is a sudden change in attitude. He is summoned to a circle that has formed in the centre of the room. The C.I.D. Sunday ritual has begun and he is invited, some would say commanded, to participate. Someone may ask his first name. They may even use it.

"Can you play crib?" he is asked without any apparent interest being displayed in the answer.

The answer does not really matter because he is going to play and he is going to lose. Hands are dealt, and scores announced, with all the tenseness and excitement of a speculator putting his life's savings on the stockmarket. No simple round with the worst hand losing; a long process of elimination of one per hand, with much shouting and debating of misfortunes at the final head to head. Those who have been eliminated from the contest take a renewed interest in the proceedings, speculating on the luck, or otherwise, of various colleagues who continue to battle against being the sole survivor—that costs money.

The aide has heard of, even seen, these rituals before and he knows that escaping the role of overall loser does not eliminate him from the object of the whole affair—paying for something. There is a second round: as it begins the first round loser leaves to buy tea for all, grumbling at reoccurring bad luck. The second round loser pays for the biscuits and aides rarely escape both risks, even if they can play the game.

It was possible to achieve some rapport between the higher orders and the aides and attachments to the department, or even in some cases the lowest of all, the Cadet, but it was dependent upon individuals. The Cadet was an obvious target for C.I.D. humour and a certain incoming

*A sudden change in attitude*

Cadet was warned by the outgoing youngster to be on the look out for particular formulas, one of which was an instruction to look for the crime register keys; they were as mythical as the skyhooks that building trade apprentices were dispatched to find. It happened, inevitably, and it came from Tom whose friendliness to newcomers was greatly appreciated but had to be watched carefully for a mischievous streak of humour; in fact this particular Cadet had already been the victim of a diversion that had resulted in his newly purchased jam tart moving from a plate to a fixed position beneath the C.I.D. clock. A possibility of revenge by the lowest denomination in the department? Why not?

"Get me the crime register keys, urgently" says Tom laying the groundwork. The Cadet exits the department and the elders turn to other business, satisfied that he is now well into a series of exhausting enquiries. They would have been less satisfied if they had known that his enquiries were to take him to the ground floor and include Stumpy, the General Office Inspector, Station Sergeant and, eventually, because of the intensity if the enquiry, the Deputy Chief Constable. The aim was to cause some concern that might carry back to the originator, but, when the General Office Inspector became irate at the failure to find the keys and the Deputy Chief Constable came upon a collection of disturbed officers, it had gone further than intended. The Deputy Chief Constable vowed to get to the bottom of the whole business and, if the keys could not be found, someone should be in trouble. He asked the Cadet who actually required them and became slightly thoughtful at the reply.

Returning to the C.I.D. the artful Cadet made himself available for the obvious question. "No", he told Tom, he had not found the crime register keys, but the Deputy Chief Constable was looking for them. A startled Tom did not pursue the conversation.

Newly arrived officers who engaged the elders in conversation had to be extremely careful as one friendly, but unsuspecting, aide found to his cost. He made the mistake of knowing all about the intricacies of the one man band, and, motivated by apparent incredulous enquiries and looks of what he thought was interest, he enhanced his explanations by marching up and down the office with flapping arms, knocking knees and blowing until he was red in the face. Then the dawn of realisation and real redness in the face.

The aspiring detective who had to write a report describing the larceny of a quantity of eggs was an attentive listener when advised that the Detective Inspector would be impressed by use of the Latin word for eggs, which was apparently 'ova'. The result was a report headed 'Larceny of Ova', a very irate Detective Inspector and a much wiser Constable.

Amongst the mischief there was kindness and help, but not always recognised or appreciated. Dick was an experienced detective of kindly disposition with an eye to opportunity and a love of a small tipple, or even a large one if it was available. He was rarely found without a smile and ready quip, and never without a buttonhole, even in January. Aides, or probationer attached officers, were often grateful for his interest and freedom of speech, for he was indeed a man willing to impart information on the ways of local criminals, a scene of crime investigation and the likely winner of the 3.30 at Kempton. He was cheerful, chatty and friendly, even if his choice for the 3.30 lost. Attending the scene of a burglary in Drayton Road he had in his company a very young officer, who was being shown the department as part of the learning and character building process of establishing himself as a policeman—how he managed to get to the scene of a crime instead of feeding circulars to local dealers probably owed much to Dick's magnanimous attitude to other souls in the department, even if they were only passing through.

Arriving at the house it was quickly established that the gas and electricity meters had been forced. Dick made a thorough enquiry of both complainant and scene before deciding that house to house enquiries might be useful. His decision in this respect was possibly influenced by one of the nearby houses being a public house.

It was a wide eyed impressionable young officer that accompanied Dick into the 'Galley Hills', and responded to the invitation "What will you have?" with a concoction that did not require a licence to justify its sale. This was of no consequence to Dick who ordered his favourite tipple and engaged the landlord in conversation. It is a known fact that landlords speak more freely to paying customers and Dick pursued this fact quite enthusiastically, obtaining in the process the interesting information that two young men had been in the pub the previous evening with an unusual amount of shillings to spend. Yes, the landlord did happen to know who they were and roughly where they lived. The upshot was that Dick returned his fledgling officer to the station and later collected two local men, who, in the face of unfathomable detective work—that means they were not bright enough to work out how they had been caught—made full admissions to the Drayton Road burglary, and a few others for good measure.

Dick was rather pleased with himself and he answered the Detective Inspector's summons expecting praise and commendation. What he actually got was a lecture on leading a young and untainted officer astray. It appeared that the lesson had failed at the public house stage, because when the protege was asked by a senior officer to evaluate his progress in the department, he responded by indicating that he had not previously been aware of the amount of time C.I.D. men spent in pubs, and he thought it rather surprising. He was crossed off Dick's showing around list.

'Smudger' was a Detective Sergeant who proved that informants existed by receiving information that the Co-op on Hall Road was to be burgled. It was his information and, therefore, it was to be his prisoner; he just needed someone to accompany him on the observation. Terry (remember the Maddermarket) was on attachment to the department and consequently did not have a voice in proceedings; he would do admirably for corroboration of the capture. Accordingly, on the night in question the observers became ensconced in the rear store room of the premises. They waited, and anticipated, from closing time until about nine thirty p.m.: at which time a scraping sound was heard and the silhouette of a man blocked out the light filtering through the skylight. The skylight was then lifted and a rope dropped into the store, following which a man descended hand over hand before dropping lightly between the interested watchers. At Smudger's command Terry threw the light switch and Smudger made his presence known by clamping his hand on the intruder's shoulder. The sudden illumination revealed a number of things. Firstly, from the appearance of the intruder he was about to have a heart attack, secondly, from the noise and smell emanating from his direction he had lost control of his bodily functions, and this was very quickly confirmed by visible evidence on his trousers and plimsolls. The stench was quite nauseating and Smudger hesitated in the act of formal arrest; stepping back from the terrified stinking burglar he gave Terry what may be loosely interpreted as a smile and said, "There you are young Terry, you've got yourself a prisoner". Never let it be said that young officers were not helped by senior members of the department.

Selected detectives received extra training in the special arts of fingerprint detection, fibre removal, photography and other scientific and impressive aids to detection. They became known as Scenes of Crime Officers. Not always necessary though. At the scene of a burglary in Magdalen Street the offender had dropped his wallet with his name and address therein. In another case different identifying evidence was left, and it did not need a Scenes of Crime Officer to find it. The excitement and adrenalin rising suspense of breaking into another person's property could lead to other indiscretions, evidence of which has already been provided at the Hall Road Co-op. The detective attending the scene of a burglary near Queens Road was disgusted to find that the perpetrator had lost control of this bodily functions, leaving the evidence for all to see. He brightened a little when he saw that the substitute toilet paper was an envelope with the name and address of a well known burglar on the front. He declined to retain the exhibit but promptly arrested the subject, who wondered as to the deductive powers of the detective rather than conducting an in-depth examination of his own limited reasoning processes.

The Scenes of Crime Officer was required to attend suicides, fatal accidents and sudden deaths of an indefinable nature in which the Coroner was likely to ask many pertinent questions in the process of making them definable. It was, therefore, important that the body was not moved before photographs were taken, and distinctly embarrassing to have it taken out of the front door, preparatory to loading it into a vehicle, only for a face at an upstairs window to plead for its return because he has just realised that there was no film in the camera when he took the pictures. Two struggling corpse carriers are moved to a critical assessment of a certain Scenes of Crime Officer as well as a return of the body.

The raising of fingerprints required black powder, a soft brush and a delicate touch. A certain Scenes of Crime Officer had the first two but such was his industry at the scene he became known as the one with the wire brush. "I can't seen any prints" he would mutter, scrubbing with all the feverish intensity of a Victorian parlourmaid.

So where is our aide within this maelstrom of C.I.D. mischief and intensity? He has moved from doorstep watching for milk thieves to changing rooms. If he is not branded a peeping tom by misplaced and inefficient observations organised by the uniform branch, he now has a further chance by the requirement to investigate numerous thefts of wallets from clothes left in social and sports club changing rooms. His spur to success is persistence and the Detective Inspector's reference to the state of Norwich traffic and his possible involvement in the future. A thief is caught and numerous wallet thefts in the city centre changing rooms are admitted. The aide would have liked to have translated the Detective Inspector's muttered comment as "Well done" but on reflection it sounded like "About time".

The aide continues his efforts in the face of a perpetually missing crime car (he is well down in the pecking order), mythical bus passes, mounting paper and the failure to find 25 hours in a day. He was, however, supposed to find the extra hours and home life was something that belonged to other people. The C.I.D. worked a split shift system two or three times a week, which on paper showed that the detective went home at one p.m. and reappeared at six p.m. In reality it meant a straight 13 hour shift. Probably much more if he arrested anyone or got involved in continuing enquiries.

An aide, who was going down the main staircase from the C.I.D. shortly after six p.m., was stopped by the Detective Inspector's voice from an upper landing demanding to know where he was going. The Inspector knew because he had just seen the booking off book.

"Home Sir" was the involuntary and only possible reply from a husband seeking to recognise an anniversary and the wife that went with it. There followed a lecture, delivered over two floors, upon the need for dedication and keenness, which meant not going home when there was crime to solve. That was not the way to become a Detective Constable, according to the lecturer. Later in the officer's career (when crime had rocketed) he would be ordered from the Police Station because he had completed his eight hour shift. The difference was the transition to paid overtime.

Juveniles and shoplifters were often the lot of the aide and quite often they were one and the same. Both categories presented more problems and less kudos than any other form of prisoner, and for these reasons they were unpopular. Juveniles had to be interviewed in the presence of a parent and experiences in uniform may be recalled.

Mortified shoplifters would sit on a chair at the end of the C.I.D. main office apologising for their mental aberration in not paying for the jar of marmalade, packet of soap powder, piece of prime steak or whatever. Sometimes, the Sergeant or Inspector would reveal their greater experience of human frailties by commanding the officer in the case to accompany the supposedly previously upright citizen to their home to check whether the magpie instinct was apparent in the contents of their abode. Sometimes the Constable would report back that the person concerned had every reason to be distraught at their capture, and could they send the van for the Aladdin's Cave that had been discovered.

A young, and very ambitious, aide found himself dealing with a middle aged husband and wife who had been caught stealing clothes from a city centre store. They were very upset over the hideous mistake that was now being made over their absent minded behaviour and they expressed complete co-operation in any enquiry that would prove their innocence. Yes, they would be pleased to show the officer around their home.

Administrative procedures, including bail, were completed, and they set out to the address, a few miles from Norwich. The aide would have preferred to be doing other things, most of which related to the pile of paper that was in his drawer. He did, however, admire their picturesque cottage, approached by a gate and long winding path, but he was rather disconcerted by the couple's transformation from slow moving and chatty companions to distant sprinters heading for the cottage door, especially as he was still in the act of chivalrously holding the gate open for them.

The slamming of the cottage door, and vigorous bolting noises that followed, left him with a sinking feeling, which was emphasised when a previously clean chimney began to produce clouds of smoke. He circled the cottage vainly calling for admission, but his cries only served to increase the volume of smoke and scurrying activity of the inhabitants who chose to ignore the face pressed against the glass. Retiring to the garden he debated the alternatives of forcing an entry, the cottage catching fire or waiting for some kind of conclusion. He waited and, as the smoke lessened, he made his continuing presence known to the stokers inside. They acknowledged his patience but declined to allow him admission whilst they were sorting out their "rubbish", and in any case, the whole affair was concluded as far as they were concerned and would he like to get a warrant if he wished to continue his enquiries. He had lost, and he knew it. Searching the overheated cottage was going to be unproductive. He might as well withdraw to advise the Sergeant that he had been outwitted by two sprinting pyromaniacs. The Sergeant's views were interesting and time consuming.

Shoplifters did not have to travel very far to cause maximum embarrassment, in fact they did not have to travel at all. A soldier of fortune or gentleman of the road, some would say a vagrant, was collected from a city shop after attempting to depart the premises with an unpaid tin of salmon. He was placed on a chair at the far end of the C.I.D. main office, so often occupied by prisoners awaiting some kind of administration, and his meagre possessions were laid on a nearby desk, including the principal and only exhibit—one tin of salmon. Memory recalls that this particular wayfarer was reasonably clean and presentable, by the standards set by a proportion of those of no fixed abode, but it may have been that closer contact revealed otherwise, or the reputation of those that had gone before curtailed the normal efficiency of the searching officer. Whatever the reason, the arresting, searching and lumbered officer parked his charge in the corner and left to pursue other matters, such as name and previous conviction checks. The rest of the C.I.D. got on with the business of typing "enquiries were unsuccessful" reports, answering the telephone in slow motion and avoiding the eye of any member of the public who strayed into the doorway.

The timescale of events, or in this case an event, cannot be recalled, but the Constable returning to the itinerant shoplifter was aghast to find a visible indicator to the period he had been away. The tin of salmon was open, and empty, and the prisoner's few possessions had grown by one item—a tin opener.

Varying emotions were on view in the C.I.D. office at the time of discovery of the missing evidence. Consternation from a certain Constable, puzzled interest mixed with unconcern from the prisoner, and much back slapping hilarity from other officers who would not have to explain the circumstances to the Sergeant. The decision, reached after the Sergeant had again expressed his views, was that you cannot charge a person with stealing something he has eaten whilst in custody. Some questions might be asked, and no one would want to answer them. As for the stolen property, which had to be returned to the shop, it could have been worse, it could have been something that was expensive and difficult to replace. One tin of salmon looks like another.

It will be seen that officers who arrested people were liable to increase their experience through calamity and embarrassment. Such was the lot of two aides who were ordered to take a female shoplifter home to check her address, but failed to get there. They didn't even get out of the station. In this case it was not the exhibit that disappeared but the shoplifter. They placed her on a chair in the ground floor corridor whilst transport was organised, and then found she had organised her own and disappeared. She was never seen again and, of course, the name and address was false. Another speech by the Sergeant.

Eventually, the aide learns whether he is to return whence he came or remain as a permanent aide waiting for a Detective Constable vacancy. If he stays he may have an extraneous duty, which is a specialism requiring his regular attention, and for which he is answerable to whosoever chooses to make an enquiry, or in the case of the Sergeant or Inspector, demand a result. Scrap metal dealers, aliens (foreigners not extra-terrestrial) and stolen vehicles were examples of extraneous duties, with the latter showing up as a brighter future for one young aide in the 1960's. Not too pleased at being saddled with this extra work he asked why so many Minis and 1100s had disappeared and was assured "They gone a'lunnon boy". Apparently, anything of value that was not recovered had gone to London, especially if it had wheels, but not long after he had posed the question the Watch Committee had to rent premises to store sixteen stolen and recovered Minis and 1100s, none of which had gone to London. The Chairman of the Watch Committee was heard to remark that he thought "ringing" only applied to pigeons.

For those that were not wanted, or did not want to stay, leaving the C.I.D. was not, perhaps, such a wrench. There was always the mobile. At least there was no trouble getting transport in that department; and it came with walnut and leather. Wonder if there will be another summons to the Chief's office.

# Guided by the Circumstances

THE VARIETY of police work was both its attraction and complication. It is all very well saying that every day is different, with fresh challenges presenting themselves, but all the anticipation and preparation in the world can come to nought in the face of elements of the unexpected. An imaginative mind can foresee all sorts of difficulties and there is no reason why they should not be projected for examination by older and wiser minds; in other words, ask the Sergeant or the Inspector, bearing in mind that this course of action could lead to a degree of unpopularity because senior ranks did not like pessimists, a lack of confidence, or policemen with too much imagination. Neither did they like being stuck for an answer.

Asking a senior Constable was a recommended route to further knowledge, although the choice should be arrived at with care; it was not unknown for an immediate and brutal answer on the lines of "You'll have to find out like I did". Sergeants and Inspectors were required by their very position to be a bit more forthcoming and they generally used a standard form of reply that had evolved from an inborn caution against commitment in any form.

"You'll have to be guided by the circumstances" was about as helpful as the senior Constable's retort.

Describing the anticipated circumstances could bring the dead bat response, "It all depends", following which the questioner learns that "depends" means the circumstances and he is back where he started, except he has gained an irritated supervisory officer who cannot understand the interest in something that has not happened.

Circumstances could leave very little room for guidance. The Constable entering Ketts Hill Mortuary paid scant attention to the white sheeted recumbent figure on the slab, until it slowly sat up and extended its arms. Resurrection was not covered by any police manual and this potential heart attack scenario was only defused when the sheet fell away to reveal to a colleague with a macabre sense of humour. Cruelty reached an advanced stage when the same ruse was directed against the civilian who delivered petrol to the building. On this occasion there was a moan from the rising dead. The poor civilian left at olympic speed and, even after an explanation serving as an apology, refused to enter the building ever again.

Ghoulish policemen were known to inspect the shelves of the Ketts Hill Mortuary, motivated by a desire for a gruesome update on the inhabitants and their final state of unhealth, even though their own visit was totally unconnected with the mortuary side of the building. One such Constable created his own unwelcome circumstances when he investigated too vigorously and pulled a drawer from its compartment. He found himself wrestling with a corpse that he had only wished to view. That was the least of his problems, for reuniting corpse, drawer and shelf was almost beyond his physical capabilities and did little for his own immediate health.

Coping with the dramatic, traumatic—expected or otherwise, and other non-routine events, received plenty of practice between 1939 and 1945 when circumstances became acute and life threatening. The Second World War overshadowed everyone's life—and took some, including a Constable in Oak Street.

The day war was announced there was a foretaste of abnormality and changing times. The sounding of the air raid siren created an immediate response in St. Stephens Street where pedestrians began rushing to and fro, mainly in the direction of the Chapelfield shelter. The Constable standing in this narrow street thought that scurrying activity was beneath the dignity of the uniform and remained rooted in a doorway, although he did wonder when an old lady rushed past with a gas respirator perched on top of her head. Later, the Sergeant visited and coldly imparted the information that there was a light on his beat—showing through a skylight in Surrey Street, apparently observed by a spotter on top of the City Hall. The Constable's disadvantage in elevation was not taken into consideration. It was obviously going to be a difficult war.

War meant different things to different people. New routines, changing circumstances, adventure, alarm, sorrow, despair, grief and death—they all appeared, with direct or indirect effects upon the policemen and policewomen who shared emotions and adapted themselves to dealing with a new criminal, one they could not arrest but whose presence caused trepidations in the city. Never was the police and public relationship closer or more meaningful. Morale was all important and when a local fortune teller advised a fearful customer that she was going to be bombed the Chief Constable took swift action to prevent a queue of customers seeking information that lay more within the power of Herman Goering than a crystal ball: local fortune tellers were visited and advised of the limits of their perceptive powers.

On and off duty officers were required to telephone the station after the air raid siren had sounded and this caused a blaze of summoning lights on the switchboard, each signifying an impatient skyward glancing caller demanding an acknowledgement from a frantic plug stretching operator. Originally, the beat Constable was supposed to stand-by at the calling-in point until the conclusion of the raid, but this caused stagnation due to the Luftwaffe regularly passing over Norwich en route to the Midlands. Policemen were among the observers who saw them flying north above the railway line from the City Station.

The frequency of alarms on one night so disrupted the conscientious property checks of Ernie (later to be a Sergeant) that he was forced to partake of refreshments with an unfinished beat. This unheard state of affairs caused consternation in upper echelons until logic eventually prevailed and the stand-by order was amended to "Wait for ten minutes", and, if nothing happened—such as alterations to the beat from above, then continue as normal.

During blackout the city slipped into pitch darkness of interminable depth, only occasionally lightened by German flares, and much less by pale Wootton lamps. The Inspector and Sergeant who stood at Eastbourne Place wondering as to the whereabouts of the beat man found that he was standing next to them, listening to their conversation. It was that dark.

The black crosses did not always pass over and at the height of the Baedeker Raids (named after the German's use of the travel guide) the city was subject to regular bombings with great destruction and loss of life. The sight of a dishevelled Police Surgeon standing in Bethel Street Police Station visibly moved after visiting a bombed shelter was an indelible memory and vivid example of the immediacy of disaster caused by war.

Policewomen had a vital role to play in wartime, both regular and auxiliary. The regular establishment was one, increased to three in 1943, and she was usually attached to the C.I.D. During the war her duties became more comprehensive necessitating an almost constant appearance at Bethel Street Police Station. Margaret had obtained this post in 1941 and was to serve during the most fearsome of the air raids upon Norwich. At the height of the blitz, she wended her way through scenes of great devastation to report for duty. Stepping over continuous fire hoses, crunching through glass, avoiding scattered debris, changing direction because of blocked streets, passing smoking ruins and dazed homeless groups, she eventually arrived at the station amid scenes of frenzied activity. Such was the disruption caused by the frequency of the raids she stayed at the station and slept in a cell.

If police officers thought they had a life of their own a World War was to prove otherwise and a policewoman sleeping in a cell was not a solitary example. As bombing raids upon the city reached fresh peaks of intensity it was decided to employ a stand-by force and single men were deposited in the basement corridors of the City Hall. Blankets and bunks were provided in this subterranean incarceration and the fetid atmosphere of togetherness was a constant reminder of the restricted area and the numbers present. It did not escape the notice of some people that a direct hit on the City Hall could substantially reduce the size of the Force.

Shrapnel hunting became the pastime of local schoolchildren, who, in between hoping that a Teutonic bomb aimer would line up their school, gathered souvenir parts of bombs, shells, aircraft and anything else that came to pieces during those momentous days and nights. Policemen pursued these juvenile collectors and gathered their own collection at Bethel Street, which included a piece they were rather proud of: a fragment from the bomb that had made a large hole in the Carlton Cinema. This was logged as an exploded bomb until, several days after the event, and many large audiences in the cinema, a Bomb Disposal Officer visited Bethel Street. He noted the fragment and asked "Where did that come from?"

"Oh, from a bomb that went off in the Carlton Cinema".

The next statement from the Army officer caused some activity.

"Be damned for a yarn, that bomb is unexploded". And it was. The Police Station had a bomb ring fragment. The bomb was still nestling under the cinema. The rest is history and well documented.

The bombs that hit the Goods Station at Thorpe exploded without any doubt. One of the warehouses was stocked with baked beans and they were scattered over the iron structure, where they baked in the sun for several weeks—causing a most unwelcome aroma.

Some Constables had been recalled from military service to assist in dealing with the increasing frequency of the city air raids. They were trained to take charge of air raid incidents and carried Sergeant's stripes in their gas masks. As soon as they arrived at the scene of a bombing they put on the stripes and became Acting Sergeants. Self and instant promotion, courtesy of the Luftwaffe.

Examples of dedicated duty were not exclusive to the police. The night the Bus Station was bombed brought the usual road closures as Constables attempted to seal off the area. Everything appeared to be under control, except that some buses were not what they were and at least two unexploded bombs were believed to be amongst them. A chain was prudently placed across the entrance to the station. There was no moon and visibility was very poor as a cyclist approached. He was stopped and duly advised that he could not go through the station, and why. Ignoring the Constable, alias Sergeant's, account of events he suddenly rode furiously towards the station crying out that he was "Home Guard" and he "Had to go". The darkness closed over him but a crash signified that he had found the chain. Cycle pieces were added to bus pieces. Where he had to go is unknown. He was not seen again.

Some Norwich City officers saw war service on the home front and some in military service abroad. When the travellers returned a reception was held and the Lord Mayor said, "They are a jolly good, genial set of fellows". He meant all of them—home or away.

The Norwich City Police returned to what passed for normal with some of the jolly fellows revealing a streak of eccentricity. A very well known and popular Constable was notorious for parading late for duty on early turn, always with effusive apologies for the slipping chain on his cycle. The morning he arrived, long after six a.m., at Magdalen Gates

Police Station, he could not apologise enough and he displayed two well greased hands to prove that once again his cycle had let him down. The Sergeant was unimpressed but did not really care, pointing out to the greasy apologetic Constable that he had made a mistake and was day off on the rota.

Police work was not altogether solitary in its application and the Constable could sometimes obtain assistance from colleagues. If it all went well they could jostle for the commendation, but in the event of Murphy's Law prevailing (what can go wrong, will), the blame could be shared or even shifted. It was called teamwork. Examples abound but one example related to a Constable carrying out his duty and his Sergeant helping him.

The setting is the declining era of the horse and cart, 1949 the attributable year, when a significant section of the public subscribed to the view that horses were great assets. (See earlier for some police views). Opinions were qualified to some extent by the degree of contact with these fine animals and whether you rode, drove, merely admired, or put money on their anticipated turn of speed.

Whilst some were disillusioned through financial losses, caused by an overestimation of a particular animal's capabilities, there was also a section who saw the horse as a working animal, a beast of burden designed to further the progress of its owner and his goods. Overestimation of equine capabilities in these cases was potentially distressing, and cruel. Such was the case that came into the view of Jock, a beat Constable.

Jock was a large, well built, and conspicuous figure, with an aura of imposing authority. When he confronted two scruffy men leading a horse and cart, substantially loaded with wood, up St. Andrew's Hill, they had no option but to stop. The men were shifty and unhappy but the horse was only too glad of the rest for it was emaciated, tired and struggling to keep the wood cart moving up the steep incline.

The scruffy men were clearly in the overestimation group, or probably an uncaring sub-order, for there was little consideration for the forlorn and worn out animal. Jock told them so. He then reinforced his statement by having the horse unhitched from the shafts, much to the disgust of the scruffy men and relief of the horse.

Jock ensured that the cart was angled into the kerb and a wheel was blocked. A grateful horse was then taken off to the ever welcoming 'Buff Coat', and the disgruntled owners were booked to appear at the Magistrates Court to discuss the provisions of the Protection of Animals Act. There remained one problem—the wood cart. What to do with it? The owners had lost interest in what was now essentially a horseless carriage. Their view was that it was the police's problem. The police had rendered it horseless. They would have to move it.

Duke was the Sergeant who arrived to join this laudable horse saving enterprise. He was of even larger stature than Jock and the two officers standing at the side of the road made an impressive and substantial obstruction to pedestrians. The real problem was, however, another obstruction standing inconveniently at the side of the road, in the way of both traffic and pedestrians—a cart loaded with wood. It had to be moved.

A plan was devised. It comprised the laws of weight and propulsion. Reduce one and increase the other. Two very large and powerful policemen would equal one skinny horse. To make absolutely sure, some of the wood could be removed from the top of the cart. The reasoning was faultless, a triumph of improvisation and initiative.

The planners were satisfied with their initial assessment, but the incline that had troubled the horse might lead to a pulled muscle or hernia in the largest of policemen, therefore, it would have to be a downward braking journey, which was very convenient because once they had crossed the main St. Andrew's Street at the bottom of the hill they would be onto the plain of St. Andrew's Hall: this imperious building stood well back from the busy road, offering considerable parking for horseless wood carts. The whole operation would have to be performed with decorum and dignity because of the busy main road, not to mention the busy 'Festival House' public house opposite their destination.

The plan could not be faulted. After some of the wood had been moved positions were taken up. Duke was the Sergeant and would take the responsibility of piloting the cart. He inserted himself between the shafts and prepared to kick away the wooden block retaining the wheel. Jock took up a rearward position, taking a firm hold on the rear section and leaning confidently backwards in his role as a brakeman.

With the anchor man in place Duke removed the block and swivelled the cart in line with the chosen route. He shuffled forward, Jock leant back, the cart moved slowly downhill. They were on their way; it proved that positive thinking and action would solve most problems.

Duke's shuffle became a little quicker as the full weight of the cart and load sought to obey the natural law of gravity. Fifteen stone of policeman at the rear attempted to delay the inevitable progress but found himself moving at an ever increasing pace with heels scoring along the road surface. Progress was being made rather more swiftly than had been envisaged, but everything was under control and the main road was getting closer. They would have to judge the traffic when easing the load across: it, therefore, followed that the pace should be reduced prior to meeting the junction. What was obvious was not always enforceable.

Duke found that he was moving faster than he would have liked and his legs were keeping up with the speed of the cart rather than dictating it. Jock was not doing anything with his legs other than wearing out the road, or more probably his boots because he was stiff legged and inclined backwards as he attempted the necessary de-acceleration.

All was lost. The cart was in charge and speeding towards the main road at an ever increasing rate. Neither policeman dare abandon his position, one because he did not want to be run over by a load of wood and the other because he was now running so fast he was out of control,

151

*Progress had been made rather more swiftly than envisaged*

with or without the cart. His stiff legged pose had gone and along with it the danger of his boots catching fire. He was now running behind the cart, holding on and desperately trying to match his speed with the runaway.

How much the traffic in St. Andrew's Street swerved and braked is not known, for the policemen were concentrating on staying upright and the relevant drivers did not come forward afterwards. Probably still recovering from the dramatic appearance of a cart full of wood hurtling across the road with a large uniformed policeman running frantically at each end. It is certain that they were noticed, and that traffic stopped to savour the sight. It is also known that patrons of the 'Festival House' rushed to the doors and windows to cheer the flying squad as it thundered by with clanking wheels and rapidly pattering feet.

Duke, Jock and the wood cart survived the main road crossing but their troubles were far from over. As they reached the plain of St. Andrew's Hall speed was still increasing, albeit the slope had now decreased. Duke was hanging on to the shafts with windmilling legs and Jock was trying to change a running rhythm into a braking stance, with little success.

The main doors of the hall loomed up. They were made of stern stuff and would have, and indeed may have, repelled a Cromwellian invasion. Of great height and width, made of solid and ancient wood with metal bracing, they presented a formidable obstacle. Whether Duke viewed this as an advantage or not is debatable.

The shafts of the cart arrived before Duke. They slammed into the door (knowledgeable locals can still point to the marks). A split second later Duke met the door and promptly subsided from view as he went downwards and the wood went forwards. Jock would also have gone forwards but the cart was in the way.

Jock's enquiry after Duke's health was met with a scuffling amongst the wood now piled up against the door. Duke emerged casting doubts upon the braking prowess of his partner who was himself wondering about the steerage and speed control of the pilot, but was in no position to comment in depth. Rank had its advantages.

The officers, now imbued with a healthy respect for a certain skinny horse, set about restoring dignity which commenced with the dispersal of an interested group of onlookers and followed by reuniting the wood with the cart.

Of one thing they were sure—being kind to animals was a dangerous practice.

There were other occasions when teamwork produced the desired result, but not in the manner intended. A salutary example of enthusiasm combined with Murphy's Law occurred as the night shift prepared to go off duty and the early shift was assembling.

There was excitement in Bethel Street Police Station as it was announced that a stolen car had been observed moving through the city. This in turn produced an array of flashing pillarphones and furiously cycling officers. Some actually got into a police vehicle heading towards

153

the appropriate map reference in search of adventure and conquest.

The information was simple and to the point. A stolen car, containing two men, was heading out of the city towards the Newmarket Road, The fact that it was in no particular hurry hinted at a measure of defiance or casualness that was seen as a challenge.

The Newmarket Road ran through an area of pleasant stockbroker belt, with the Eaton golf course on one side, before it terminated by going downhill towards the city boundary. At that point it should have been all over for the car thieves, for Smudger (late of the C.I.D. and Hall Road Co-op) lay in wait. He was now an Inspector and with the Inspector's car he formed a road block in anticipation of the capture of two thieves and one car. He was partly successful, although there were others who later wished he had been completely so. He certainly got the car because it rolled down the hill and onto the verge in front of him. The fact that it was empty somewhat nullified his triumphant rush forward. There was, however, some activity on the golf course.

Smudger was now an also ran in the catch the car thieves stakes. Officers were heading onto the golf course from various directions, fired with the sense of occasion and revelling in the escape from routine. The targets were well aware of running policemen and probably regretted abandoning their illegal transport at the top of the hill, although Smudger's sense of anti-climax was of no concern to them as they legged it across the greens with one showing a greater turn of speed than his partner in crime.

The police chase across the golf course was simple and direct. It was a case of there he is, he went that way—get him. Once line of sight was established the fugitives were doomed for policemen with the relevant view were converging from different directions. Their straight line progress showed little sensitivity for the hallowed game of golf, but it was effective. Fairways, greens, rough—it was all the same; a direct line was the shortest distance between two points.

The short winded car thief was captured with some differing views as to who actually laid hands on him first. Neither does history record who handcuffed him to a convenient tree in order that all those present could continue the pursuit of his more fleet footed accomplice.

On this latter account there was no need to worry. Kenny was a slim, fast moving Constable with his sights set firmly upon fleetfoot. (He was also good at truncheon throwing—at Wolseleys). He was gaining as his intended prisoner tired. An arrest was imminent and that arrest was going to be Kenny's, or he would know the reason why. A probable reason was looming up rather quickly.

Johnnie was a large well built Sergeant (as previously described), who, whilst unable to match Kenny's speed, had an advantage because he was closing fast from the opposite direction in a single minded charge designed to cancel any further progress by the fugitive. He concentrated on his target as the intervening distance rapidly diminished.

Kenny won. He grabbed the fleeing man who swerved in a last

154

desperate attempt to evade the restraining clutches, or was it because he saw that Johnnie was almost upon him. He was not going to give up easily, which must have been the opinion of Johnnie as he thundered in swinging a punch, forearm smash or something similar intended to finish the tiresome running part of the operation.

The impact of Johnnie's arrival was without question, but the accuracy of his swinging arm left a lot to be desired. It flattened Kenny who immediately lost all interest in the proceedings.

The astounded prisoner found he was in no position to capitalise from this collision of opposing forces because Kenny had claimed his prize by handcuffing himself to him, this preoccupation probably being the reason for the failure to observe an apparently out of control Sergeant coming in at high speed.

The embarrassment of an unconscious policeman attached to a prisoner was matched by the realisation that no one in the small circle of concerned and out of breath policemen could remember where the first prisoner had been left. It was a well wooded golf course and somewhere in there was a man handcuffed to a tree trunk. Trees and greens meant little to the impromptu council of war that was hurriedly convened. A retracing of steps was obviously necessary, but this required some recollection of routes taken—it also required a measure of mobility now lacking through exhaustion and the insensibility of one of the party. Never has one golf course had so many handicaps.

The problems of a misplaced prisoner and another attached to an unconscious policeman were not insurmountable. Kenny recovered after some ten minutes and offered Johnnie an on the spot analysis of his arresting technique. A search party found the other prisoner, who had some views of his own on arresting techniques, and various assisting officers left to go off duty, or return to the station to recount the adventures in suitably garnished form.

All had been satisfactorily resolved and everyone agreed that it had gone rather well, two gentlemen in handcuffs dissenting, except for some minor hiccups of which Kenny's sore head was obviously one. It only now remained to unlock number one prisoner from his tree and convoy back to the police station.

Where the handcuffs came from suddenly became very important. There was no key available for the pair that embraced the prisoner to the tree. A further conference was obviously necessary and by this time the prisoners must have been wondering how they had been caught by this lot in the first place. After much discussion there was common agreement on the current position. The prisoner could not be removed from the tree. Various solutions were contemplated with the unfortunate man straddling the tree being suitably alarmed at facetious references to amputation.

The most obvious answer of obtaining keys from the police station was quickly discounted on the grounds that no Inspector should be aware of the circumstances, especially a thwarted Smudger. He would be particularly sensitive to any comedy of errors by those who had snatched

*It had all gone rather well except for some minor hiccups*

both excitement and glory.

What followed the final emergency conference in a series of such conferences, made necessary by a chapter of misfortunes, is not in dispute, but memories are cloudy on certain issues. Did the greenkeeper volunteer the saw from his hut or was it obtained and returned without his knowledge? Did someone notice the tree sawn down on the golf course? It was suggested that one of the conferring officers knew the greenkeeper, but that may be coincidental.

Those with practical minds will ask how you saw down a tree, albeit one with a slender trunk, with a person wrapped around it. The answer is—with great care.

The final analysis? Best qualities to the fore and two under par after a record round.

Searches and raids were examples of teamwork. Some were fairly straightforward but had built in problems and, in this context, an eye opener, in more ways than one, was the investigation of offences under the Obscene Publications Acts.

The first step in bringing to heel the targeted bookshop, usually named in a letter of complaint from 'outraged ratepayer', was to divert the Cadet from shopping for Stumpy's oranges to seeking something "a little bit special" from a seedy shopkeeper who is glowering over a display of 'Health and Efficiency' and 'Playboy'. The Cadet's brief is to appear in his best suit and recite with fresh faced innocence the key phrases. If the "something special" brings no immediate response it will be the "under the counter" or "back room" stock that is requested, accompanied by a knowing wink, which in the Cadet's case came out as a contorted grimace.

Having spent the ratepayer's money, and returned to the station with his brown paper bag, the Cadet is dismissed from the growing circle of experts on pornography on the grounds that he is "too young for that sort of thing". His purchases are quickly identified as illegal and a decision is made to obtain more of the same.

The searching team is assembled with no shortage of volunteers despite other pressing commitments. The leading light is a Sergeant, and he enters the offending shop clutching a Magistrate's Warrant, granted by a local businessman who has recoiled from viewing the Cadet's purchases with exclamations of disgust, although he did persevere and not sign the warrant until he had reached the last page of the proffered book.

The entry of four reasonably dressed, fairly ordinary men arouses no interest amongst customers furtively browsing the display shelves; and a semi-comatose shopkeeper remains sprawled over his counter. There follows a short announcement of identity and purpose of the visitors, with an accompanying flourish of the search warrant, which is in turn followed by a crush of humanity in the doorway as the customers remember urgent appointments.

As the last customer disappears a member of the search team ominously locks the door, and prospective customers, seen to be anxiously tapping the glass, quickly vanish as the word "police" is bawled in their direction.

A tea chest is acquired and placed in the centre of the shop floor, and a spluttering, protesting shopkeeper is asked, "Where is it kept?". The question is, however, rhetorical and the emphasis switches from objective to subjective as books and magazines are pulled from shelves and scanned with dedicated interest. Material that fails to pass the perusal of the locust like censors is hurled into the tea chest. The back room and depths of the counter receive extra special scrutiny with any doubtful material winging its way towards the all consuming tea chest.

Through this hive of industry and flying paper there are comments of "Cor, look at this", "That's disgusting" or "Must be a bloody contortionist". Films are seized on the grounds that the unknown is suspect.

Eventually, a resigned shopkeeper watches a substantial part of his stock disappear through the door via the tea chest, knowing that half will be returned; but he will pay the penalty for the other half. His only consolation is the stock that he is keeping at his house. In later episodes he finds the police take out an extra warrant—for his house. Anyone know a good lock-up garage for rent?

The seized material is stored in a secret room at the Police Station. Over the next few days this is visited, on some pretext or other, by nearly every officer in the station. The designated readers and viewers begin

157

brightly but finish in a wearisome and resigned manner. You can have too much of some police duties.

The shopkeeper is duly fined, protesting that the public has the right of choice and the beat man needn't bother to call in for a cup of tea again. The police return the hired film projector, and what was originally transported in a tea chest is taken in two cardboard boxes to a local incinerator where a stoker risks burnt fingers and a headache trying to look at photographs that are being shovelled into a furnace. A successful conclusion to teamwork.

The Norwich City Police was a team, in war, in peace, adverse circumstances, Murphy's Law, or whatever—but the end is in sight in the 1960s. There is talk of new methods and a new word is being used— amalgamation. Remember Norfolk County? Remember Norwich City!

It is the beginning of the end. Changes are afoot, some coincidental, some related to the impending extinction of a City Police Force, but all representative of a new policing age.

In 1964 traffic lights are installed at St. Stephens point and recruits are regaled with stories of how it was: actually standing in the middle in the pouring rain—they were the days.

In 1966 new uniforms appear on the streets. They have caps with distinctive yellow bands and the wearers apply themselves to the vehicle parking laws with a previously unseen ferocity.

Pocket radios are issued to replace the need to respond to pillar-phones. No longer the observant ratepayer, but policemen who put the batteries in upside down. "Sorry Sarge, have you been trying to get me?"

Everything happened so quickly adjustment sometimes lagged behind. The Inspector who saw the advent of the personal radio as a means to address the whole shift made a stirring speech from the Operations Room during a tour of night duty. This was the first and last time he sought to inspire his troops in such a manner for he had only just finished, or it may have been a pause to draw breath, when a large raspberry sounded over the air and he immediately realised that his men had an anonymous means of reply. Perhaps the pillarphones were not so bad after all.

The C.I.D. moved with the times as trenchcoats and trilbys gave way to anoraks and bare heads. Sports jackets were seen, and one aide ruined his chances of progress by insisting on wearing a flat cap. A Clerk Constable was appointed to talk to the public twitching in the doorway. In later years detectives were issued with radios, but reception was poor in the 'Walnut Tree Shades' and 'The Plough'.

A well known local criminal found it difficult to adjust to the new radios and stopped the beat Constable to complain that whilst he did not mind being interviewed as a suspect for theft, he did object to the interviewing detective leaving his radio on the kitchen table: it never stopped chattering, and, please, "how do you turn the damn thing off?" One embarrassed detective, not used to carrying these new contraptions around, returned to the address at high speed.

Observations became a thing of the past; they became surveillances, mainly the prerogative of a new and mysterious organisation called Regional Crime Squad. The law makers followed this trend with sweeping changes in the criminal law, probably working on the supposition that the existing legislation was becoming understandable. Burglary—only between nine p.m. and six a.m., became a twenty four hour offence and was no longer reserved for dwelling houses, which only created further questions—such as the status of a potting shed. Larceny, false pretences, fraudulent conversion, embezzlement, and other legal niceties ingrained upon police officer's minds, were replaced by newly described offences— theft, criminal deception, pecuniary advantage and other fine sounding titles. And an amalgamated city Constable would have to check whether the Diseases of Animals Act was still around, Form D and the bucket of disinfectant could yet come his way. Moriarty, of course, became out of date.

The new recruit was to be launched without knowledge of Stumpy, chocolate, Wootton lamps, pillarphones, capes, and other integral aids to a career in the police service. Neither were senses to be sharpened by the competitive urge to obtain tea in the face of hunting supervisory ranks: something called 'community relations' was abroad, officially! The beat Constable had been practising it for innumerable years.

Values and priorities were changing and the joining with Norfolk County, and Great Yarmouth, was coming. The rapport and camaraderie within a city identity was to be lost. Intermingling with the neighbour was not viewed with enthusiasm. Some thought the downgrading of the importance of door handles only emphasised the slide into the degenerative pit of amalgamation. Never mind dark green Rileys and black Wolseleys, they'll be having white police cars next.

Coincidental with amalgamation the word 'Panda' takes on a new meaning and the beat man no longer has to find warmth and shelter. It is provided, with wheels. The beat Constable becomes a 'mobile' officer, but without the leather; and a Hillman Imp did not have quite the same image as a Wolseley.

And so to the end. From 18th January 1836 until 1st January 1968. Amalgamation, or takeover as some unkindly referred to the change, cannot be blamed for changes that were inevitable through a transition to modern policing methods but it can be said to have begun a gradual process of removal of a police heritage, loyalty and identification with a fine city, replacing it with a more impersonal less knowledgeable application based on the wider concept of the County of Norfolk. Who will compare, comment and tell of what went before in a bygone era of policing when a whole way of life differed considerably from more intensive times? Perhaps this book will serve such a humble duty for it is truly a record of a city's finest and, hopefully, both it and the city will endure long after the subjects have gone.

# APPENDICES

Extracts from the Confidential Norwich City Police Beat Book,
dated February 1957.
(Reproduced by kind permission of the
Chief Constable, Norfolk Constabulary).

**Appendix One**
Beat Book Pages 4 and 5—**General Instructions**

**Appendix Two**
Beat Book Pages 7 and 8—**Police Boxes and Pillarphones**

**Appendix Three**
Beat Book Pages 14 and 15—**Two Beat 'A' and 'B' Night Schedules**

**Appendix Four**
Beat Book Pages 26 and 27—**Nine Beat Boundaries, Instructions and
'A' Night Schedule**

**Appendix Five**
Beat Book Pages 44 and 45—**Fourteen Beat Boundaries, Instructions
and 'A' Night Schedule**

**Appendix Six**
Beat Book Pages 54 and 55—**Nineteen Beat 'A' and 'B' Night
Schedules**

## PATROL SERGEANTS.

Patrol Sergeants will parade at their respective Divisional Stations or as instructed by the Duty Officers. The senior Sergeant parading at 'A' Division Headquarters will march the reliefs from the Police Station via Bethel Street, St. Peter's Street, Gaol Hill to London Street Corner. If more than two P.c.'s are continuing through London Street, the Sergeant will accompany them.

Patrol Sergeants will ring in at intervals from Police Boxes or Pillar telephones.

The Sergeant on No. 1 Section will relieve the Station Sergeant for refreshments.

## BEAT WORKING.

All Beats, with the following exceptions, will be worked discretionally:—

Beats Nos. 1, 2, 7, 8, 9, 13, 14, 15 and 19 will be worked according to schedule from 10 p.m. until the times stated on the beat schedule for refreshment periods. Constables will follow the routes laid down. Although not specifically naming all streets, alleys, etc., Constables will ensure effective coverage.

Constables working a beat on a laid down route will, if delayed, resume working the route as soon as possible and work late, informing the Station Officer of the period of time lost and the reason.

A, B or C Schedules of Working will be operated at the discretion of the Duty Officers.

## DUTY TOURS.

Time-tables have been prepared on a 24 hour basis, so far as Beats are concerned, and Constables commencing duty will ring at the appropriate time in the time-table concerned. Constables changing beats during tours of duty will pick up on the time-table at the appropriate place for their new beat or beats.

4

## RINGING-IN TIMES AND POINTS.

Constables on beats and patrols will ring-in from boxes and/or pillar telephones as laid down in the ringing-in schedules for each beat or patrol. Constables will remain at ringing-in points for a period of five minutes after making the requisite ring irrespective of the time the ring is made, except when working a single inside night duty beat to a specified route. Constables will make the points laid down for each beat and patrol at the times stated unless delayed by a matter of duty. In all cases when scheduled rings are made at times other than those shown in the time-tables, officers concerned will inform the switchboard operator of the reason for such change. A Constable held up by a matter of duty and unable to make a scheduled ring from the appropriate box or pillar phone will ring in from the nearest Police telephone point, giving the switchboard operator the reason for such ring.

## IMPRACTICABLE RINGING-IN TIMES.

The first and/or last ring-in will, in some instances, be impracticable owing to the distance to be covered from or to the parading on and off points. The requisite ring will, in such cases, be made as soon as possible after commencing duty or as late as possible before terminating duty as the case may be, unless varied by the Duty Officer.

## RELIEF POINTS AND ROUTES TO BEATS AND PATROLS.

Routes to all Beats and Patrols as shown on the beat schedules, will be adhered to when commencing duty. Constables going off duty from inside beats and patrols will remain at the relief points shown until their relief arrives at the point in question.

5

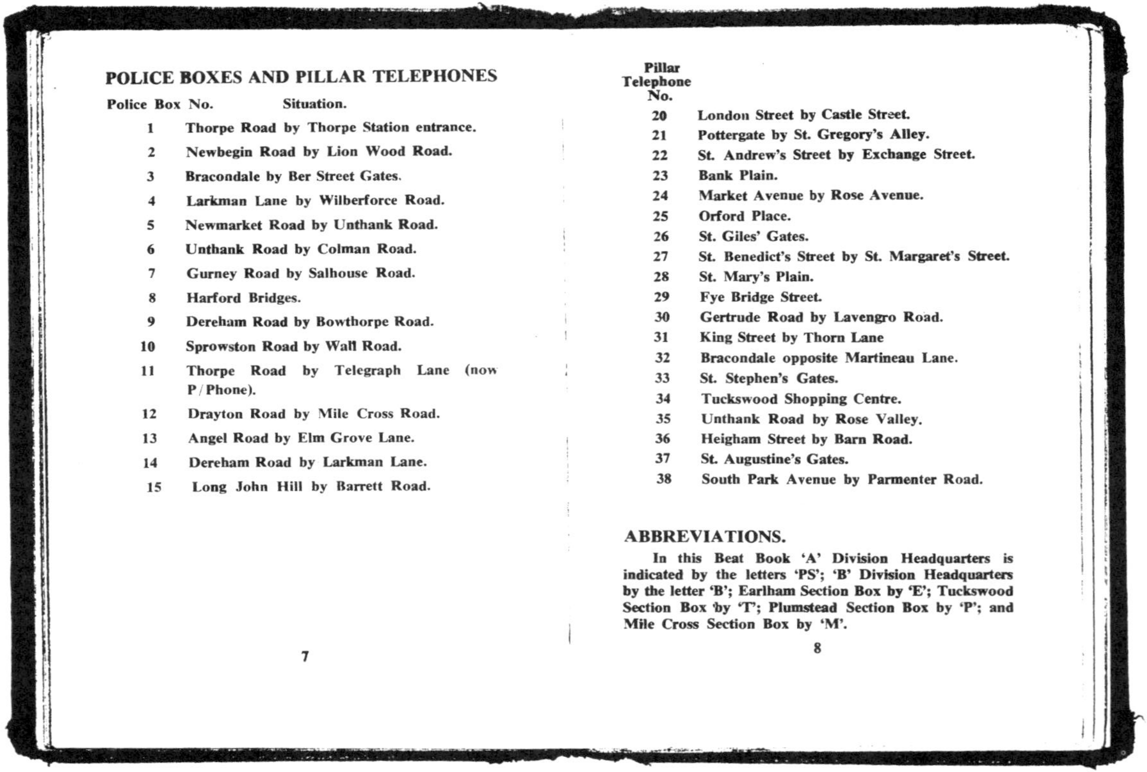

## POLICE BOXES AND PILLAR TELEPHONES

**Police Box No.**   **Situation.**

1  Thorpe Road by Thorpe Station entrance.
2  Newbegin Road by Lion Wood Road.
3  Bracondale by Ber Street Gates.
4  Larkman Lane by Wilberforce Road.
5  Newmarket Road by Unthank Road.
6  Unthank Road by Colman Road.
7  Gurney Road by Salhouse Road.
8  Harford Bridges.
9  Dereham Road by Bowthorpe Road.
10  Sprowston Road by Wall Road.
11  Thorpe Road by Telegraph Lane (now P/Phone).
12  Drayton Road by Mile Cross Road.
13  Angel Road by Elm Grove Lane.
14  Dereham Road by Larkman Lane.
15  Long John Hill by Barrett Road.

7

**Pillar Telephone No.**

20  London Street by Castle Street.
21  Pottergate by St. Gregory's Alley.
22  St. Andrew's Street by Exchange Street.
23  Bank Plain.
24  Market Avenue by Rose Avenue.
25  Orford Place.
26  St. Giles' Gates.
27  St. Benedict's Street by St. Margaret's Street.
28  St. Mary's Plain.
29  Fye Bridge Street.
30  Gertrude Road by Lavengro Road.
31  King Street by Thorn Lane
32  Bracondale opposite Martineau Lane.
33  St. Stephen's Gates.
34  Tuckswood Shopping Centre.
35  Unthank Road by Rose Valley.
36  Heigham Street by Barn Road.
37  St. Augustine's Gates.
38  South Park Avenue by Parmenter Road.

### ABBREVIATIONS.

In this Beat Book 'A' Division Headquarters is indicated by the letters 'PS'; 'B' Division Headquarters by the letter 'B'; Earlham Section Box by 'E'; Tuckswood Section Box By 'T'; Plumstead Section Box by 'P'; and Mile Cross Section Box by 'M'.

8

162

**Beat Book—Police Boxes and Pillarphones**

## Div. 'A' Sec. 1 Beat 2 Night Duty

### 'A' SCHEDULE

START—London Street Corner, Exchange Street both sides to Bedford Street, Exchange Street left side to St. Andrew's Street, St. Andrew's Street left side to St. John Maddermarket, return St. Andrew's Street left side to Museum Court, Museum Court to Duke Street, Duke Street to Bridge and return to St. Andrew's Street, St. John Maddermarket, Pottergate both sides, St. John's Alley, Charing Cross left side, St. Gregory's Alley, Pottergate to Dove Street, return Pottergate to Lower Goat Lane, Lower Goat Lane to St. Giles Street, return Lower Goat Lane to Pottergate (21 P.P. 10.55 p.m.), Upper Goat Lane, Guildhall Hill, Dove Street, Lobster Lane, Exchange Street left to St. Andrew's Street return Exchange Street, Parsonage Square to end and P.H 11.35 p.m.), Exchange (C.P. Post Office Tavern P.H 11.35 p.m.), Exchange Street, Bedford Street, School Lane to end and return, Little London Street, London Street left to London Street corner, return London Street, Swan Lane, Bedford Street, left to Little London Street, return Old Post Office Yard to end and return, Bridewell Alley, St. Andrew's Street, St. Andrew's Hill, Bedford Street right side to Swan Lane, return Bedford Street, London Street right to (20 P.P., 12.15 a.m.), return London Street, left to Bank Plain, Queen Street to Old Bank of England Court, return Redwell Street both sides, Princes Street right side to Tombland, Tombland right to Queen Street, Queen Street right to Old Bank of England Court, return, Tombland, Tombland Alley, return, Tombland, Waggon & Horses Lane to Del Ballroom, return Wensum Street to Fye Bridge, return Wensum Street to Elm Hill, Monastery to end and return, Elm Hill, Princes Street right to St. George Street, St. Andrew's Street to Redwell Street, return St. George Street to Bridge and return, St. Andrew's Street, Stamp Office Yard to end and return. St. Andrew's Street (22 P.P. 1.35 a.m.).

14

### 'B' SCHEDULE

START—London Street Corner, Exchange Street both sides to Bedford Street, Bedford Street both sides to School Lane to end and return, Bedford Street, Little London Street, London Street right to London Street Corner, return London Street, Swan Lane, Bedford Street to Little London Street, return Bedford Street, Old Post Office Yard to end and return Bedford Street, Bridewell Alley, St. Andrew's Street, St. Andrew's Hill, Bedford Street to Swan Lane, return Bedford Street, London Street, right to Swan Lane, return left side to Bank Plain to (23 P.P. 10.55 p.m.), Queen Street, left side to Old Bank of England Court, return Redwell Street both sides, Princes Street, right to Tombland, Tombland right to Queen Street, Queen Street right to Old Bank of England Court, return, Tombland, Tombland Alley, return Waggon & Horses Lane to Del Ballroom, return Wensum Street to Elm Hill (C.P. Wensum Street by Elm Hill 11.35 p.m.), Wensum Street to Fye Bridge, return Elm Hill. The Monastery to end and return, Elm Hill, Princes Street right to St. George Street, St. Andrew's Street to Redwell Street, return St. George Street to Bridge, return St. Andrew's Street, Stamp Office Yard to end and return, St. Andrew's Street (22 P.P. 12.15 a.m.), Museum Court to Duke Street, Duke Street to Bridge and return to St. Andrew's Street, St. Andrew's Street both sides to Exchange Street, Exchange Street both sides to Lobster Lane, Dove Street, Guildhall Hill, (C.P. Top Lower Goat Lane 12.55 a.m.), Lower Goat Lane, right to Pottergate and return to St. Giles Street, Upper Goat Lane, Pottergate both sides to Dove Street, return Pottergate both sides to Dove Street, return Pottergate, St. Gregory's Alley, Charing Cross, St. John Maddermarket, Dove Street, London Street, (20 P.P. 1.35 a.m.).

15

## Beat Book—Two Beat 'A' and 'B' Night Schedules

163

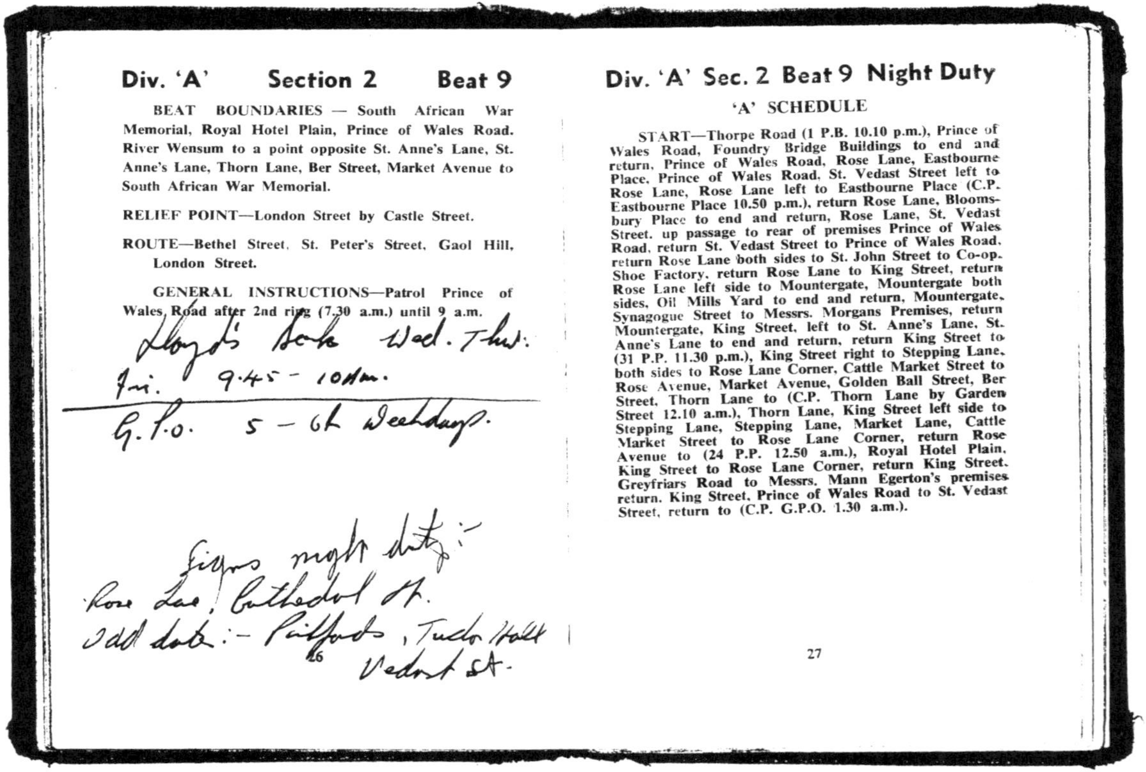

## Div. 'A'    Section 2    Beat 9

BEAT BOUNDARIES — South African War Memorial, Royal Hotel Plain, Prince of Wales Road. River Wensum to a point opposite St. Anne's Lane, St. Anne's Lane, Thorn Lane, Ber Street, Market Avenue to South African War Memorial.

RELIEF POINT—London Street by Castle Street.

ROUTE—Bethel Street, St. Peter's Street, Gaol Hill, London Street.

GENERAL INSTRUCTIONS—Patrol Prince of Wales, Road after 2nd riga (7.30 a.m.) until 9 a.m.

*[handwritten notes:]*

*Wed. Thur.*
*Fri. 9.45 - 10.0m.*
*G.P.O. 5 - 6t Weekdays.*

*Signs night duty*
*Even due cathedral St.*
*Odd date :- Pilford, Tudor Hall*
*66 Vedast St.*

## Div. 'A' Sec. 2 Beat 9 Night Duty

### 'A' SCHEDULE

START—Thorpe Road (1 P.B. 10.10 p.m.), Prince of Wales Road, Foundry Bridge Buildings to end and return, Prince of Wales Road. Rose Lane, Eastbourne Place, Prince of Wales Road. St. Vedast Street left to Rose Lane, Rose Lane left to Eastbourne Place (C.P. Eastbourne Place 10.50 p.m.), return Rose Lane, Blooms-bury Place to end and return, Rose Lane, St. Vedast Street, up passage to rear of premises Prince of Wales Road, return St. Vedast Street to Prince of Wales Road, return Rose Lane both sides to St. John Street to Co-op. Shoe Factory, return Rose Lane to King Street, return Rose Lane left side to Mountergate, Mountergate both sides, Oil Mills Yard to end and return, Mountergate, Synagogue Street to Messrs. Morgans Premises, return Mountergate, King Street, left to St. Anne's Lane, St. Anne's Lane to end and return, return King Street to (31 P.P. 11.30 p.m.), King Street right to Stepping Lane, both sides to Rose Lane Corner, Cattle Market Street to Rose Avenue, Market Avenue, Golden Ball Street, Ber Street, Thorn Lane to (C.P. Thorn Lane by Garden Street 12.10 a.m.), Thorn Lane, King Street left side to Stepping Lane, Stepping Lane, Market Lane, Cattle Market Street to Rose Lane Corner, return Rose Avenue to (24 P.P. 12.50 a.m.), Royal Hotel Plain, King Street to Rose Lane Corner, return King Street, Greyfriars Road to Messrs. Mann Egerton's premises, return, King Street, Prince of Wales Road to St. Vedast Street, return to (C.P. G.P.O. 1.30 a.m.).

27

Beat Book—Nine Beat Boundaries, Instructions and 'A' Night Schedule
(Note the officers reminders of other duties)

## Div. 'B'     Section 3     Beat 14

**BEAT BOUNDARIES**—Fye Bridge Street, Magdalen Street, Bull Close Road, Silver Road, River Lane, River Wensum to Whitefriars' Bridge, Whitefriars' Street, Palace Street, Wensum Street to Fye Bridge.

**RELIEF POINT**—Magdalen Gates.

**ROUTE**—Magdalen Road to Magdalen Gates.

**GENERAL INSTRUCTIONS** — Patrol Magdalen Street from 7.30 a.m. to 10 a.m.

P.c. will take refreshments immediately after 10 a.m.

When there is no Policewoman available, assist schoolchildren at Magdalen Gates 12 noon to 12.30 p.m., 1.40 p.m. to 2 p.m., 3.30 p.m. to 4.40 p.m.

---

## Div. 'B' Sec. 3 Beat 14 Night Duty

### 'A' SCHEDULE

START—Magdalen Gates, Magdalen Street left side to Cowgate, Cowgate to Peacock Street and return Magdalen Street to Fishergate (29 P.P. 11 p.m.), Fye Bridge, Wensum Street left side to Palace Street, Palace Street, Palace Plain to Whitefriars' Bridge, return Palace Plain, Bedding Lane, Quayside, Fye Bridge, Fishergate to Cowgate, return Fishergate to (C.P. Fye Bridge 11.40 p.m.), Magdalen Street right side to St. Saviour's Lane, St. Saviour's Lane, Peacock Street to Barrack Street both sides to Cowgate, Cowgate right to Fishergate, return Cowgate, Barrack Street both sides to Silver Road, Silver Road, Bull Close Road left side to Magdalen Gates to ('B Div. 12.20 a.m.), return Bull Close Road, Bull Close, Cowgate right side to Peacock Street, return Cowgate both sides to Willis Street, Willis Street, Peacock Street (C.P. Peacock Street by Fishergate 1 a.m.), Fishergate, Magdalen Street to Police Station for refreshments at 1.40 a.m.

---

44

45

**Beat Book—Fourteen Beat Boundaries, Instructions and 'A' Night Schedule**

## Div. 'B' Sec. 4 Beat 19 Night Duty

### 'A' SCHEDULE

START—St. Augustine's Gates, Bakers Road, Oak Street to Sussex Street, Sussex Street to Chatham Street, return Oak Street both sides to Station Road, Station Road left side to (36 P.P. 10.45 p.m.), Barn Road, left side to St. Benedict's Gates, St. Benedict's Street left side to St. Margaret's Street, St. Margaret's Street to Westwick Street, return St. Benedict's Street to Charing Cross (C.P. Charing Cross by St. Swithin's Terrace, to Westwick Street both sides by St. Benedict's 11.25 p.m.), Westwick Street both sides to Westwick Street, New Mills Yard to Messrs. Hare's premises and return, return New Wincarnis Works, and return, Westwick Street to Station Mills Yard to Westwick Street both sides to St. Martin's Road, Station Road, Oak Street both sides to St. Martin's Lane, St. Martin's Lane to Quakers' Lane, return Oak Street to New Mills Yard, New Mills Yard to end of City Laundry premises, return Oak Street both sides to Colegate, Colegate to Duke Street, return Coslany Street, Westwick Street, St. Margaret's Street to St. Benedict's Street (27 P.P. 12.05 a.m.), St. Benedict's Street, Charing Cross left side to Duke Street to St. Mary's Plain, St. Mary's Plain to Oak Street, return (C.P. St. Mary's Plain 12.45 a.m.), St. Mary's Alley, Pitt Street, St. Martin's Lane to Quakers' Lane, return Pitt Street, Gildencroft to rear of premises in Pitt Street, return St. Augustine's Street, Sussex Street to Cross Street, return St. Augustine's Street to St. Martin's Oak Wall Lane, up lane to rear of Clarke's Shoe Factory, return St. Augustine's Street to (37 P.P. 1.25 a.m.).

### 'B' SCHEDULE

START—St. Augustine's Gates, St. Augustine's Street to St. Martin's Oak Wall Lane, up lane to rear of Clarke's Shoe Factory, return St. Augustine's Street, Sussex Street to Cross Street, return St. Augustine's Street to Gildencroft to rear of premises in Pitt Street, return Pitt Street, St. Martin's Lane to Quakers' Lane, return Pitt Street to (28 P.P. 10.45 p.m.), Duke Street to Colegate, Colegate to Oak Street, return Duke Street to Cole-gate, Charing Cross, right side to Westwick Street, return Duke Street to St. Swithin's Terrace to Westwick Street both sides to Westwick Street to Wincarnis Works, return Westwick Street to New Mills Yard, New Mills Yard to Messrs. Hare's premises, return Westwick Street, Barn Road to St. Benedict's Gates, St. Benedict's Street, to St. Margaret's Street to Westwick Street, return St. Margaret's Street to (27 P.P. 12.05 a.m.), St. Benedict's Street to Westwick Street, Westwick Street, Coslany Street both sides to St. Mary's Plain, St. Mary's Alley, return to Oak Street, Oak Street right side to Station Road, return Oak Street right side to New Mills Yard, New Mills Yard, Westwick Street to Barn Road (C.P. Westwick Street by Barn Road 12.45 a.m., Station Road, Oak Street both sides to Sussex Street, Sussex Street to Chatham Street, return Oak Street both sides to Bakers Road, Bakers Road, St. Augustine's Street, Pitt Street, St. Martin's Lane, Oak Street, Station Road to (36 P.P. 1.25 a.m.).

Beat Book—Nineteen Beat 'A' and 'B' Night Schedules